THE 'SOFTWARE' OF YOUR PERSONALITY

The Meaning and Purpose of Your Life

Dr ET Todd

Published by Blue Stone Publishing 2016
Melbourne, Australia

Copyright © 2016 Dr ET Todd

The moral right of the author has been asserted.

All rights reserved. Without limiting the rights under copyright restricted above, no part of this publication may be reproduced, stored in or introduced into a retrieval system, or transmitted, in any form or by any means (electronic, mechanical, photocopying, recording or otherwise), without the prior written permission of the copyright owner and publisher of this book.

ISBN: 9780994591920

CONTENTS

Hello Reader 6

An over (under, or sideways?) view of the human condition .. 10

How we shall proceed 17

The meaning and purpose of life and consciousness? 24

My brain/mind and body is the 'me' I know 39

Some thinking/feeling about feelings and thoughts 46

It is essential to be able to conceptualise your self. 51

Metaphor and analogy 56

How we are now. Accepting or rejecting: an intention to change or not? 62

'As if' thinking is not good thinking/feeling 78

Understanding: 'reading' others and yourself 83

Features lead to outcomes that are beneficial, or the opposite! 92

Psychology, philosophy, therapy, feelings and thoughts 118

The 'software' of your personality 124

You and your consciousness are your memories and narratives 130

Narratives 138

Narrative, meaning, personal identity and narrative conflict 154

The brain/mind as a preprogrammed PC (computer) is hardware and software 164

The world and you. 183

What can be learned? What is the 'new'? 188

Reprogramming your self is possible..196

Choice vs. determinism (yet another look)................................205

If you don't know where you are going then you are liable to end up nowhere 216

Are you no more or less than your 'editable' memories? 225

Present pasts? Confusion, discrimination, decisions and revisions... 234

The 'software of our personality' is necessary, useful, unavoidable, beautiful, marvellous...and can be a problem ...241

Self-actualisation 246

Self or selves? 252

Introducing 'sub-personalities' (SPs) – some ways to conceptualise your life, self and others...258

Several 'selves'? But I 'feel' like I am just me 266

Beliefs, values, ethics, morality and other suspicious issues! 289

Creative living is meaning and purpose. 300

Finally 309

Bibliography...313

A diamond is a piece of coal that has achieved its ambitions.'

(Abraham Maslow)

What is a person though? What is the meaning and purpose of life?

HELLO READER

What follows is about life, personality, meaning and purpose and how all that may be said to be human 'software'. Quickly, here is the good news: the above being the case, you can have more control of it. It is not that hard to improve or understand one's life. If you decide to bring about change, say, a better working life or improved relationships, then this book may supply you with some easy and practical tools. Someone said that *'Sex is better than logical thinking, but they can't prove it'*... It's an old joke that's seriously funny. In the meanwhile, I am passionately interested for this work to investigate, explore and improve human lives. So, reader, now that you have launched into this book, we shall become a sort of 'dialogue', I hope, just as happens between friendly debaters about life and things that matter.

My main aim then is to be of some help in improving lives, be they good already, or less than satisfactory; cultivating clearer ways of living and achieving can always stand improvement. My other and naturally attached aim is to make people *think* differently about certain 'ordinary' and 'extraordinary' life issues; this in turn will also help improve the lot of humanity.

This book has been long in the works. I had to learn, test, experience and evaluate many ideas and methods. I examined what life had brought to me via all that in a personal way and also in the wider sense, referring to human lives in general. This was sometimes enlightening or at least interesting, even fun, or else dreary and miserable, in various ways. I believe anyone may find some of what follows useful, exciting – and yes, at times perhaps frustrating as well, but I hope never boring. I do not ask you to agree with me on everything, but I do ask that you examine and consider what is offered. Then, perhaps – if you so decide – take some action on it.

My aims with this work are 'modest'? (Maybe not...)

- To clarify the meaning and purpose of human lives, clearing away any out of this world mystery about YOUR meaning and purpose, which you already have to a degree, whether you know it or not. You could greatly profit, in various ways, if you were even clearer about your purpose and meaning.

- To clarify and improve what and how an individual thinks and feels, chooses and acts on, and what starts and stops good thinking and feeling.

- To develop a clearer idea of who or what your 'self', that is, your consciousness, is. Most people think that consciousness is a huge mystery, and yet it need not be so.

- To practically improve intimate and daily relationships, in order to enhance and improve your career, success, and wellbeing in life.

If I fail at doing all this perfectly (which is likely) and if all I achieve is that you develop more interest in the sometimes unusual, intriguing and/or well-known ideas I shall present, then I still hope that you will have taken more focused interest in your life, and that shall be my reward.

ॐ

I will be taking some liberty with the English language and with certain concepts:

- The brain and the mind I shall call 'brain/mind'. For my purposes the two can be treated as one (although some will disagree).

- Sometimes I refer to a person as 'hardware'; your entire body/self is hardware. When I refer to 'software', I mean your consciousness or brain/mind or self.

- At times I roll several concepts into a brief nomination for simplicity and because they do not at that point *need* to be more complex.

- Feelings and thoughts: throughout this book I use the idea of thought/feeling as one total movement. I think that there is never one without the other. Some will argue for pure feeling states, others for pure thinking ones, and I don't mind considering the possibility of those, but this work does not need such complexities. Rather, for most of us, the feeling and the thought are barely, if at all, separable in practical ways. Yet it is good to be aware of which is which and how thought and feeling attach and follow one another.

- And, dear reader, I shall move from one topic to another and back again like a free range chicken – repeatedly laying eggs…not by accident, but because I think it works better in a book such as this. That is for you to judge, of course, but please abide with me.

ॐ

To begin with, I have decided to offer some views of a dear old mate, Russell Atkinson, now over 85 years of age, still bright and sharp and even more cognisant of the human condition than he has ever been. Russell was probably the first Australian yoga teacher ever (Sydney) and possibly the first practising naturopath in Australia. He is a student and disciple of the Vedanta as well as other similar lines of thought. He has written several books and many articles on naturopathy, Vedanta, the human condition and the meeting of Eastern and Western thought, scientific and metaphysical. We do not entirely agree on some things. I am, for example, an atheist, Russell is not. I wish to stay firmly on the ground with my belief system, which is that of a Western-style academic. What we do share is a quest for better understanding of the human condition, and to be helpful in improving the lot of being human.

AN OVER (UNDER, OR SIDEWAYS?) VIEW OF THE HUMAN CONDITION

by Russell Frank Atkinson

Considering the really important questions of life – what is it all about? Was it created by some extra-cosmic being? What is the purpose of life? And my particular ones especially – How best to live it? Who am I really?

Whatever the questions that you may feel important to add to this list, they all have one thing in common, whether singly or all together – there is no consensus of opinion, for there is no way to irrevocably prove the various answers.

It could also be argued that it is no business of ours and our attention had best be taken up by humbly appreciating the wonders and mystery of life instead of attempting to satisfy our curiosity with speculations. In any case, most of us prefer to ignore these big issues, spending our lives in the pursuit of pleasure and satisfactions until some rude shocks, illness, trauma, or old age cause us to wonder if our life has been wasted. If a life has been spent only chasing the many forms of pleasure, it has indeed been a waste of time. Many turn later in life to seek verities when the gilt has worn off the plastic lily, but by then the body and mind are too compromised to make the most of either. Some rare ones set out early in life to do just the opposite, denying themselves pleasure and comforts in pursuit of verities, but may find that this too has been a waste of time of another order, though they may have lived a less troubled and troublesome life. Many others try to find a compromise between the two extremes and so may live compromised lives in a sort of twilight zone.

But this does not mean that no one alive or who lived in the past knew the answers to the big questions. Those who did became the founders of religions or philosophical and scientific systems of belief and all have one thing in common – they need a priori acceptance of some basic principles. This acceptance without confirmation from within one's personal experience is called faith. It is one of the most important factors in life. Faith is required in some measure in all scientific disciplines and all belief systems, even if it is only a faith in the possibility of ultimate success. Faith in the vast possibilities of our own innate potentials is probably the most important of all.

As to all those big life issues, life itself shows us that pursuing answers is likely to bog us down in a morass of concepts or entangle us in a briar patch of one sort or another. It is also possible that the intellectual pursuit of answers to the big questions is powered by personal dissatisfactions, confusions, problems and conflicts. Children don't bother. They are too busy being alive. Nor do mature happy adults bother much with fretting at answers. Maybe the answers to most of the big questions will emerge from your innate being as an aspect of your best potentials!

Getting a leg-up.

Here is a newish idea for you to think about. What we call a mind is subtle sort of stuff, and matter is mind-stuff in a coarser vibration. When you get the idea, the images you see in your mind-stuff are not subjective realities, but are appreciated as objective things to the real subjective principle that is you yourself. That makes dealing with them so much easier. Here is an exercise that might make the idea of mind-stuff clearer for you. Close your eyes and imagine a cat. You are seeing it in your 'mind's eye', as we say. Now, tell me, what are you looking at? You might reply, 'A cat!' but this is not really correct, for what you are actually observing is your mind-stuff taking the form of a cat by the power of your will. Not only that, but you can do what you like with it, giving the cat horns, making it as big as a house or as small as a mouse, or deleting it altogether. The particular type of cat you imagine depends upon subconscious impressions. Everything you think is an image in mind-stuff, heavily tinted with subconscious impressions. So are dreams. There is much to be learned from dreams though not by attempts to decipher them, for what is a dream but an experience in, of and through mind-stuff; you are the cast, producer and director. Everyone and all objects in a dream are comprised of your own consciousness; therefore, you are everything in your dream. In dreams you are making images in the same way as you do while awake. Imagination is making images, as you do when you dream.

When you become aware, you will realise that there is a constant stream of images playing in your mind, in much the same way that projected images play upon a movie screen. As you experienced in the 'cat' experiment, what you were actually seeing was your image of a cat made out of your mind-stuff, impelled by your will, and experienced in the final analysis by a witnessing consciousness. Contemplation of these facts helps one to be aware of the source of thoughts, as well as their nature, and to be in control of the content of the mind. Experimenting with these ideas reveals how attached we are to the inherited images in our mind and how deep impressions in the subconscious mind determine our actions and outlook. A group of such deeply held items manifests as an attitude, and when fixed, a prejudice, program or conditioning. There can be no freedom to manifest our best potentials while such images dominate our consciousness, but when such freedom is obtained, images can be manipulated, used or disposed of according to our will and/or the need of the moment, just like you did with your mental cat. Such ideas can be a great help in achieving a harmonious balance of emotional, intellectual, spiritual and active aspects of our nature.

So whatever you choose to believe or not believe, the fact is that you have a life to live and that you can give it great meaning by spending the time freeing your mind from useless clutter that is getting in the way of you being at your very best – joyful, creative, balanced and free of chains.

Many people seek to achieve these ideals and fall into another sort of briar patch – pop psychology and self-help gurus who might live in the same confusion as you might do, but write books about it. Or New Age teachers who promise all sorts of wonders for the cost of a weekend workshop. They all have one thing in common – they all require faith to some degree as acceptance of basic premises. In this book the only basic premises are very obvious ones that require no beliefs but a simple observation of facts. This brings us to consider what the factors might be that hinder us. If they can be unearthed and eliminated, or at least reduced, one can then be free to develop one's unique creative abilities and so manifest the best potentials. That's the main idea.

The major factors.

Some programming or conditioning is not only inevitable but essential. (This is what the major push of Ted's book is about.) We are programmed (or conditioned) to adopt methods of driving a car according to rules. The various and different conventions of manners and speech are aimed at making relationships easier and so on. Most of them are useful and worth keeping but without thinking we are apt to change actions and intonations of speech and manners according to the company we are in, conditioned by an equally automatic process of conditioning – the need to seem to belong and to be one of a group. Society dictates the former, psychology the latter. Those programs we adhere to, imposed by society as manners, laws and by-laws, can be a practical necessity, but those acting through our shared psychology can be downright disastrous.

There is a difference between what is meant here by programs and conditioning. As pointed out previously, the idea of programs is taken mostly from computer-software speak, and as in a computer, one program can cover a range of possibilities. In my context a 'program' spans a range of many possible attitudes and actions, whereas the term 'conditioning' has perhaps a more limited range – or it may be in relation to specific issues. The good news is that although we are and have to be conditioned and programmed, we do not have to be entirely manipulated by programs or be conditioned by our conditioning! You are greater than they. Potentially at least. As an individual, you love, hate, get angry and frustrated, know sorrow, feel and think; all that is part of the personal you. Yet there is also a, may I say, 'impersonal', fundamental you that once unearthed can use what is useful and delete what is not. To be trite, this impersonal you is the real you, not the one that is conditioned and programmed and twisted way out of potential shape. You are not just those feeling–thinking states. You can do what you like with them. The realisation of the truth of this is immediately freeing; it is the passport to a creative and original life.

The 'Software' of Your Personality

To remain conditioned by our conditioning and run by our programs is to live a dreary mechanical sort of existence. A bird born and bred in a cage is so programmed that it stays there even with the door open wide. In the same way, the restricted and therefore inadequate response to the issues and challenges of life creates errors of judgment and thus erroneous actions which lead to dissent, conflicts, suffering and strife of all kinds.

We have no problem with the errors conditioned by the nature of the senses, such as the fact that the sun rises in the east and sets in the west while the truth is that it does neither. It is a fact that the earth seems flat though bumpy but the truth is it is round; that the moon waxes and wanes, comes and goes, though we know that it doesn't. It is a fact that the earth seems stationary and fixed but the truth is that it is whizzing through space and spinning like a top. Knowing the nature of the delusions as such, we live with them unconcerned. In the same way it is possible to live with and use programs and conditioning in a practical sense where needed or to override them if redundant. That is real freedom. There will always be limitation of one sort or another by the very nature of life, so complete freedom is impossible. These facts suggest that freedom is the expression of our natural potentials which arise without manipulation or according to our personal notions, when the limitations imposed by false programs and conditioning are removed. Ideally, it is not change according to a preconceived pattern.

Beliefs of whatever sort are the most limiting form of conditioning and are the most difficult to let go. They are rarely the outcome of our own enquiries or revelations but almost always imposed by others: society in general, religious indoctrination, parents and teachers. There they sit (beliefs), largely uninvestigated and accepted as right and proper. What we call conditioning might be relatively harmless but nevertheless should be carefully watched, noted, and our use of it modified according to whether it is really useful at the present time. Belief systems are of another order and like a net are intertwined to capture the unwary. Ingenuously constructed by your own life situation, they are the product of religious academics, philosophers or even scientists.

How can a person become free of all these redundant layers? To show a possible way is the intention of this book by Ted, and though there may be many ways, they must all start with seeing and acknowledging the existence of all the redundant beliefs, notions, programs and conditioning we have accumulated over the years. The author's wide experience, training and personal confrontations with his own ghosts make him eminently qualified to show the way.

RF Atkinson

NSW, Australia

HOW WE SHALL PROCEED

My aim in this chapter is to explore a subject that will have a large influence in the discussions, suggestions and arguments that make up this book. Coupled to 'purpose and meaning' is always the issue of good communicating. Is it? Yes, once you dig in and see how communicating with others and your very own self is all there is to deliver better life meaning and purpose. How human beings communicate their aims and goals, and how they constantly think and feel is also a somewhat metaphoric affair.

In this work, I am going into all this and more, to clarify and even (humbly) offer practical ways of making lives better. Making improvements in life in the areas of careers and personal relationships can bring to individuals peace of mind and a more meaningful life.[1]

The preceding undertaking is made cautiously. I tend to be realistic. I don't have a magic wand. And, dear people, I admit, writing about how to live better is often easier than doing so. Yet it most certainly is possible to do better and have fun improving one's life. I know that, for that is my own experience of my life. It is after much living, experiencing, and a great deal of studies of humanity in the varied areas of philosophy, psychology, the sciences and social sciences that I attempt to synthesise some

---

1 Sounds like a huge undertaking and I feel inclined to edit it, reduce it, for it does seem a huge ask for me to offer all that: an improvement of personal lives in all ways. Part of me wants to delete my offer, but another 'part' of me wants to have a go, so I carry on.

of the many schools of thought offered. Some of my own ideas come from, and are blended with, the thoughts and wisdom of many great thinkers (why be too humble about it?).

I differentiate myself from the millions of others who write this sort of thing by saying, even promising, that the philosophy and psychology of successful and practical living that I shall offer will be jargon and pretension free, as far as that is possible. And, that what I suggest in practical ways can be put into practice by anyone willing to focus in these directions. Nor should it take you 50 years (or even one year) to reach some improvement, for I believe smaller steps are virtually instantly attainable.

I spell it out again: my end aim/goal is to improve lives.

This can't be done in just one area of life endeavour; you can't be a great parent but be lousy at work, or build a huge career but be alienated from your children and partner etc. Oh yes, all right, you can, but at a great cost to your and their lives. In my book, all the major strands of human living and action have to work together.

I am not offering:

'Enlightenment' (in its usual meaning), emotional or intellectual get-rich-quicks, spiritual practices, instant satisfaction, health cures etc. However, I think that what I do offer may even help with some of the above – if that's what you truly want. I may as well also admit here that I do not believe in Santa, the tooth fairy, reincarnation, a personal God of any sort, or outdated tales from over 2000–5000 years ago. I do, however, believe in a kind of 'self-actualisation', a term popularised by psychologist Abraham Maslow, and that it can happen here on earth now, ASAP. I trust humanism, science, the brain/mind, and the good earth. And I believe in doing it all, getting more of it all while we are alive and kicking, having fun and drama too. For me that's enough.

The 'Software' of Your Personality

Through the ages there has been much searching by humans for what amount to miracles, out of this world rewards, inner peace, outer success and so on. A great deal of those searchers were bright human beings who acted in utter error, considered outdated data or belief systems such as religions, and yet they were people of their day and often had great insights into life.

As for me, I am trying to be satisfied with what can be had rather than believing in promises of after-life, out-of-body and after-death experiences and many other wonderful fictions.

Immediate questions:

More than anything, it is important to actually find out a few things about yourself in a practical way, before you act on anything hands-on:

1. What do you think you really want?

2. Do you have what is needed to achieve that?

3. Is what you want a truly good, i.e. positive, thing? And is it realistic and reality?[2]

4. Are you open enough to learn and experience new ways of being?

Most people answer quickly and often glibly. At workshops I have run for many years, I posed such questions and I mostly heard people saying that they want more money. That's OK, and can be useful. I also heard the desire for all sorts of other things. Some more serious, some less. The voices were often notably embarrassed, or glib, and small giggles accompanied many. I

---

2 'Positive' is a subjective term. But we all know that positive living is what we mean and that this is good for you and others: healthy, sane, and balanced. This should suffice for my use of 'positive' and it needs no further elaboration.

firmly believe that most people have trouble knowing what they **really**, really want. And they have even more shyness about putting that out on the table. Then again, what people think they want is not always necessarily what they really need, or even truly want. I mean that nearly everyone wants more money, say... Yes, that would perhaps help, but is it really the money they want? Or you think you want peace of mind. Yes, but what exactly is that for you? Or you need love, or youth or...

To achieve anything some change is needed.

In my experience working in psychological areas, I have come upon the curious fact of people being afraid to change because they were actually worried about what it would mean in their lives.

> *A famous Zen story tells us about a young man who visited a young, but by reputation a very wise, Zen practitioner. The wise man looked up and said hello, and went on chopping wood. Shortly he was finished chopping and picked up a pail of water, carrying it into his humble house. The visitor was disappointed at the sight of such an ordinary life, for the visitor believed that he was here to see how a very wise man's life looked. He said nothing and left.*
>
> *50 years later, he was passing by the same Zen house and he had heard that the same enlightened man lived there. Curious, he stopped at the gate. There was the same Zen practitioner of 50 years ago, older, frail, but still recognisable, carrying water and chopping wood just as he had 50 years ago. The curious visitor could not resist asking why an enlightened man still had to do all this work.*

The 'Software' of Your Personality

The old man, clear-eyed, shrugged and smiled. 'Before enlightenment chop wood and carry water, after enlightenment chop wood and carry water!'

Zen and all similar schools frustrate me as much as they instruct me; they do have a great deal of wisdom. The truth of the above tale in the end is simple: life is life; there are things you will need to do no matter what happens or in what way. Don't let that get in the way of doing better in at least some areas of your living.

If our human and individual purpose is known and is positive, then true meaning is (likely) attached to it. Let's look at what purpose is and how it might work by investigating what drives and facilitates your purpose(s) or/and what works against it. You might ponder and consider what your purpose is, or if you have one or perhaps several by which you live. Also, whether your purpose(s) drive most, or any, or none of your actions. (Now there's an odd thought, yes?)

We will consider and outline consciousness and contents and hook this up with various possible change frames by using metaphor and analogy. One such will be today's amazing technology, the PC (computer) hardware-software metaphor! The not so humble and amazing PC/Apple Mac can be used as a representation or comparison for human thinking, feeling, actions and behaviours. The PC and other metaphors and analogies will help to *conceptualise* you as yourself, complete with what or who is currently pulling the strings.

Then, we shall tackle the more than one self – indeed the many selves – idea as another method of exploring yourself. Our lives can be altered and improved in easy and practical ways. There are means and schemes for that, even if many are so silly that...I won't mention them. The analogies/metaphors I will offer shall speak of self-exploration leading to awareness and change you can achieve by yourself or with others. Those chapters will be followed by some ideas on your personal creativity.

※

I declare that I am an atheist, though that is emphatically not what this work is about. I make this clear because exploring and discussing the intended issues would be on very, very different grounds if some sort of God formulation, faith or belief system was involved. I accept no such things. However, I do accept that nature is awesome. Still, whether you hold on to pure science, maths, or to a God and religion as your way of life – whatever – that will not lessen what you might gain here, if you are open to thoughtful ideas. Whatever human lives are about, we, each of us, can have clearer direction and better choice making. Such direction and power is, however, only within each of us, according to my thinking, and not anywhere else, nor given by grace or anyone else.

※

I will draw on a wide range of disciplines that interplay, as I intend making this work available to anyone. Often, I will shortcut explanations and reduce elements to the essentials to keep within the (my) boundaries. Too many otherwise excellent and helpful works of similar intention are far too verbose and complex. Thus, at times, you will find me entering an area of thought and then saying 'we need not go any further in this direction'. That does not mean you should not go there; it is simply not needed for my exploration.

I am not selling anything here other than the above stated: to assist people to have better lives. I must be a very brave man to offer that and mean it in a practical way. You and I both know that we want to do well, live well now, not after 40 years of meditating or prayer. Do it ASAP, and if you can't do it perfectly – and no one can – then still, the process itself will improve and add to your life.

Before I launch into a brief but to-the-point exploration of purpose and meaning, I feel compelled to explain one more issue.

This is not an instruction book. Or is it? I will be offering some actual practices and ways of doing-being. The very consideration of this material can bring about change and possible life improvement. To what degree, if at all, is up to the reader.

THE MEANING AND PURPOSE OF LIFE AND CONSCIOUSNESS?

So, what is the problem?

Why people struggle (unnecessarily) with the purpose of life is a question as puzzling as the time and energy involved on it is wasted. This is a strong opinion of mine, but please consider what follows.

Might it be true that everything in the universe appears to have a purpose, except for poor us humans? The word 'purpose' has a heavy connotation. For me the sense of 'purpose' is something like a commitment, a determination of sorts, a drive, or an intention...a striving, by whatever word. Do our lives have meaning and purpose? I see Joseph Campbell's answer as simple, elegant and correct:

'Life has no meaning. Each of us has meaning and we bring it to life. It is a waste to be asking the question when you are the answer.' (Joseph Campbell 1993.) Now this simple and brief message ought to be the end of this book or chapter! Except for finding out what and who is that '...you are the answer...'

Still, this way of seeing yourself is hugely healthy and very smart. Now, if life has meaning, then it has purpose. Equally, if there is purpose, then there is meaning. The two are inseparably the two sides of the one coin. Yet for thousands of years, people have been pained by the question and have looked for the meaning and purpose of human lives. Campbell supplied it: meaning and purpose are what you make of your life. The process of living itself. Abraham Maslow offered the other salient words I paraphrase: be what you can be, and do it as best as you can.

The issue then is not the question of whether there is purpose and meaning to our lives, but recognition of it as a simple enough fact. Yes, there is and it is You, which also brings with it the need for awareness of and constant exploration of your life. I suggest that such a survey need not be hugely complex if one applies questions that can be asked, such as these: what are your givens, features, programs, feelings, thoughts, and abilities? These questions can be easily and simply explored and understood. They are very important questions needing answers that are as precise as possible.

Striving.

'Conatus, our essence, which dictates that all of our intentions derive from our concerns with our own selves, leads us, if we truly attempt to fulfil ourselves, to see ourselves from the outside, as it were...' (Goldstein 2009)

'Conatus' is Latin for effort, endeavour, impulse, inclination, tendency; undertaking; *striving*. (Wikipedia) It may be said that Spinoza thought it is the innate inclination of a thing to continue to exist and enhance itself. One of the meanings of the word 'conatus' – '*striving*' – suits me in explaining my aims.

I believe, and I have learned this from many great thinkers, that the purpose and meaning of humanity and individuals is indeed to 'strive' to become the best they can be. Such striving is what brings purpose and meaning to human lives according to Campbell, Spinoza, Metzinger, Plato and Maslow, just to mention a few great brains. Plato's idea was one I have taken to heart but with my particular explanation of it. My understanding and usage of the Platonic 'perfect forms' is brief and simple (probably not welcomed by academics, I think) and it is this: things, people too, are in reality mere 'copies' of what Plato calls the only true 'reality' and those are the 'perfect forms'. That is to say that everything, people included, may have a form that would be the perfect form of that particular thing. It is not to say that one needs to be perfect, but rather that one ought to strive to become the best possible version of one's self.

Again, therefore, the aim of life of all things living is to **strive** for the best possible version of their individual kind.

We are built from genes. They form and deliver us as we have turned out to be... *'Genes, and in particular the molecules of DNA that constitute the physical genes, are merely the carts that are loaded with information. It is the information that is struggling unconsciously for survival'* (Atkins 2003) and the 'information' is us. It was Richard Dawkins' book *The Selfish Gene* (2006) that powerfully presented the idea, indeed the fact, that basically everyone, every living thing is a complex bundling of 'selfish genes' that just wish to, indeed must, survive! This is accepted as true by most thinkers, but one must note that the genes do this determined 'striving' unconsciously.

So there we have it. If you are one of those who always wanted to know 'what it's all about', or if you have not found enough meaning or purpose in your life so far, then read on. The previous few pages have already covered it in a simple sense so hooray! If you already have both purpose and meaning, dear reader, then still read on for there is much (and some of it is unusual) stuff to be explored in the pages to come. I still believe in the idea that being happier and successful is better than not being so – and I do believe that it is attainable. Thus, given it won't fall out of the sky, I figure that improving life needs an effort of some sort.[3]

Any attempted explanation or discussion about human meaning and purpose is likely to be made either based on science or on religion (or some mix of the two). Fortunately, for our purposes in this book we need only the common sense of the term and usage of 'meaning and purpose' to fulfil my aims. Thus, religious, overly scientific, or heavily philosophical ideas about 'purpose and meaning' will be left out of my discussions.

I shall suggest various ideas, and ask merely that you explore them if, and only if, you wish to have more purpose/meaning and success in your life. Or if you simply have an intellectual curiosity about them. Therefore, although I will approach certain issues that may be arguable (what isn't?), I won't always debate, explore, or go out to totally convince you – because to do so is not necessary for my message.

Purpose and meaning?

'I suppose it is tempting, if the only tool you have is a hammer, to treat everything as if it were a nail.' (Maslow, from several of his books.)

To most people, the idea of needing or having a purpose/meaning does appear to be intuitively acceptable. Many people struggle to find such; some people never think about it. As a rule, it is at best foggy, seemingly mysterious, an 'out there' idea. Usually we think we have no idea of the purpose or meaning of human lives unless we have religion. It is worth endlessly repeating the paraphrased words that Abraham Maslow gave us: *the meaning and purpose of human lives is to become the best possible sort of*

---

3 Contrarily, I also understand that one of the best ways to improve life is to stop wanting to improve it. More about this later.

themselves. And Campbell's words: you are the purpose and meaning of your life.

It is a touch worrying for me to be seen as big-noting myself by offering that I have understood PURPOSE and MEANING as such, given most people appear to admit that they do not. Why am I even telling you this? Because I wish to be different in this book from most other writers. And one way for me to do that is to allow you some insight into my process of thinking/feeling. As for my version of 'purpose and meaning', I do find myself relatively satisfied with it, although I am very open to getting further input.

It is my hope that a deeper and yet easygoing understanding of the purpose/meaning idea will create the recognition that human lives, yours and mine, do in fact have meanings and purposes – and note the plural. Such purposes are not airy-fairy, not up there, not out there, not later on, not so dependent on this or that. If plural, then purpose/meaning is not one big thing, but likely several things that adhere and make sense. They are possible here and now, while you are alive and are a doing-being! Practically, successful human lives are not entirely[4] an accident but are achieved by committed purposes!

A word of caution: aims or goals, which we more easily recognise and usually relate to, are not to be mistaken for Purpose with the big P. Goal setting is the thing we will need to do in order to activate the self in an effort to fulfil our purposes and achieve meaningful lives. That is, if we know what they are or might be... and if we have the will and energy to do so.

---

4   Nevertheless, much of what happens in life is a chaotic undetermined chance, what we usually call good or bad luck.

Let us go deeper.

A broad, light and yet salient discussion that everything in the universe appears to have some sort of purpose is my focus right now. A 'broad and light' discussion, says I, slightly philosophical yet common-sense dialogue it will be, because it is not my intention to offer hard-core scientific proofs or arguments. Mostly because there aren't any conclusive ones! Not really. Science is closer to the truth and I think religion has no place in such a discussion. The thing is that people in all areas of thinking are still wondering why we humans are here and what the point of it all is. My aim is to plainly address those old questions with some old and yet I think newish – and dare I say, streamlined – answers, bringing it all into a comprehensible sense.[5]

As far as anything other than people goes, we can fairly easily see the purpose of many living things if we think about it. The idea of 'purpose and meaning' seems to be a nature-driven something. A something that is the 'operator' of all living things: people, animals, plants. Yet, people are hesitant when considering the purpose and meaning of us, human beings.

One small sidestep at this point is to see that the driving energy for purpose and meaning is supplied and controlled by the 'features' of various living things. As it turns out, this is as true about, say, a flower as about a human being!

Living by chance – as it were – is what most people experience as life. We all 'intend' many things, and yet so many experiences just happen to us unexpectedly. That's life folks, unavoidable

---

[5] I shall not bother too much about why humanity even goes to the trouble of wondering about the 'why are we here, etc.' question for that is, it seems to me, unnecessary and comes from longstanding religious-style thought that truly now belongs in the past.

things happen and have done so since the big bang...I mean the day of our birth! Much of what occurs to us in life appears, and I believe is, accidental. Life comes at individuals in great or small chunks, often, if not always, undetermined, good and bad luck, surprise, whatever. All this happens even if and when we try to take the wheel of life in our hands and drive it towards various goals and aims. Accidental birth is the start, for we did not choose our parents, place of birth or situation, let alone the time or the setting of the world we are born into.

Let us first discuss the intuitive, known, provable and marvellous fact that all things living do show a 'purpose/meaning' towards which they grow. Then, on a common-sense basis, I will move on to compare human purposes and meaning to other living things. I will be asking what human purpose and meaning might or could be, and how it operates in lives on a daily basis. Doing this sort of review will mean a consideration of those factors that either facilitate your personal purposes or block them. To know what facilitates or stops us is a big step – and not an obvious or an easy one to take. This I shall explicitly tackle later in the book.

The idea of 'cause and effect' is simple, obvious, and amazing... and most people agree with the notion. It is what makes the world turn around. Everything is caused by something and the outcome becomes the cause for the next outcome...and so on and on. We need not go too far back, or forward. Merely, keep in mind that all is cause and effect. In a moment I will add to that some logic of the sort that cannot be doubted. Perhaps the best known logical argument ever is the one below:

> *All men are mortal*
> *Socrates is a man*
> *Therefore, Socrates is mortal.*

The 'Software' of Your Personality

Or this one:

A bachelor is an unmarried man.

These are samples of undoubtable logic, just the way I like them, but of course not all arguments and propositions are this easy. Still, keep the idea of such unassailable logic in the back of the mind as we move on.

People are keen to have the best possible life and perhaps at times even assist others in that direction. What we do, how we are, in what ways we strive, hope and aim depends on genetic givens, environmental input, and on the ad hoc amazing life situations we find ourselves in. Knowingly or otherwise, whether we are clear or not about what our individual purpose is, we struggle, feel, grope towards some sort of understanding of the purposes and meaning of our lives.

Simple unassailable logic

Flowers grow and 'aim' to be what they are and nothing else: a rose never turns out to be a daisy. Animals and plants all follow the cause and effect of life, and of what they are supposed to be, can be. They all instinctively aim, struggle and strive to be the 'best sort' they can be of their own kind. *They all fulfil their pre-set unavoidable biological purposes.* Simple and easy. The biologically driven programming of what a living thing will be directs and makes absolutely certain that a cow always looks, acts and is a cow and is never like a tiger. A gum tree grows gum leaves, fish do not talk, and so on.

Obviously, then, living things have certain givens, what I mentioned before: the 'features' that bring about inevitable outcomes, at least up to a point. Plant a flower and never water it, and it will be a poor specimen or it will die. Eradicate the environment for tigers and they die out; poison the rivers and fish begin to mutate and so on. But basically, the wheat you plant will turn out to be wheat, of better or lesser quality, but wheat, not apples. You may get a shorter than usual gum tree or a lush one, a healthy large cow or a skinny, small one, and so on. I repeat: animals and plants have the simple straightforward imperative of being nothing else other than what they were *biologically preprogrammed* to be.

Why would the above not apply to people? It does. In some ways it is obvious that it does, even if we immediately assert that due to our consciousness we can and do change the perimeters of being a person, have some available choices and perhaps we can even control some of our in-built imperatives. So now let's simply add a small touch of what I above called undoubtable logic:

1. All living things are programmed and appear to strive to become the best of their kind; that is their purpose.

2. Humans are living things.

3. Therefore, humans are also programmed and strive to become the best of their sort. That is human purpose/meaning.

Ah, oh, and gee-whiz, the question that immediately hangs in the air like a cartoon character coyote that had jumped off the cliff is this: what is the best sort of human being? How to know it? Is it the same for everyone?[6] What exactly is the 'best sort' that plants, animals and particularly people are looking for? I believe I have answered that question sufficiently for living things other

---

6   The 'best sort of being' – in the very end – may well be about beauty, truth etc. for humans. All rather up and out there even while we know there is truth to this. But examining such high philosophical ideas and ideals is not where I wish to go.

The 'Software' of Your Personality

than humans by simply suggesting that each tries to become its best sort.

Now, let's look at that tricky question of 'best human life'. The religious will say that the best and proper way for humans to live is in finding the one God set for them. (I reject that as too far off the ground with no scientific or actually any proof as its basis. And which God would be the right one, etc. etc.) I sometimes find old philosophies clarify issues further. So allow me to mention Plato, that Greek genius of better Greek times, again. He spoke of the 'perfect forms' of everything. The ideal of the 'perfect form' of a rose or of a chair or of a fox...does not exist here on earth, said Plato, it is simply an ideal of the really real...

I won't go far in a Platonic direction, but wait...never mind perfect, let us just call it a 'very good example' of a cow, apple, donkey etc., at least as compared to poorer versions. Well then, why not an ideal human being? No, that too is not right, we are not considering a master race or any such thing! We are only searching for the most real true YOU actually. Never perfect, but a clear, sane, successful and able human being. It makes sense and it can be done here on earth, without any mystical, religious or other beliefs. To me it seems intuitive and logical. Readers, don't we all actually try to go for as good a life as we can? The real and only drama, I repeat, is that often we go for the erroneous versions of our so-called ambitions. It is obvious that people can and do act in much error.

We have crossed plums and...and made nectarines. We have improved many foods, flowers and animals. (Some may not agree that it is an improvement.) We cannot make a new genus out of homo sapiens though. It does not matter who you 'cross' with whom, you still get the same human genetics, although – and this is important – with variously different features and givens.

So if all living things strive to become their best possible version given their circumstances, then we can safely propose that the rules apply to humans as well.

Again we must note that the 'best' each of us can and should strive for will always be a somewhat individual ideal-best, for we are all born with various givens and into various circumstances and opportunities. We can all strive towards ideals: a better, saner and more successful life, but what that will actually be will be mainly a 'personal' best. Yet it will also have much resemblance to all other human lives, for so much of being human is shared givens, features and values.

So I repeat: all things strive to be the best of their kind. To do this striving is the only and proper Purpose and Meaning of being human. No mystery, no overcomplicated, vague, out there aims are needed.

You can argue further about what is meant by 'best'. I won't do that here for fear of getting lost in unnecessary debates. Let me just grasp the idea of the 'best' human beings can be in a general and in a practical sense. Statements and thoughts about human 'best' always contain a great deal of current day ethical morality, opportunity and situation. A great deal of that gets outdated as time goes by, and was possibly always. Ethics and morality can also be very much a local affair. In fact, it is, partially. I am addressing the more universal 'best' or 'better': the 'best' cannot be achieved at the expense of other people. That would not be the true best.

Back here on earth – *'nanoo nanoo'*, as Mork used to say to Mindy in that old TV series – it is a fact agreed on by many scientists, and even by some religious thinkers, that inevitably and essentially all living things are in the same system. All of us and all else are the world system, all needing one another to survive. 'You are the world and the world is You' (Krishnamurti 1972) is a nice and sharp way to put it.

If everything is in the world, if all is connected, then all is likely to follow this imperative of becoming the best of their sort. That imperative would then incorporate automatically that living things ought to help and promote one another (even the tigers eating the gazelles may just be adjusting the ecosystem to best balance). In the end though, I think it is clear that this 'striving' – human or otherwise – is also all about evolution. The thing built into living things is to survive, procreate and evolve towards ever better versions of themselves. Richard Dawkins in *The Selfish Gene* points this way and the idea is greatly accepted by many thinkers.

For now, we have covered purpose and meaning sufficiently. My point is simple:

If, as it seems, all living things strive to be the best of their kind, then so do human beings. To do that striving right here in life on earth IS the very Purpose and Meaning of being human.

What about the idea that there is no sense, no purpose in the universe at all? That is not a discussion I need for this work, yet I must touch on it somewhat. So let's consider that there is no human purpose, is all then chaos? I quote now a discussion from an eminent professor of biology Peter Atkins' book *On Being* (2011). At first Atkins appears to argue against the idea that there is purpose to human lives. I think he is doing something else in fact.

> '...Some hold that evolution...is driven in a purposeful direction as organisms strive towards perfection (us), but as we shall see, even frantic sniffing there will come up blank.

I need to justify some of these remarks in more detail before turning to the question of whether our local experience on Earth is relevant on a cosmic scale to a universe. To do so, I need to introduce you to that great liberator of the human spirit, the Second Law of Thermodynamics, my favourite law. The centrality of this law to our discussion can be appreciated once we know that it explains why anything happens at all. In broad terms, the Second Law asserts that things get worse...'

'Frantic sniffing', huh? A great image but perhaps there is too much frantic sniffing? Poor us humans are confused and thus doubt our own becoming. Only humans can think about a blessing and/or a disaster when we get things wrong or need to overcomplicate. The second law states that things left to themselves degenerate into disorder. (Atkins' explanation of this law is the best and easiest I have ever come across; note that the underline below is mine.) However, disorder and ceasing to be is a necessary part of renewal as well. Again, I need to add that 'striving for perfection' may be a mistaken idea. We struggle, yes, and it can be hard work. I say 'strive' for the best possible version of you, not for a 'perfect' one. That, I think, is all nature asks of living things. Particularly given the bleeding obvious, that we do not know what perfect of anything is, let alone of people.

Atkins explains that renewal happens... *'Although matter and energy tend to disperse in disorder, <u>that dispersal may be used to drive organized structures into being</u>. Information is organized structure, especially when it is embedded in a physical entity, like words on a page and strings of atoms in DNA... Thus, although every event is accompanied by a net decrease in order of the universe, locally order may be generated without the need for an agent.'*

Here, Atkins points out that there is no need for a God or a whatever agent in order to do or to be. The second law of thermodynamics, which initially sounds like a destructive one, is a huge part of the in-built drives of nature and existence. It is also important to be a little familiar with this second law of thermodynamics because it does suggest the never-ending chain of changes. Changes are inevitable on the cosmic and on the personal levels. Just as cause and effect is. Am I suggesting then that the very 'purpose' of nature or of you is change? Perhaps, but we need not move further in this direction for this exploration. Enough said, I am uncertain and need not tackle the idea of whether evolution itself has a part in the nature-driven striving of living things, but probably the answer is yes.

Now back briefly to an earlier question about 'what is the best' sort of human being. Before that can be answered in general, and specifically by yourself for you, you need to become even more aware of yourself. Before you can truly know what your 'best' might be, you need to know your **givens and features**. Then you can work out and decide what to aim for, what can be aimed for.

Thus, we need a framework that is quick and easy to use to **conceptualise** ourselves. Past methods of doing that were (and still are) sometimes all right, or bloody dreadful. They are often heavy, dreary, long-term affairs where much expertise and study is needed. Neither philosophy, psychology, religion nor science has so far delivered an easy way to see the 'what, where and how' you are in your situation, at this point in your life. My suggestions about how to best conceptualise and understand yourself also won't be the last word on it...to put it mildly. The methods I shall offer are a fast and user-friendly rethinking of how our psychology works.

Some of the main points in this chapter:

- Much of what happens in life is a chance, an accident.

- To really know what facilitates or stops us is a big step – and not an obvious or an easy one to take.

- The meaning and purpose of human lives is to become the best possible sort of themselves, so for You to become the best possible version of you.

- The driving energy for *purpose and meaning* is supplied and controlled by the *features* of various living things.

- We can all strive towards an ideal: a better, saner and more successful life, but what that will actually be will be mainly a 'personal' best.

- I say 'strive' for the best possible version of you, not for a 'perfect' one. That, I think, is all nature asks of living things.

- Before you can truly know what your 'best' might be, you need to know your **givens and features**.

MY BRAIN/MIND AND BODY IS THE 'ME' I KNOW

Many of the details of early life input are mostly forgotten, or concreted over by layers of experiences, feelings/thoughts, time and life. Most of the early input works, in any case, below our daily consciousness and memory. But that input 'acts' out on us, just the same. You know the phenomenon when you kind of surprise yourself by something that suddenly and surprisingly floats up from within. Thus you are aware of and know some things about yourself, suspect others and have no available knowledge of yet other areas of your being.

In the early years of human life, we have great potential and ability to store, process and increasingly integrate information. I've said this before, but here is another way to look at it. Our brand-new body/minds (hardware and software) are not blank paper or an empty computer; our genes incorporate and offer various facts and features, instincts, certain levels of ability, various mental and physical givens. We write (program) into our non-blank computer, what we call the 'self' we know, receiving incoming stimulus of which our sensory systems make some sort of understanding, sometimes only at a slight (or no) level of awareness.

Some of this early sense-making is basic because our understanding of the world as a three-month-old or even as a two-year-old is partial and undeveloped. More and more impressions, information and experiences come to us. Much of it is explained by all that has gone before and by our experience of the world around us. Alas, again, often this can happen in a flawed way. In fact, it is unavoidable that it happens in an imperfect way! 'Who' actually does the explanation and integration of what life brings? Mostly 'they' do it. Most of the explanations come from out there, from other people and circumstances. Also, increasingly this sense-making and explaining of the world to myself happens by the growing 'me' that I get to know increasingly as myself. 'Who' actually does the explanation and integration of what life brings? Mostly 'they' do it... Again, the process of input from out there, and interpretation internally, forms a circular system. The 'me' I get to know increasingly does become a more and more sophisticated and complex information processing system. Officially, this way of looking at human development makes me a 'constructionist', that is one who builds and is built by the world around me (Neisser & Fivush 1994).

All this is good, simple and complex, and can be troublesome too. I say 'can be', but in fact it is always troublesome to a degree; that is human nature and life – concern is never far away, and it is inevitable. New people are not clones; each person has their own more or less unique givens and situations. Yet each new fellow has to rely on, accept to a degree, and use what previous life forms and situations confer upon it. No wonder life can be confusing and unpredictable. Or as some clown said, life is confusing because one of your parents was a man and the other a woman...(??).

To round it up: no one is perfect or trouble free. Everyone experiences good and bad feelings/thoughts. Everyone has and IS also a story. We have memories of a great deal of things. We have no memories of some things important. We know much about ourselves and yet so little.

The 'Software' of Your Personality

'The purpose of brains generally is to organize the waves of sensory phenomena that nature's cerebrally gifted creatures experience. Their job is to filter the world's chaos effectively enough to avoid, for as long as possible, the disagreeable experience of death. A direct correlation exists between survival and how well a brain maps the world around it.' (Walter 2013) Yes, folks, but that word 'survival' is very loaded and big. Instead, I would just say a good 'life' and those brain maps.

You are – rather than just have – indeed an essential core/mind that may also be called your observing and perceiving 'self'. In older days we called the essence of an individual the soul, but these days, it's better and more simply nominated as the 'mind'. A person is the body/brain/mind, the so-called self, and the sense of self is there from early on until you die. This mind/core self changes, develops, grows all through life. Your essential self observes and perceives everything you do, and all else in the world around you. It is always there, whether you are aware of it or not. One feature, amongst many, of your essential core/mind is to know and accept yourself as a self, the 'me' that you recognise as an ongoing entity. Another feature is to actively discriminate about your experiences in the world and about your responses to it, that is to say, to be aware of how you live your life/story.

What or who is the 'self' I call Me?

A little digression follows into the idea of the 'self'. I strongly suggest that the nature of the self is purely experiential. And that 'self' is an experience housed by memory that brings the two together (Metzinger 2009; Neisser & Fivush 1994) into what I call Me. Thomas Metzinger is an eminent German philosopher.

In his book *The Ego Tunnel* he talks about the self and thus consciousness, as an 'ego tunnel'. He tells us that '*...experience is not so much an image of reality as a "tunnel" through reality. Whenever our brains successfully pursue the ingenious strategy of creating a unified and dynamic inner portrait of reality, we become conscious.*' By and large, I think many, if not most, thinkers would agree with much of that. '*We possess an integrated inner image of ourselves that is firmly anchored in our feelings and bodily sensations.*' Meaning that: '*the world-simulation created by our brains includes the experience of a point of view.*'

Our self-models are not recognised by ourselves as simulations. Such models are 'transparent', meaning that we are not conscious of the medium through which information reaches us. '*We do not see the window but only the bird flying by.*' (Metzinger 2009)

I don't wish to go too deeply philosophically, but the ego – or self, as already noted – is an abstraction, not an actual physical place. The same goes for the 'mind'.

The self is just an experiencing continuum that experiences itself and relies on itself to be in the world it (you) finds itself in. In any case, selfhood seems to emerge when the human organism becomes aware of itself as a whole. As a 'whole', would mean the body and its place in time and space, in the here and now moment and as a continuing thing. It also means that the awareness is of both body and mind as separated from other people, particularly from the parents. This separation and individuation process is both real and necessary. It arrives mostly at some point in childhood and early adult times, but many adults carry an insufficiently unseparated self into their old age.

Now some would argue that the separation is illusory and in some ways I agree even with this. We are not separating from the human race or from all else in the universe after all, yet we are constructing a 'self' that becomes uniquely ours. Such a me does, however, incorporate the universe... Enough said, but those who do not complete the early individuation process from parents, and to a degree from society even, tend to get stuck with outdated data about the world that is not of their own, but their parents'/society's/culture's making – situations they were accidentally born into.

This much is sufficient for now and for most of our story, although we will be adding to the larger picture later. To reinforce it all and given I equated the brain/mind to 'self', let us take a short further look into the mind.

The idea of 'mind' is also an abstraction that is indeed facilitated by the brain. We're not leaving out the body though, since the brain is housed in the body. That is why for my purposes writing brain/mind with a slash is sufficient. Mind is, in essence, not easily or fully knowable by itself, and thus seems mysterious. This thought, simple as it is, likely gave birth to the idea of what we termed as the 'soul'. Again, mind is not an actual thing, a body part, or something one can measure, though it appears to be – indeed it is created by your body/brain. Your mind has no physical properties, your brain does. Examining your own mind is done by itself, so it is pretty much a closed loop – but possibly not entirely so. Old wisdom says that you can know the mind only by direct experience – whatever direct experience of the mind is... Usually this is a meditative and long-term path and can be a variously torturous affair, although perhaps it does not have to be that way.[7]

---

[7] Such is not my path in this book, much as I have a great deal of respect for it.

The structural genome we inherit continues through life via a never-ending construction of our own 'software' and hardware, complete with our specific talents and predispositions. *'Just as some of us may inherit stocky bodies and others long, slim ones, our parents can also issue brains that incline us to be gregarious or shy, a leader more than a follower, mathematically, musically, or verbally predisposed. This part of us is a genetic crapshoot, and we have no control over it.'* (Walter 2013)

Fortunately, we are not entirely stuck with our genetic directives. People are 'programmable' and 'editable'. Not entirely – up to a point! How far? As far as I know, this is not known at this time. So this editable brain/mind is a great bit of luck and yet at the same time the facility can also be a disaster. Later I shall propose several further ideas on this. You are not unlike the 'internet' in some ways, except you have limited time, capacity, memory and so on. The internet has only the meaning we bring to it. It serves up what we ask for; it has neither emotions nor ability to think like a person. It serves our purposes in many ways if used carefully. This is also applicable to the self you know; you can bring more or less purpose or meaning to it, use it or not, waste it, or develop it.

In the next chapter we need to have a look at 'feelings' and thoughts and the inevitable mixing of them.

- 'Who' actually does the explanation and integration of what life brings? Mostly 'they' do it.

- *You are* – rather than just have – indeed an essential core/mind that may also be called your observing and perceiving 'self'.

- That 'self' is an experience housed by memory that brings the two together into what I call Me.

The 'Software' of Your Personality

- People are 'programmable' and 'editable' and this is potential for good or for disaster.

- The ideas of 'self' and 'mind' are abstractions, not physical entities.

SOME THINKING/FEELING ABOUT FEELINGS AND THOUGHTS

What is a feeling? No, I am not joking. Many people say it is obvious, but I think not. When it comes to it, at times we *think* we *feel* something, not because we do but because we think that we 'should' or 'ought to' feel that way. We are talking about emotional feelings here rather than, say, hot or cold. A bit of an examination of 'feeling' and 'thinking', and then the two together, will help to facilitate several issues yet to come.

We have 'meta' feelings, which are feelings about feelings. There are only a few so-called primary feelings, such as love, hate, anger, fear, and so on. Much of our feeling/thinking tends to be these 'meta' stances; we think/feel something about how we feel that is often a 'learned from others' feeling/thinking situation. Have you ever not felt grief at a funeral though you thought you should have? Or perhaps had a sudden rush of feeling that seemed to have not much to do with the current situation? Or felt less than loving on a Wednesday to the partner you know you love? To genuinely feel is easy and happens often and may not be always explainable at the time. But when I say easy, that does not make what and how we feel clear. This also applies to thinking but perhaps less so.

Can others make us feel?

'He/she made us feel bad...or great...whatever.' Can we **make** others or ourselves feel anything? I have been told by most of the psych community, and learned through my studies of it, that what I 'feel' is my feeling and no one made me feel that way. Hmm. On the one hand, if you tell me that my book is crap, I will feel bad and think that you have at least stimulated me to feel that way. Yet I also acknowledge that my response, my feeling, is mine. You possibly did or did not intend to hurt me, but that is beside the point; my response of 'feeling bad' or 'I don't care' or 'anger', or whatever, is mine. In any case, I must accept responsibility for how I do feel and actions resulting thereof. For us on the ground and for our practical purposes, I think that we can indeed make others and thus ourselves 'feel' some things.

Feelings are learned and programmed into the self. We have been through that several times already, but we are certainly born with the capacity to feel and think. Some feelings border on and couple with instincts that come via our biology. Physical pain, like a baby's upset tummy, makes them feel bad and cry. It seems no one likes to be yelled at – that feels threatening and thus scary. Some young children appear tactile or cuddly, others less so. Some people grow up having tried to be open, to expose their feelings, others keep them to themselves. The environment and the socio-cultural and family situation have dictated how 'feelings' are or are not expressed, shown or shared. If repeated tries of expressing feelings are met by hostility one time and acceptance another time, or sometimes both, it is confusing, and will reduce taking chances on being emotionally open.

We need not go too far in this direction, except to clear up some matters that fit with our overall story. In any case, feelings come from deep within a psyche that was 'built', 'programmed', constructed, swallowed whole – as has been said too many times – in our early years. Feelings do not settle at a reliable list or degree, but can continually change throughout life. The whole feeling thing is still a mystery of the brain/mind. For us all, our feelings rarely, if ever, arise without a thought. Thoughts appear more often to rise without a feeling – perhaps, but I think not. It is just that many rational mind movements, for example, carry less powered and obvious feelings. Suffice it to reiterate that feelings mostly carry thoughts and vice versa.

Feelings/thoughts are changeable, as most of us know. Things you felt strongly about 20 years ago perhaps are not so important now, while some others are. New feelings and thoughts come and go. Maybe you are even more aware of strong feelings about some things in the past now than you ever were, or maybe not. Sometimes we catch thoughts clashing with feelings. People mostly do not like nor cope well with inner (or outer) conflicts. One instance of using the 'as if' stance is to find firmer ground in order to avoid conflicts. This not only does not work, but also can confuse and even escalate the conflict. Often the 'as if' drags others into our conflicts, usually incorrectly so.

Blame and claim

The next important thing about feeling/thinking is to realise that whenever we do not like what is happening in our life we tend to flick into the 'blame' or/and 'claim' mode. In these modes we look for whose 'fault' things are, who or what has caused ill feelings and events. We set out to find either that it was someone else's fault, or our own. In fact, things as they turn out may not be anyone's fault. Perhaps it is just the way life happened.

The 'Software' of Your Personality

We put blame and claim onto others, or on ourselves, or both those. We might blame others for what should have or ought not to have happened. As if anything else could have happened, which clearly was not the case... (except maybe as a theory of what now is hindsight). It is an odd but strong statement to note that whatever has happened to you is absolutely what did happen, and therefore nothing else could have happened differently... the proof being that this, not something else, did happen. But no, folks, it was not God's will, bad karma, or a reward from the universe.

Things happen in our chaotic world often by accident, some of which we call lucky and others bad luck. It is best to blame and claim as little as you can. But do not fool yourself about it. The Holocaust and the Nazis had taken much from me in 1945 in Hungary. I do blame them still, but that does not mean I don't buy their cars or hate them or whatever. And I still have to accept responsibility for my life, feelings and actions totally. I also think that I should have done more in the world than I have, but I shall have to settle that 'claim' by accepting what I have done. Amen to this section, brothers and sisters? Sort of but not really. Stand by...

In *Unlimiting Mind: the Radically Experiential Psychology of Buddhism* (Andrew Olendzki 2015), we are told that damage is caused not by change itself, but by our resistance to it. This is now a greatly accepted thought, and not just by Buddhists. Olendzki offers that personal suffering is a psychological response to feeling, rather than a feeling itself. Suffering consists of the disappointment felt with the passing away of pleasurable experience, or the annoyance and discontent felt in the face of unwanted or unpleasant experience. This means that if we have expectations other than what we find to be our current reality, then we suffer. The suffering is caused by our wanting things to be different from what they are. This important truth of Buddhism sounds right. According to many schools of thought, only wanting less or nothing can combat it. While I see a great deal of logical and undeniable truth here, I worry about it because I do not see the human race as capable of following such a total ideology. So, rather, I think that thinking/feeling creatively can combat personal and basically all suffering. (This sort of creative thinking also covers the Buddhist ideas.)

Some important points from this chapter:

- 'Meta' feelings are feelings about feelings.

- We put blame and claim onto others or on ourselves or both those.

- No claim, no blame is good medicine.

- No, it was not God's will, bad karma, or a reward from the universe.

- Suffering may be a psychological response to feeling, rather than a feeling itself.

- Feelings are learned and programmed into the self.

Now we move to a very important and salient idea, that of being able to 'conceptualise' how you operate. What follows is not about your so-called 'self-concept' but a rather different notion.

IT IS ESSENTIAL TO BE ABLE TO CONCEPTUALISE YOUR SELF.

To conceptualise an abstraction? Yeah, that's right. I paraphrase Albert Einstein saying that science cannot move forward until, and if, a new idea has been **conceptually** envisioned. This is exactly what we need to know ourselves better personally and as human society. We need an easy, simple and logically intuitive way in which we can conceptualise our lives as individuals within the community of the wider world. We need to see that one of the problems of human lives is that most of us do not possess a coherent process of what and how we are, one that imagines, envisions and thereby understands ourselves. Only a clearer and immediately available concept of our psychological make-up will lead to more awareness and better practical lives, not that the two are in any way separate. Now, just as homo sapiens has evolved through time, each of us does personal 'evolution' through our lifetime.

Evolution has brought us this far and there is no reason to think that it has stopped operating. The more we have managed to comprehend about our evolution, the more we are able to also personally understand what people and individuals are like as acting agents. Professor Atkins has wonderful turns of phrase to plainly explain high thinking:

'Evolution is not about the purposeful acquisition of complexity: it is about the random generation of successful junk. Instead of thinking of ourselves arrogantly as the apotheosis of creation, it is perhaps more humbling to think of ourselves as currently top junk.' (Atkins 2011)[8]

Yeah, well, I don't think I am junk, but I get the idea and agree. An exciting idea is contained in that quote. It is not at all dismissive of potential human excellence, rather the contrary. Atkins merely suggests that neither a 'maker' nor a 'shaker' was needed for human evolution. So, we need not think that we are a lesser copy of God, nor that we count not at all. We are part of LIFE EVOLUTION, that is for certain.

I wanted to connect this kind of thinking about human beings into the idea of conceptualising your own personal self, the how you as you operate and evolve. Interconnected, and yet ambitious, striving to be and to do what you can for yourself and others.

Psychology has its place as a study of humans and certainly as therapy when needed. The science of psychology, however, is and has been a 'thin' science (oh dear, they will get me for this) when it comes to the ordinary punter in many ways. Psych finds itself – I think – a bit lost when it comes to human angst, or practical problem-solving of sometimes simple or else more complex individual and social issues. Psychology has a long way to go in order to help those people whom we might call 'nice everyday neurotics'. Or people perhaps like you and me, who function well enough, in worldly terms. Yet so many people live

---

8   Darwin's idea was that evolution is neither intentional nor directed. That it is simply the 'unconscious competition for resources; in brief, evolution is the result of natural selection.' (Atkins 2011)

with much angst, emptiness, puzzlement and dissatisfaction in their lives. In my opinion one of the greatest problems is, as already stated: psychology does not offer the ordinary person a readily usable, easy to comprehend framework of life and living it. No way to 'conceptualise', to grasp the self and life as your process in a way that can be applied to everyday living.

Unfortunately, the odd fad or half-baked psychological get-rich-quick scheme gets on and into lives. Some brought disasters, some were used to lousy ends, and many are badly misunderstood.

It is not possible to 'program', reprogram, or improve something that one does not understand. Therefore, we need a better concept of the process of being a self.

Therapy of various sorts can be helpful, particularly at times of trauma or great personal upheaval. Yet many therapies fall short of the mark, because they are, or seem, complex and hard to comprehend. I am certainly opposed to over-complexification, if it can be avoided. I do not advocate reductionism either, far from it. I am convinced, however, that if we could better understand our inner workings, then we could call upon that for saner and more successful life solutions. If individuals had this clearer comprehension of their lives and inner workings, then the whole human race would move on to better personal and social lives.

To suggest easier and simpler ways of conceptualising the self, I will go in for some 'reduction' and simplification of how people operate, think/feel. That people are immensely complex is obvious. Still, I insist that first we need to have some ability to quickly and relatively correctly understand what and how we do-are as people. (I like the word 'process' for all this because that word is dynamic, a happening thing.)

It is a curious fact that a car mechanic understands the parts and the totality of a car (likely) better than he does his own human 'factory' that is his body/brain/mind: his self. The same is also true for many who have expertise in other areas of endeavour. In fact, most of us have little idea about the working mechanism of our bodies, and even less of our built-in computer, the brain/mind, which in turn is the self, emotions, thoughts.

I will be suggesting easy and immediately usable ways to conceptualise yourself, your life, and your purposes, whoever and however you are at this time. Such a framework will help to explain how or why you function in your world just as you have done until now. It will also offer a practical way to personal change, if that is wanted or needed. Taking all that on board, or even part of it, will make things happen by themselves

> *Consider: Emotions, boredom, purpose, cause and effect are not brought together or explained sufficiently in current psychological thinking. Such ideas are not a coherent everyday concept known to us all. Does boredom, angst and negative emotions, or the lack of emotions, cause suffering? How and why do they happen? If your purposes are strong, angst and boredom appear further away as an issue, and yet can lurk in the background.*

Oh, aha...IF?

I said 'if change is wanted or needed', because here we have one of the possible misunderstandings of at least Western thinking. We think we must change, or want more, or want less, or whatever. Well, amigo, it ain't necessarily so. You may well decide that what and how you are is OK as it is. Good on you, if you are genuine.

The 'Software' of Your Personality

Meanwhile, let us take a look at how human lives work and how they can be better 'seen' and understood via understanding *The Metaphors We Live By* (Lakoff & Johnson 1980).

- I said: if change is wanted or needed.

- One problem of human lives is that most of us do not possess a concept or understanding of the process of what and how we are.

- Just as homo sapiens has evolved through time, each of us does personal 'evolution' through our lifetime.

- Imagine your life, your self, and the process going on.

METAPHOR AND ANALOGY

To better 'conceptualise' yourself, let us consider some of the underlying thought/feeling patterns of being human by exploring the very 'language' of human lives: metaphors, analogies and the like. When that mental coin drops (a metaphor), whenever you go 'aha', when an explanation works, one does *'feel the key turn in the lock'* said American philosopher CS Peirce. Metaphors are often the 'key' that open the mental lock of our brain/mind.

I assure you that looking at metaphors is no diversion; rather, it's the sharp point of the pencil (another metaphor). Much of what I discuss and offer in this book is presented as **metaphors** or metaphoric ways of understanding actual things. Mostly I am concerned with metaphors – and note that analogy and simile, while often sounding somewhat similar, are not the same. An analogy shows a similarity or at least a relation between two objects that allows implications to be made about one, based on the other. Both 'metaphor' and 'analogy' are special language usages pointing sharply to something other than themselves.

A metaphor is a figure of speech in which a term or phrase is applied to something with which it has no direct relations. For example, 'The prime minister put the ship of state on its feet', has nothing to do with politicians, ships or feet, and yet the meaning is clear and obvious. Metaphor means to 'transfer', 'convey' the transference of an often figurative illustration from one idea to another in order to make for more clarity. A metaphor can be evasive and amazing as it points to things so unlike itself that there is mostly no actual similarity between the metaphor and what it explains. In *The Metaphors We Live By*, Lakoff and Johnson explain the importance of the fact that so much of our lives (not only our words) are in truth 'metaphoric', and are spoken of in such a vein that perhaps all our understanding of things has a metaphorical edge. As they had argued, our ordinary use of language is largely structured by metaphoric and metonymic principles that exhibit 'directionality'.[9] I ask that this brief explanation of metaphors is accepted as enough for my usage of the idea.

Human beings systematically – we might also say automatically – characterise abstract ideas, thoughts, values and beliefs, political and ethical situations often in terms of bodily movements and bodily functions. For example: 'he or she gives me the shits' or 'I was running away from my feelings'...and so on, are obviously not about faeces or exercise. To make an idea, particularly a complex one, easier to comprehend, it is often of great value to construct and use metaphors and analogies. To make them? That sounds intentional while in fact mostly we seem to use metaphors automatically. It is rare we actually set out to make one, except when struggling to make another understand what we mean. When we use a metaphor it seems to come out as a surprise at times. However, chances are that a huge percentage of the metaphors we use we have most likely learned from other people and culture in general. This fact is immensely significant and important for my later explorations.

There are of course limits to using metaphors, whether we employ them by accident or on purpose. We need not 'dig too far into that tunnel' either (another metaphor), except to say, yet again, that unless we have a method of theorising/conceptualising/imagining something, we cannot truly understand it, be this people, situations or even ourselves. All conceptualisations tend

---

9   In their work the whole metaphor idea is brilliantly exposed and explained.

to employ many metaphors, and other special language features. Metaphors can also be thought of as an image that gives concrete coherence to even highly theoretical thought.

> *A metaphor may be used in loose ways; it can be misconstrued and thus badly misunderstood. There is no guarantee that a metaphor will always deliver what it was meant to.*

To simplify: a metaphor brings together, explains and explores ideas, feelings, thoughts, words, or objects in terms that mostly have no obvious relationship to the issue at hand. In usually novel ways, a metaphor illuminates and points at something that may be a new and creative approach to old (and often boring) issues and problems.

Another aspect, that of 'metaphoric associations' from common experiences, might be things like hearing a song that reminds one of 20 years ago in another place etc. *This* ***'memory'*** *that each of us* ***is*** *–* ***rather than just has*** *–* the '**me**' that we know, is tremendously important to ourselves. The human memory bank has a great deal of metaphoric associations. Memory is always association with something – tangible or otherwise. When I hear a melody from, say, my childhood, I may also recall feelings, thoughts, and places and people, and even perhaps the smell of fresh bread. (For me this last one recalls my place of birth, Budapest, for example.) Possibly much of memory is metaphorically constructed, most likely not by direct intention, but by a creative mind on autopilot, one that uses metaphors as a device of recollection.

Metaphors thus – I muse – may offer us the possibility of a real tool, an intentional one, via which we may become more creative. This would help to somewhat free the intellect and feelings from past conditioning.

The 'Software' of Your Personality

Our learning from the moment of birth has forced upon us a set of spoken and unspoken rules/ideas/morals, programs by any other word. The individual cannot avoid adapting most of the conventional standards, values and beliefs of their surrounds. Indeed, a lot of it is necessary, but not all, and never unquestioningly. (More about that later.)

❧

Let me interpose what I think is an interesting metaphor that fits in with the above: the 'parents' are the already given *narrative*, the 'child' the *self in becoming a story* (McAdams 1993). My suggestion: parents and society are a universal living 'memory' with all its stories. The child is the new 'myth' yet to be 'written, read and spelled out'. As we progress through this book you will see and taste that a great deal of what is offered is somewhat or entirely metaphoric. For example, *The 'Software' of Your Personality* is clearly not about computer software – the offered analogy to computers is actually about people – and you will meet 'Voice Dialogue' which is not about sounds or voices. The 'internal family' is an imagination, and 'literary editing of yourself' – given you are not a book – is also a metaphor. Yet all these are tools for deeper understanding and transformation. Many more examples could be given, but this shall suffice. Keep this whole idea of metaphors and their power in the brain box, ready and tuned, for it will help not just to understand better but also to live more creatively.

You think you know what you want?

To move on, we need to go deeper into the ideas so far presented. We need to be able to conceptualise self, and/or another person's self, and incoming experiences. Then we couple this with what we want, need, can have, and can do. For as that very sane man Abraham Maslow said:

'It isn't normal to know what we want. It is a rare and difficult psychological achievement.' (Maslow)

It is a truly rare achievement to know what one really, really wants. Or, I may add, needs even! That wraps it up well, for if you really knew what you want/need, **and** really knew what you can do/and have, then you'd be near perfect and perfectly happy. I don't know anyone like that, do you? But to aim in this direction is not only right, but it **actually is the meaning and purpose** of being a human – a life form that reaches out to be the best of its kind that she/he can be, under whatever the circumstances are.

We believe earnestly that we need, want, or even must have certain things; we set goals, and we live as if it were forever... And we often choose badly, in some error, what we want – *or can have*! NOTE this 'can have'. Some people believe they have the power of choice, some see none of that; the truth may be closer to the middle of the argument, but such a huge question as freedom of choice etc. we need not tackle at this stage, not for this exploration.

Thus, I now turn towards where we are going, for otherwise we would be going backwards, yes? At the same time, we will take a step slightly sideways but deeper into the vital issue of acceptance of self, others and life. We shall return to conceptualising the self as we go through other ideas.

Some important points from this chapter:

- In fact, this one is the MOST important!: *'It isn't normal to know what we want. It is a rare and difficult psychological achievement.'* (Maslow)

- *'Usually we know what we do not want better, though often we can be wrong about that too.'* (Todd)
- To aim in this direction is not only right, but it **actually is the meaning and purpose** of being a human.
- No, you can't have or be anything you want.
- A metaphor is a figure of speech in which a term or phrase is applied to something with which it has no direct relations.
- Even memories are (or can be) a sort of metaphor.

HOW WE ARE NOW. ACCEPTING OR REJECTING: AN INTENTION TO CHANGE OR NOT?

Hannah Arendt: 'Prepare for the worst, expect the best and take what comes.'

In the novel *The Eternal Wonder*, by Pearl S Buck, something curious happens at the start of the story. Obviously, but only so after reading a few pages, the reader realises that we are reading about a new baby. The narrator does not tell us that it is a newborn baby she is speaking of:

'He did not know that nothing is permanent. Everything began with not knowing. He had to learn that he could try again and this began by instinct impelling him to continue to try.' (Buck 2013)

The human condition is to learn and try this or that, again and again. This applies to a baby, a child, and for adults too, perhaps at a different higher level. We do not learn without acquiring something from the last try. Of course, adults can become a stick-in-the-mud and lazy, unless we remain very vigilant.

The 'Software' of Your Personality

'Most people, the professor said, are merely adaptive. They learn as animals learn – a chimpanzee rides a bicycle; a mouse follows a maze. But now and then a man is born who is more than adaptive.' (Buck 2013)

The professor was right. Now and then, there are a few people who seem to have been born with...but what exactly? More brain power, more ability, talent and opportunity? Yes, perhaps all those. Still, we must add that all people are also greatly affected by their parents and socio-cultural situation. (How many potentially great singers have not had the chance to become Pavarotti?) In any case, the great majority of people vary in their given abilities. Many of us are not born specifically talented. Or were we? Was our talent lost or buried as we grew up? Did we never have any? These and the like are just some of the mainstream questions we are addressing in this chapter and book closely and sanely.

Right now, I wish to add again that finding out who, what and how you are, and what you 'have' or 'have not', is the key to becoming the best of your kind. The best Tom or Tammy. Again I warn that when I say 'the best of your kind' I do not mean the best person ever, but simply the best Ted, Sharon or Lesley! Again I repeat it because it is so important: you don't have to be the greatest person ever. Just work towards the best that YOU can possibly be. Now that would actually make you, as it happens, a very, very good human being anyway. Are you asking what exactly constitutes this 'best' thing again? Ah, friend, then you have not read me right. There is no best or perfect – only your personal best.

The human situation is such where, as philosopher Jim Holt put it, *'mediocre possibilities are common, truly excellent or awful ones rare'*. But I hasten to add, things can usually be improved. *'Yet, the middle path is the hard path for humans.'* (Holt 2012)

> *I suggest, that this middle path, the one most of us seem to live, often does not feel entirely satisfactory even if we are reasonably sensible about it. This is part of what we commonly refer to as the 'existential angst'.*

So, what about change? Do you really want change in some aspects of your life or daily living? In a small or maybe in a major way? Or change your career or intimate relating? Or maybe you do not want change because it seems scary? Or perhaps you see no need for change? (And that too is fine, if it is real, or as we say in Australia, 'fair dinkum'.)

The story of our lives keeps being 'written' and rewritten. Mostly, the writing is done by yourself, with outside experiences being the plot fuel for what you 'wrote'. There is a certain 'construction' going on unceasingly from the start to the finish of our lives. If we are not so pliable, if we are locked into one written version of our self that comprises our learned and already programmed behaviours, then change is much harder or near impossible. If you have 'written' your story into stone, then it will be harder to change it and your chisel will be blunt by now. *'Contrary to all appearances, the world is causa sui: the cause of itself.'* (Holt 2012) People do not cause themselves though, do they? Not initially, but we do construct-cause ourselves as lives unfold (Niesser & Fivush 1994, 2006).

> *In Catch-22, Joseph Heller said that some men are born mediocre, some have it thrust upon them and some achieve mediocrity...*

Everyone agrees that change is inevitable and that it happens whether we want it or not, and that seems true. Change can seem good, or at times bad. You get fired at work. Seems bad. You find a better job...hmm. You win the lottery and invest the money in bad deals... Your wife leaves you, your mum dies... You decide not to live in the city anymore, or you are sick of farming... There are many banal and also huge potential changes in everyone's life. There are practical changes, as I just listed, and there can be internal, mental, emotional changes also. One brings and affects the other. The internal changes usually bring practical ones, but not always absolutely necessarily.

What can we do about change? Or, if all is well, do you have to change? Some say yes, some say no. In the end though, many people mostly resist change anyway. Yet, change will happen; it is inevitable, and we all know it. Strange that we have so much trouble embracing the idea of change. Everything is in constant flux after all, and obviously so. Your body, the economy, the weather, etc. etc. all change constantly. I am uninterested here about debating the obvious and ordinary facts of change any further. What I am exploring is whether there is an alternative to *wanting* change, to wanting your life to be different. 'Surely', I hear the reader say, 'the alternative is accepting the way things are.' Paradoxically, that would be the biggest single change one could ever achieve; it is perhaps the greatest desire one could ever ask for.

The great Buddha declared that 'desires' are the root of all evil, and this is hard to challenge as an end point. I personally wonder whether it is possible to stop having cravings and aspirations, or if doing that may be akin to stopping being human. Worse still, as I had said, the biggest desire, the greatest ask a human being can desire is to stop having desires. That is a curious paradox. As for me, for now, I both agree and conflict with the idea. There is something heady, wonderful and impossible in what the Buddha wants us to do, and his aim is right in the end. Very few people, if anyone at all, have managed the big quest. For most of us, conceivably for all of us, life is not desire free, and I doubt that it can ever be – or should be – entirely that way.

I suggest that it is ho-hum to tell people that we need to spend 50 years in contortions of yoga or in the silence of meditation to get 'it'. Meditation or yoga are brilliant in some ways as an addition to your healthy and sane living, aiming in the right direction, but are not all that they are sometimes cracked up to be.[10]

Sometimes we do aim for and desire what for us is impossible; we want that which we cannot do, or cannot have. We try to choose something that is not within our range of possible choices! Or we want that which will 'cost' us too much... Often we even try real hard to go for something that turns out to be totally unsatisfactory! We commit 'category errors' as it were, say, when we change jobs instead of finding an intimate relationship or vice versa...and so on. Yet we do this all the time. Retail therapy, constant entertainment, adverts like 'Impossible Is Nothing' or 'Just Do It' all rate a mention as suggesting far too much.

So there is the necessity to reduce desire, want, ambition, by any name, most particularly the sort of want that you may not be able to achieve. But, and a big BUT it is, note that to realise/actualise the best possible version of yourself is a positive movement (even if we call it a desire), for it is real enough if honestly followed. Eventually, the body winds down and makes us give up things anyway. That is how human life runs – that is how nature conducts itself and us; entropy is unavoidable. Birth, growth, fulfilment of biological and social purposes, and death. All of which equals wanting, complexity, sharing, helping others, and death. Amongst many people 'wanting more' is celebrated; 'greed', they think, is good. Not all of those people ever finish

---

10   Yet, folks, dear oh dear oh me, no matter what I just said: in a way that I shall go into later, the aim to reduce cravings, to aim in that direction is, it has to be, a good one.

their own race so well. Fortunately, many others care less about money and power. Happy poorer folks and desperate rich ones... you know the stories.

So, having said what I did, do we just accept what there is right now? Accept the way things are in our lives, or fight and improve and get more of whatever we want or need? There is no way I or anyone can actually answer such a question for another person. I am, however, offering an answer you may care to explore. Again: there is first the asking, the conceptualising of yourself. Then getting to know what you really want/need. Then the questioning of what you **can do** and be. This step is the one that asks whether you do or do not have certain givens necessary to reach your now intelligently chosen goals and thus your purposes.

Oh dear, here I go again: once it is grasped that we need an easy and readily usable framework to understand our self-lives, then we can look at what ways or methods there may be to effect personal, sensible and possible change. Then, and not before.

It is your decision whether you want change, and I am speaking now of doable human changes, internal or practical, like changing your job, or being a better father or going back to your studies, or dancing...or whatever. Or finding a wonderful intimate partner.

One must do all or any of this with real **'commitment'** – not by accident, not waiting for the 'roasted pigeon to fly into the mouth' (as goes the translation of an old Hungarian adage). Once one is clearer about what needs to change or what you do wish to change, then we need to make choices about our priorities. Commitment to one or several choices is a must. But do not get confused about what you really chose. How many young people do you know who are working hard spending 60–70 hours at work and complain that they can't find an appropriate partner. What is their priority? Where is the appropriate focused commitment?

What exactly do they really want? I am not suggesting that one cannot build a career and a great relationship at the same time. Far from it. Most of us need both. But life, energy and opportunity are limited, so commit to what you truly need/want and focus on it, at least for the time being.

❧

We are not going around and asking for any spiritual or metaphysical clouds, not asking for the impossible, in fact the contrary: to find out what is potentially achievable for you. That is base one. You already know what is or is not changeable, don't you, because you have done the work to find out a great deal about yourselves?

Aha, maybe yes and likely not, for *'Most people never run far enough on their first wind to find out if they've got a second.'* (William James)

'To change or not to change is the question', with many apologies to Shakespeare. But I think my line is more practical than his was. In this idea of 'change' I have also included the biggest single change: the huge transformation of deciding on acceptance – and thus no change. This, as already stated, is accepting what there is – and choosing no change (or little of it, since some will be forced upon you anyway). A decision not to change is legitimate and it may be as hard or harder to do than deciding to change. No, it would be a gigantic adjustment and commitment to choose no change; I know no one who accepts all there is. It seems that the contrary is correct, given all the human suffering, unfairness, and tragedy that is present in our world. And a lot of it need not be so. (All this sounds a bit like a dog chasing its tail but it's not.)

The paradox of acceptance

Enchantingly enough, the idea of 'acceptance' is the very first step towards effective and committed change. And vice versa. So, whether you decide to make changes in your life or not, once you make a commitment to a decision, you have an almost equally hard (or easy?) task. For what we need to do to start with is to see, comprehend and accept what and how things *actually* are for each of us RIGHT NOW as individuals. To do that, one needs to seriously comprehend what and how you are and do so deeper than most people suspect. Therefore, the very first step is to become more aware of what and how we think/feel at the forefront of your brain box. Start to note your ordinary everyday thinking and feeling. Heard much of this before? I know I have, but endure with me for a short while.

Once a 'right' or sufficient level of awareness is reached, then we can speak of acceptance or otherwise of the 'now' – the what there is now. If not totally, then to various degrees. After that, we can embark on shifting our inner and outer feelings and behaviours: our thoughts, beliefs, relationships, communication patterns and actions. All this is easy to say and not that easy, or very hard, to achieve. I mean that if you do nothing, then nothing much will be done! (That's a good aphorism.) Nothing will change. And yet the world will do 'it', change that is, to you to a degree. Change is unavoidable.

If you are reading this book, then chances are you have read other works of a similar ilk. You are probably reading this for the same reason that I have read and now write this sort of thing. It is certainly part of my and I imagine your quest to live as well as possible. To be my best possible version. I need not go into it again, but basically you know what 'living well' feels like. (And have accepted that your living well should never harm others.)

To change or not...was, I said, the first question and decision you need to make. To strive or not to strive as much as possible. The first question, if we do want change, was **what** is 'it' exactly that we want to change and from what to what. Skies and clouds above, 'exactly' is asking too much, even approximately will do. Never mind for now the 'why' questions, though those might well get some curious answers along the way. Whether to change or not is not an easy enquiry to answer; so I keep saying, though it is often responded to in various glib ways by many people. There are times when one simply has to change. Right now I am tackling the situations when we have a specific target for change.

The readiness to address this question simplistically by society has not worked to bring good change of a satisfying, lasting and real nature to individuals or to humanity at large. The second part, once we have answered the what to change to, is the **how** to do it. My methods offer (later) a way by which we can decide to either go for, or decide against, major or minor personal changes of self – or aspects of our selves!

There are three kinds of changes to be had, as I see it:

- Changing outward conduct and thus behaviour.

- Changing inner feeling and thought patterns.

- Changing both.

Clearly, any of the above will affect the other two. Yet changing internally is a deeper and more profound transformation. Sometimes this is necessary, sometimes it is not, to begin with. Depends on what you aim for and how you are currently. Thus, I am moving towards the idea of effective and speedy transformation by at first changing more of the outward-bound behavioural actions. Need I say that one sort of real change always brings with it deeper others? This sounds like the cognitive behavioural mode; however, I am not a behaviourist as such. Nor am I an analyst, a chaser of what your mum did to you. I am not of any one particular persuasion, but I do have my own take on lots of it. I think we can and should take aspects from many schools of thought and practice to build our lives. Which, once again, does not mean we keep every tool forever or discard it after one use!

Finally: change can be had and needs commitment. It is OK to decide not to want to change. But be very careful. In any case, you need more practical, conceptualised knowledge of yourself and how you operate for decision making. Whatever you decide, fool yourself not, for your mind is likely to want to entertain you to a degree.

Abandoning excuses and discovering reasons is part of the solution for better lives. Some 'excuses' were programmed into us, and some we have put there later when things in life got a bit tricky. So, do people always or easily know they are using excuses? I think not, and that is what we are exploring and questioning in this book.

Moving deeper into the idea of 'acceptance' is a very tricky issue. Unless you know everything about everything, the whole idea does not make enough sense.

Many schools of thought have had a lot to say on the need for self-acceptance. Most of this is either an oversimplification, or a lifelong torturous affair needing a great deal of sometimes unusual input. My view, which agrees with many others, is that accepting of the self can only happen as a result of great self-awareness. In any case, the very first question is this:

<u>*If you don't know as much as possible about yourself, then what and who are you trying to accept exactly?*</u>

A lot of self-acceptance is to do with how we feel about ourselves. But none of it is outside of active life issues and situations. But, but, but...even then, what exactly should we accept, what can or cannot, ought or should not be accepted? People have various capacities and ways of being in the world. Some often simple and sometimes complex issues include accepting that one cannot be taller, younger, and cannot fly like a bird etc. I can't sing, don't have a mind for engineering, and so on. We need to and have by and large accepted some obvious facts, for there really is nothing else for it. Yet even these we fight, and sometimes fight too far in total error. Ageing, height, the way we look, just to mention the obviously simple stuff; we fight to be otherwise. Up to a point to fight against dying, ageing, etc. would be all right, but we go too far. Real-life issues, complex and practical ones like having a divorce, the death of a loved one, changing jobs and careers, are at a higher level of complexity and affect us in various ways. These need more thought before 'acceptance' of the way things turned out can be positively integrated. We often try to change things in life, with more or less success. Have you ever seen a hair transplant that was less than laughable? Or bought a business you then found you hated (I did), or took a job that did not work for you, or met the seemingly perfect partner who was a disaster, or whatever?

The usual offerings on self-acceptance suggest that all we need to do is to see what there really is; that's a huge ask already. Then we are told to simply accept that situation, thought, feeling! Terrific, go ahead and do it if you can. Well, all right, maybe if you really could see the total truth of the matter, it may even work, acceptance might just come on automatically by itself. But I can't see how it is possible to 'see' or comprehend or take in the whole truth. Yes, we can work towards it. This book is aimed at doing such work, for what I propose is living more positive and successful lives, ones that will be easier to accept...

The 'Software' of Your Personality

'Choose what you did so you might do what you have chosen.' (I'm sure someone has said this before me, but who?) Many a time we either mistake what there 'really' is, or miss the real point of it. Here, right now, we are talking about self-acceptance, accepting ourselves as things, as we are, rather than accepting all and everything else in the world. I hasten to add though that one is hand in hand with the others, people in the world who always affect our lives. But let's start at home, with self-acceptance, before broadening out.

Accepting the who, what and how you are is the issue. Caution: recall that the self, or selves, the you, is not an isolated thing that you can crystallise out like salt. You cannot leave other people and the world out of your self-concept and self-identity, yet this totality is what you know as you. Now then, is there a need to accept unfair, unfortunate or bad things the world brings to you or to others? The answer is – unfortunately – yes and no, and even maybe, as is usual for such unsolvable propositions. But!

I mean, folks, it'd all make sense if it did, don't it? No, it doesn't. If you could truly accept that this is how you are, and this is how the world is, and this is how things are, then you would be... terrific, or even better! Buddha managed it and perhaps a few others, so we are told. On one hand, it would hurt you less if you could accept what there is now, how you are now, how things are, no matter how bad that is. On the other hand...but, as I think Tevye, the hero of *Fiddler on the Roof* said, is there another hand? I mean, why accept lots of what is truly bad, unfair or dangerous? Why accept that you cannot feed your children? Or that you are being underpaid, or the lies politicians and others would have you believe? Or female genital mutilation? Or total lack of freedom...or accept that some people kill each other because they think you have the wrong beliefs.

We are asking the personal acceptance question as well: should one accept all, even one's worst bits? Should the average crook accept that he is how he is? Clearly there are things more or less acceptable depending on what each of us has been programmed with. Some things are acceptable to all of us, some really are not so, and jail, for example, is not a nice way to live. Crooks create havoc in innocent lives. Let's say that you have accepted your own crooked actions, stole a car and got caught. Here now is a point where acceptance of your own behaviour may be the first step. Accept that you are now in jail. Accept responsibility. Watch and see what you are actually doing in your life, note how you feel, and then actively go and change it (do something about it) for your own enlightened self-benefit. Sounds so ridiculously simple and yet so – evidently – hard to do.

Now then folks, readers, and all: accepting your behaviour is not the same as accepting your self. You have various behaviours, all of which add up to the total self you are or could be. This last sentence will make more sense later when we consider what a 'self' is and how many of them there are and so on... All fun stuff.

Most of us are not crooks, but the scheme is the same. You do something, you get a reward, or the opposite. Having done what you have, you take responsibility and may as well accept the outcome. Then I hear someone in my head asking this question: if things did not work out, is it not better to learn from experience and try again? Yes, it is, but first see and accept the results your actions created. Dem's de choice, man. On many home toilet walls there is a printed copy of the 'Desiderata' that says and enlarges on what I just proposed. A wonderful document that is.

I wish to clearly say this: do not accept particularly your worst bits, do not settle for less, go and change what you can actually change. Then accept what you cannot change. But be careful to know what that is, for it is not so clear or easy to see and know that. At least consider where you are at. Behaviours is what we are taking or leaving, not SELF, OK.

On the other hand (oh yes, there is one when you need it...), there is a great deal of what we need to and must accept and cannot change, and yet we never stop fighting against. Don't waste your time and energy fighting against those things you truly can't change. I have accepted that I will never be a jazz singer, much as I liked the idea, because of the tiny fact that I don't have a voice for it. Nor a footballer, too old now to even try, etc. I have not accepted many other issues in myself or about the world around me. For certain, it would be better if I did accept some more. For example, the fact that I will never understand many things, or that I cannot change or affect the world economy, or that I cannot accept...whatever. I still fight against my own greed and against the greed of the worst sort of rabid capitalism. I still fight against many things in me and out there. I am game to say that I am a person who has deliberately set out and changed much of my life. My efforts and risks did not always turn out for the better. I have known many others who did the same; we did it because of dissatisfaction with our lives. We did not accept what there was. I can say that some of my moves worked well. Others I'd have been better to have accepted as things were. For example, I gave up my retail career to my everlasting regret.

The case for many people is that their lives are often not entirely agreeable enough. That is the very human condition and situation. People often believe that they want or need (or must have) something other than what there is. And as you suspect, so I shall now say: they may or may not be right. What people think they want or need may be good or bad for them or it may be simply out of reach. In this last case, it would be better to see that as a fact – that it is out of reach – and then to settle for what is within reach.

Overall, I agree that there is nothing wrong with 'acceptance' as an ideal to reach for; it is in fact a start point towards change. Providing it is fair dinkum real as an effort, and providing it hurts no one and nothing else, self-acceptance is usually a great place to aim at, to stop at, and to look around and relax into, before embarking on new journeys. The great Buddha had this acceptance thing correct, up to a point. He was right about desires creating problems. For me, however, accepting that you are too poor to feed your family is not on. Being abused, chased or even murdered because one is born Jewish, Tutsie, Black or Gypsy, is not acceptable. Thousands of children dying daily of hunger and disease is unacceptable. And so on and on. I cannot accept all these and much more.

To summarise the important points in this chapter:

- Acceptance of self, behaviours or things in the world is much subtler and trickier than what I have put here, for clearly it is the 'outcomes' we are not supposed to be attached to and (may) need to accept. But this is not an essay on Buddhism so I stay with my simpler model. I have used the idea of 'acceptance' loosely here, wanting to make it clear and thought about.

- Non-acceptance means, it has to, that people need and want things they do not currently have. People may wish to explore and perhaps choose differently what they do, in order to maximise their own (and perhaps others') lives and potential.

- However, people suffer lots because they are unable to reach certain goals they had set, even while they might know or suspect that those goals and aims were always unrealistic, and will stay out of reach.

- We need to be more familiar with what has been input and how that operates on and within us, knowingly or otherwise.

- We need to know what the limits of our body/hard drive and mind/software are – at least for now.

- **The self I want to be ought to be the best possible potential self I can be.** That is the point. This is a process never-ending. A rose starts as a bud, develops, opens, and reaches its best possible form in the circumstance it is grown in. That is truly acceptable.

- **Acceptance** of certain personal behaviours helps to improve the unproductive ones. It is a mighty idea and basically a good one. Start by knowing what there is now, truly. Ask what it is that you should or should not accept in your life. Once that is done, try to accept that situation for now, as the point from which to move forward.

- You are NOT just your behaviours, but they add up to what and who you are!

ஒ

The road ahead of us is curving and splitting again. I need to take what seems like another side-track. Yet it's a way of seeing more of your personal and the personal-global reality. To 'see' is to perceive, to distinguish; it is to differentiate between things inside and outside of yourself.

READ ON about 'AS IF'...

'AS IF' THINKING IS NOT GOOD THINKING/FEELING

A common cliché: 'shit happens'. The thing is though, what sort of manure happens to you and what it smells like depends on your particular individual make-up, situation and givens. And some of that dung, lots of that manure that happens, comes from unexpected sources seemingly from out there. Yet it also seems to come unexpectedly from within yourself.

Years ago the book *When Bad Things Happen to Good People* (Kushner 1978) sold millions of copies. It was not terribly revealing, I think, but the title and the kernel of the main message made it worthwhile, even brilliant. It said that bad things just happen randomly, and that not all bad things turn out actually bad, just as not all seemingly good things turn out to be good for you. Marvellously simple truths. At the time, impressed young fella that I was, I actually contemplated writing a book called *When Good Things Happen To Bad People,* but quickly concluded that the answers would be the same. Life just happens to us in big chunks. Life comes at us in big or small lots, often unwanted, unexpected, unfairly, or luckily. Sometimes good things happen, other times doubtful ones. Not all that happens to us can be controlled, sometimes very little of it.

However, some of what happens in life can be at least seen and understood for what it is. Some of it we can act on, instead of just having knee-jerk reactions. Some we can redirect or change totally. In the end shit happened (in some cases) because that is how you feel about what has happened. One man's bad luck can be good luck to another. A thing that happened to you now, turns out later to have been a lucky one, and vice versa. Such as the young fella who volunteered for the army but was not accepted. He was upset about that but remained alive; his friends did not. You missed out on that house auction and yet the one you bought, you know it is better, so it was lucky you missed the first one. And so on.

Some things that happen seem to have 'no rhyme or reason', accidents that kill a loved one, illness in the young, a partner who decides to leave you. Most of this is often not truly explainable. What you can do about it, about feeling that life is shitty, is the question to tackle. For example, grief after a loved one's death is appropriate, but after a time, one does have to move on. Some things are fixable, many others are not. Leave the ones you cannot tackle. Here is one reason why the unexpected happens. 'As if' is also the underlay for many of our learned behaviours. If it goes too deep and far, then there can be real trouble.

The 'as if' phenomenon.

One thing I think of as a marvel, and everyone is familiar with it to a degree, is the way we often act and talk 'as if' we knew or understood something well. Or 'as if' things were this or that way. Or 'as if' I was always…or never…and so on.

Many fairy tales have covered this subject, like *The Emperor's New Clothes*, you know, when everyone acted as if he had the clothes on while he was buck naked. The politicians act a lot 'as if' they knew or had the ideas. As if they have suddenly become experts overnight on the economy or the army. But we do it in ordinary life amongst often reasonable people as well.

'As if' is how we tend to react when we sort of know something, or believe something or not believe it, etc., and we then act out 'as if' we were experts, or in agreement or in opposition etc. The point is that 'as if' is actually an act, a partial or full lie or pretence, and is useless to us. The 'as if' tendency ranges through small stuff, like when someone asks me if I know who Beethoven was and I reply yes. This is already an 'as if', since I know very little about that composer beyond his fame and perhaps a recognition of some of his music. But when the 'as if' phenomenon refers to more important matters regarding your job, say, and particularly your personal and communicative relationships with others, then employing 'as if' can kick us in the head. When I understand something only 'as if' I did, and assume that I know and then proceed to act on it, trouble may well follow.

What I am very interested in is that many problems arise in life because of this 'as if' thinking, not only when relating to others, but also when relating to one's own feelings and thoughts. Imagine if that 'as if' thinking was applied to the surgeon who has your belly open; a disaster is likely. Imagine all the possibilities that may be open to you in your career, or all your potentials that you are unaware of, or that you think of 'as if' you knew. But what do we really know?

'As if' thinking is what we grow up into almost automatically, and for many various reasons. It was virtually inevitable that we grew up and owned 'as if'. Now we are adults, it is time to drop many of them. 'As if' came about, and still does, because people seem to feel that they 'should' or 'ought to' know something that they often do not really know or comprehend. Most of us are reluctant to admit to what we think of as our ignorance. There seems to be a put-down of yourself if you say: 'I do not know, or I do not understand, please explain again.'[11]

Now, here we are talking about 'as if' mainly in reference to your feelings/thoughts, for the 'as if' inevitably brings with it the 'should and ought' of life. You know, you should (or should not) be doing this or that, and you ought to be able to do blah, blah... There are no 'shoulds' in life...or so I was trained, by various therapists, books and wise men. Ouch, holy rubbish, peppery poppycock... There are 'shoulds' and 'musts' in life, of course there are, just nowhere near as many, or as heavy as we put upon ourselves. As what was put on us! More of this last one later. Suffice to say that if all you get out of this book is that you catch yourself now and then at doing 'as if', then you will have greatly improved your chances of a successful and happy life.

Some of the main points:

- 'As if' is how we tend to react when we sort of know something, or believe something or not believe it, etc., and we then act out 'as if' we were experts, or in agreement or in opposition etc.

- Problems arise in life because of this 'as if' thinking, not only when relating to others, but also when relating to one's own feelings and thoughts.

- There is no 'as if'. You know, or you don't, or you are uncertain. Whichever way, know that this is correct.

---

11 Ask children how much of what they are being told by teachers they truly understand. Half would be good. Perhaps some of this is the teacher's fault, but how can he/she be sure of what is or is not taken in by students?

- There really are some 'shoulds', 'ought tos', and duties in sane living. But nowhere near as many, or the usual ones we most fear or practise.

UNDERSTANDING: 'READING' OTHERS AND YOURSELF

I shall use the words 'reading others and self' in this chapter particularly to mean comprehending, but the word 'reading' when it comes to others and self seems appropriate to me. That is because in the end we are all 'narratives', stories. All the things that happen to us are stories, long or short. I shall go into this later in more depth.

One of the great tragedies of human existence on a personal and on a global scale is what happens to many of us and often – being misunderstood. People do misread others and themselves. Often badly, sometimes disastrously. Some of that is due to the 'reader's' ability to comprehend another person, an incorrect 'reading' of what was offered to us. Some of that is due to what I am reading (you), as it were; perhaps you are communicating badly. There seems to be a rather fixed framework via which we do our *reading of one another*. That fixed framework is what we have learned so far; it is set in virtual jelly and practised time after time. What we know and how we are prejudice our reading.

'Prejudged', bias, bigotry, discrimination all mean rather similar things. Prejudice, goes hand in hand with a great deal, including fear. Something that deviates from my 'normal' reading and expectations can be scary to a greater or lesser degree. Whether it is or is not probably depends on how open you are to things and others you are not familiar with. We need not go too far in this direction, but note that fear and prejudice always go together and form an uroboros, the snake that eats its own tail.

How else to explain murderous anti-Semitism, racism and the like? I mean, have you actually had any bad experiences yourself with some of the people or things you tend not to like? Have you actually had bad experiences personally with a Muslim, Jew, Catholic, black people or, heavens, with men or women, etc.? Or with bolts of lightning, or with sharks, or with boiled camel brain? I doubt it. And even if you had one or two such bad experiences, why apply it to the other 99.99% of that group? Just yesterday I heard a really good one that is funny enough and yet concerning. It is the 13th of October 2015 as I write, not 1685, and a neo-Nazi group in Geelong, Australia, is marching against Muslim migrants, holding placards that say that feminism is a Jewish conspiracy against men... Hmm. And aha.

All your prejudices had come to you as hearsay, as a story, as manipulation by some people who often did not even know they were placing (writing) things into you. Or else they knew very well, and also knew how to best plant it into you. People whom it serves to create fear amongst others are usually dogmatic, often fanatics, Nazis, terrorists and sadly followers of the orthodox religions as well as other unreasonable forms of lives. Unfortunately, one cannot propose that such lowly life forms are the uneducated or the poor or the rich or the clever. The pain of being a bigot is distributed amongst many people. They all share in gross ignorance and act in error. Enough on that sad subject.

So what's going on? Why is another person, belief system value, communication – all of which are narratives – why are they so hard to accurately read-interpret?[12] We shall address this further

---

12 Note that I am using 'story' or 'narrative' interchangeably for now.

later with more tools in our hands and some of it will become obvious as we move on.

※

Earlier we looked at metaphors and how that language instrument works in human lives. If thought and language are, as it seems obvious by now, extremely metaphoric, then we can say with some comfort that a person **is** and **does** metaphors within their own '**narratives**' (life-living stories) as his or her total concept of self, behaviours and being. Understanding something by using metaphors is not only a literary affair but the way minds operate basically (and of course it is not so basic either).

This is where I was aiming to get to; metaphors offer an ability to open and free the intellect from the tyranny of conditioning, if used creatively and with *reinvention and re-intention*. Due to overwhelming spoken (and unspoken) societal pressure to adapt to conventional standards of beliefs, we find it almost impossible to easily accept new ideas and experiences that are outside of the (our) norm. Some of this is needed, but it makes it harder to stay open and so it can restrict our ability to change our own actions and lives. And, it certainly can and does bring prejudice and rules into daily living, often stifling internal and external creativity. All of which then will reduce our ability to read others correctly, or to keep our fears at bay – and even to understand our own internal workings and motivations.

Let me repeat an earlier focus: once we have a way to conceptualise and understand our individual self and thus our features and givens, we can then explore what is possible for us to achieve in every or any way – for you to achieve to become the best possible version of yourself. That progress will increasingly allow you to see the processes of your personality in clearer terms, leading to better use of your personal capabilities and talents. And more – to the better use of our time, energy and relationships in your current situation. Some Indian swami once said that if you know one piece of clay, then you know all the clay in the world. I am not so interested in clay but am curious about me and you. So, my version is that you can know and comprehend others correctly only to the degree that you can 'read' and understand yourself. No separation of the two makes sense. How can I comprehend you if I do not know myself? How can I know myself and yet have little or no understanding of you?

We said that a metaphor was something that explained something else in totally different terms. We also quickly considered our metaphoric and thus 'narrative' nature and touched upon the idea of how our memory operates as our very identity.

Now, people of the revolution, friends and foes, readers of all sorts, experts and beginners…I shall explore these concepts of **memory equals self**, and that you are your narrative and **your narrative is you**, later.

First, and soon, you will have to cope with, and test-think my 'personal computer' metaphor/analogy for the self and its doings. That chapter is a metaphor in itself, a tool to help our conceptualisation and understanding of ourselves and the world we live in. The PC metaphor (or is it analogy?) is not and does not need to be very accurate, technically speaking, or operate 100% on a moment-to-moment basis. It will work, even if I am incorrect about the usage of computer features and computing buzz words. When we are looking at our complex self/minds, and all that is contained in them, us poor mortals simply cannot explain, understand, visualise or conceptualise our self and actions and behaviours (by whatever words) as such, without easier, humbler descriptions. The PC analogy/metaphor is one that is modest, and yet by these days' standards it is very understandable, as I shall offer it.

I insisted that little or no psychological or philosophical jargon is necessary to know yourself better. However, we do need concepts, words – a certain way to form a lively picture of ourselves. Before I move to the PC analogy, we will first briefly explore some errors of human judgement, and then the very important idea of 'features and benefits' (outcomes).

Some errors of history and thought

What a laugh it is to read a history book written 100 or 300 years ago. They lied, cheated, misunderstood and often had no real knowledge of what actually happened. Keep this in mind as you consider your personal history.

Now, I assume, as many others have, that what people really want is that larger purpose and meaning that leads to satisfaction/peace/happiness, by whatever word. Yet what people want or believe in, their purposes and meaning, is often turned into false and often dangerous or even terrifying actions. People seem to realise intrinsically that without purposeful meaning it is not possible to have lasting satisfaction. Fair enough. But what if you find meaning in being a terrorist who blows up innocent people in the marketplace…? Or you think that it is OK to steal, or if you believe in the worst form of exploitative (even if legal) capitalism? Or if you believe that only your version of the biblical or other fairy tales are right, and on and on the list could go…what then? How is it that some people find meaning in shooting 100 young children? Not an area I will enter further, except to differentiate it by categorically saying that madness is not 'meaning', it is just madness. Likely, it is born out of having NO properly formed 'self', no rational meaning or true purpose in life. (Remember that purpose is to become the best possible self you can be. This excludes being the best shooter, crook or drug addict, for all those activities are really bad for you.)

All life already has that overarching purpose: to become the best it can be of its nature, and to reproduce, giving further life. It would all be relatively easy to cover this whole problem of meaning and purpose if one believed in a God out there, some sort of a force that creates, drives and decides about the universe, people, nature and so on. For me (and for many), that is not the case. I neither believe nor need the God assumption as to what purpose there is for human beings. There are some interesting catchphrases such as 'God helps those who help themselves', and good advice helping yourself certainly is. The God idea, by the way, is at best yet another metaphor, and it stands for many things to many people.

Looking in the past for that one big one, Purpose and Meaning, the one out of this world or the one in the next world…it was, it seems to me, a big mistake, an error aided by ignorance, fear, superstitions and outdated data. Yet perhaps humanity had to progress and go through all that? I don't know and it does not now matter, given the past cannot be changed. Then again, the past can also be looked at, considered and honestly evaluated. I won't go into it, but so much of what we had been told was true about God, religion and various superstitions was ridiculous. Much, perhaps most of it, has now been proven to be lies propagated by those few whom it served.[13] Your part is still all wrapped up in the particular dogma of the religion you happened to be born into; it is not easy to get past that sort of programmed loading.

---

13 Just see what you get if you google modern Bible studies; there is no primary or even secondary proof for much of what we were told. No proof that Moses or Jesus ever existed. No proof for so many stories that it is a wonder why anyone still believes what men of the church sold to the masses.

We want to do as well as we can, in at least a personal way. So we say. Unfortunately, our ambitions can sometimes be horribly twisted; the strive-drive can make killers as well as positive, creative people. The 'striving' can be fuelled by the same basic needs, and yet mistaken; error-laden psyches and inner programs and beliefs can lead to awful outcomes. Enough of this, I still trust and hope that Socrates was right 2500 years ago: he said that no one truly wants to do themselves harm. So, the human monsters act in grave and sad error.

Now a brief but real sidestep is needed. What follows is a true tool of being human. It is laughingly simple, this tool – asking questions. But it is not as simple as it seems, while it is certainly easy to use.

Good questions provide good answers; therefore, bad questions will bring...

If you take nothing else from this book but this part of this chapter, and you learn to use it better and on purpose more often, you will find huge rewards.

You will have noted my insistence that one explores by asking questions, how else? Many people do not differentiate between the various forms of asking the **right** questions at the right time. Basically there are two forms: open and closed questions.

1. Open questions start with or include words such as 'how, what, who, where, when, why' and the like. What distinguishes open from closed questions is that open questions cannot be answered by a yes or a no. Try it.

2. Closed questions are such as include: 'will, or can you, does, shall' etc. All closed questions can be answered with a yes or no as they tend to call for a decision.

The point is not whether either form is better or worse, but that we use the right one for the right purposes. So, if I need more information about anything, then I am better off asking an open question. If I need a decision, then I may be better off asking a closed one. For example: 'Shall we buy this?' can be answered with a yes or no. It can also be answered by a longer sentence, but it will nudge you closer to a decision (salespeople, note). An example of using open questions: 'How do you feel about this car?' Now this can be answered with a nod of the head or a shake, but it will give you more 'story' to go on.

The correct usage of open and closed questions applies to everything from making a sale, doing a big deal, asking for a date, or challenging the kids' behaviour. I am putting it all very briefly and simply. But the crunch is this:

Ask yourself the correct questions to get better answers and possible solutions to problems, large or small

Imagine exploring yourself with a question like 'how do I feel?' This needs more than a yes or no answer. Of course, you will have to pick up on something you might think/feel as your answer. For example, my answer right now is that I am concerned as to whether this section is necessary in this book. My next question is to ask myself why, and what concerns me...and so on. Opposed to this, suppose I put to myself a closed question like 'do I need this?', and answered with a yes or no. That would tell me no more info about what's bothering me.

The 'Software' of Your Personality

I wish I knew all this when I was a young single fella. Imagine what asking proper open questions would have done for me when trying to get a date. Because open questions do something extra and terribly important – they **show interest**. Closed questions ask for a decision and could often be better couched in a more open way. For example: Do you want to go out with me? Easy to answer with yes or no and that's the end of the story. Instead, suppose I said, 'How would you feel about a date?' At least I will get more than a shake of the head yes or no.

Try using the appropriate questioning method with your spouse, at work, when making a deal, yes, all that, but the point for us is to use the idea when exploring our own mind, feelings, thoughts, problems and so on. By the way, doing this is way better in writing than just in your head.

Next, we have arrived at what I think is a most important notion that is rarely discussed sufficiently, that of personal Features leading to life Outcomes.

A few important points in this chapter:

- Truly knowing and understanding the right questions and methods of asking and listening is one easy and terribly important skill.

- Possibly the greatest skill anyone can have is the ability to 'read' others correctly. That needs very good understanding of yourself.

FEATURES LEAD TO OUTCOMES THAT ARE BENEFICIAL, OR THE OPPOSITE!

It is not necessary to go into whether the entire universe or a piece of rock has a purpose or meaning. Yet, as we have already discussed, living things, animals and plants, do seem to *strive to become the best sort* of whatever they are. Allow me to repeat that: living things strive to be the best kind they can be in the circumstances they happen to be in. Given enough water and soil quality, a tree will grow to be its maximum height, shape and colour as imprinted by its genetic material. To be the best sort of its type is – it may be said – the tree's in-built genetic, biologically innate *purpose*.[14] Given the right environment, an animal will strive to eat, live and reproduce according to its in-built, genetically determined features, instincts and imperatives. I won't stretch too far; there is sufficient scientific agreement on the idea that living things strive, struggle and 'attempt' to fulfil their biological imperatives of reproduction and to become the best of their sort.

---

14 No suggestion about the tree being aware of this; that's another unnecessary discussion for us.

Why are we here? We just are. Is the question a wasted effort?

So then simply and again, when people are looking to see what we are searching for and why, our purpose as humans, it may boil down to no more than that people also have the imperative to become the best sort each of us can be.[15] There is already a tonne of meaning inherent in looking at life this way. So, how do we do our human striving? We are looking for certain good **outcomes,** ones that we think might convert to **benefits** that are good *solutions,* leading to *happiness* and *satisfaction*. This, I suggest, will do as the specification for **'the best version of self we can be'**. However, this huge idea, ridiculously simple as it sounds, I caution, can get loose, clouded and out of control if we're not careful.

Satisfaction and meaning are on the same track as the big Purpose and Meaning, but they are, or can be, error-laden, at least on the practical, everyday level. For example, we might (and often do) mistake making money for making meaning. '...It ain't necessarily so...' as the Bible goes. Then again, to a hungry person, the lack of money will likely make finding meaning/purpose impossible.

The actual activity of finding purpose/meaning is a 'doing' thing – not only a thinking part. It is being dynamic and vigorously taking or changing actions. Discovering meaningful purpose as a personal and aimed-for goal is an actual movement, commitment and an effort. Your body biology has in-built 'striving'; it is already a well-supplied tool. By the way, I am always talking about purpose and meaning as a healthy version, one that brings true satisfaction to the individual but does no harm to others or to the good earth. Now a lot of this is common sense – I hear you

---

15 The 'why' question, by the way, is totally pointless, unless you have religious faith, and even then, what do you expect from it?

say – and it is, but stick with my line of thinking as it leads us on. You know, the guru said to the disciple, 'Follow me and I'll take you where I'm going'... (I am no guru, don't wish to be, and you must never be a disciple to anyone.)

We all know that people seem at the very least to need and want some things. Finding our goals and aims moment to moment can be up there in the clouds or down here making the next curry, or a big business deal, planting a tree, playing with the kids, or finding the right intimate relationship. All this, however, is not the deeper, big Purpose and Meaning humans are searching and crave for, though they all play a necessary part. Goals and aims are on the way, part of the process of finding the big P & M. So, on the ground, in everyday living, we might call what we actually do **goals or aims**, the things we reach out for thinking that such actions will give us the good life. All we need to understand first is that a conscious being (like you) has purposes even while you are (surprisingly) unlikely to know what they are! And worse: what they could or might be. I propose that we are not even certain about our goals and aims. Perhaps, due to our very biology, the way our brain/mind/emotional make-up is structured, we do not and cannot know all our purposes (beyond the obvious ones like begetting children etc.). Suffice to say, I also suggest that you have, can have, more than one purpose.

I reiterate: we as humanity, you and I as individuals, may be looking for ways to improve our lives. That is an activity that will, if correctly motivated, lead to finding more meaning and purpose. In this book, I am not intending to unravel universal philosophical problems, just the smaller human ones, which are big enough! Thus, let us look now at what we need to see and urgently comprehend, that being: *how to find out and understand what our individual features are.* This issue of finding out about your true individual features has been little understood or tackled.

Features?

We are looking for not the ones you already know, though it is necessary to consider them as part of the whole. Nor the ones your parents or society told you that you have (they may be correct or not), although once again you need to consider them as well. The issue is to dig down, sort out, get to know what features You Do actually have – either active or likely dormant within.

Ho ho ho, seems like a little sidetrack at first...but not really.

Everything is cause and effect, that is for certain. Choices, do we have them?

> *'The cause of anything is just everything, or is it the other way round?'*
>
> (Atkinson 2015)

Anything that occurs, or does not happen, be it a physical or a mental event, has a cause. All causes obligate an outcome/effect, so all effects/outcomes have had a cause, whether we can see the cause or the effect, or not. This is an undeniable universal scientific fact. Our personal 'purposes' (or lack of them) drive all the causes and the attached variations of consequences that we 'bring' into our life (or push out of it) in practice. Another circular rather than linear idea, for input follows output, and each causes the other to carry on loop-like, endlessly.

> *Human lives look, seem linear: we are born, get older and die. A trip from here to there. Yet what we do enact, find in science and in human affairs is that many things are not either 'this' or 'that', but rather this and that. Much in life 'feeds' on its own 'tail'; causes beget effects that in turn become causes.*

We are not about to deeply debate the cause-effect nature of the world. That appears to have no start or end, a never-ending affair that again is not needed here for us. Nothing magical or mystical there, just the laws of nature operating. A brief consideration and exploration of how this cause and effect operates on a simple everyday model for people will do us. We do need to develop a notion of it, so we can then direct our own lives a little more as we want to, living life less by accident and more on purpose! What we 'cause' will have an outcome that is inevitable, so then, can we 'cause' something with a likely better outcome? What follows that thought is the question about choices.

Choice and decision-making

Cause and effect employ – so to speak – as the underlying dynamic the three notions of **Features** leading to **Outcomes** to fulfil some **Purpose**; we shall call it FOP for short. This triumvirate drives the cause and effect in human lives, in everyday experiences.

I use 'benefit' and 'outcome' interchangeably, but please note that people are always looking for a positive outcome/benefit that actions (or lack of actions) might bring. And I press this because some outcomes can be, and often are, negative, unwanted, unplanned for and unexpected. All this is organic and straightforward, I reckon: FOP holds and works true about your body parts, organs, eyes, and so on, as discussed earlier. FOP also includes your thoughts, feelings and actions, all of which are included in your character or 'personality' that incorporates and (hopefully) integrates all your talents, features, genetic givens, disposition, attitudes and so on.

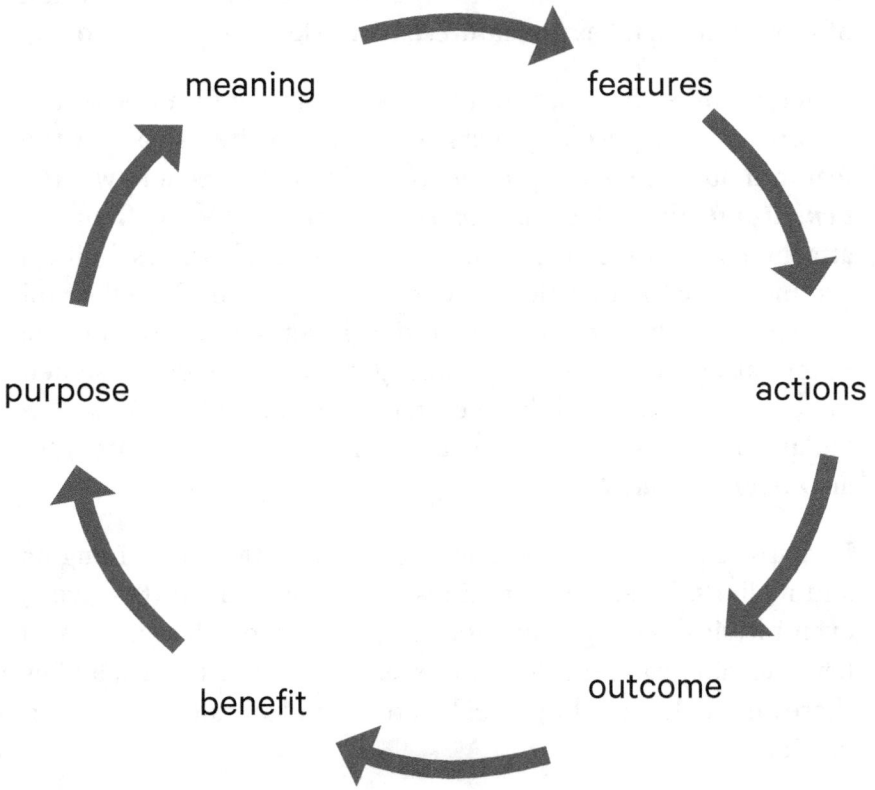

The above visually shows the steps as I see them, one leading to the other. But I have simplified the movement to just Features-Outcomes-Purpose.

Note the first step after features is 'action'. Without that we are dead-ended. Action utilises and activates your unique personal in-built 'features'. The better you know them, the more so! The dictionary meaning of 'feature' is: a distinctive attribute or aspect of something, or someone. Even if one has never thought about it in just this way, we can see that people, dogs, flowers, the stars, trees, animals, cars, pens, money, cameras and so on all have certain built-in givens, what we call features. Everything has features. All things alive or not certainly share this much: they all have several features! To me this is an amazing fact precisely because it's a universally applicable idea. (Try to think of something that has no features...let me know if you find one.)

When it comes to, say, products, like a camera or a house, the features are purposefully designed into such items so that the featured purpose of the product provides a planned and wanted ***benefit-outcome***! Such *outcomes* we call a specific **'benefit'** attached to a specific product. When manufacturers build a product, an early question will be the 'what's this for, who will want it and why' enquiry. Once that is settled and seen to be potentially popular (a money-making idea), a product is designed or redesigned, and will have certain new and old features. The end product – I say it again because it is so important – provides an ***outcome/benefit***.

Perhaps it is less obvious that even non-matter, like thoughts and feelings, love, hate, opinions and ideas of all sorts – wow, even physical feelings, like hot or cold, pain or pleasure – also have certain 'features'. Enough already, features exist; each of us shares many human biological features and we all have certain particular ones.

People are not products though, eh? And we were not 'designed' except by accidental evolution. Aha. Actually, though, are we not kind of products? Has not much been kind of *designed – programmed, constructed* – into us from the day we were born? Wait a minute now and take this in deeply. We certainly and obviously do have evidently 'given' features, the ones we were born with: height, weight, mental ability, to name a few. Also potentials for personality/character. Our very own personal features develop as they do, BUT are also added to by education and programming by parents and society. Some of my features are inevitable, like I am short and now bald; others have been involuntarily added in by my circumstances, like I am a man and a refugee. Still others I have learned from Mum and society, and some I had to modify to my own needs and flavouring. That is fine as it is, so far.

The undeniable fact is that the universe and our world is unpredictable and good or bad 'luck' can and does happen. Much of that is not foreseeable nor (sometimes) accountable. Worse still, there is not much we can do about much of it…yes? Well, yes and no. Not much at times, true, but we can certainly take some actions at other times! That is if, and only if, we are living with intent, purpose and awareness. So what's the problem? And there seem to be a lot of problems in life.

Interacting with others and our selves we employ both our known and set features, and some unknown ones. The known world and the personal situation that we live in, and the unknowable future experiences that we imagine may come our way, they all do depend (somewhat) on our features. The past and the imagined future call to us and we use what we have to meet each day. Now the point is this:

Our personal features drive and determine what purpose-benefit we can reach towards

Features and benefits touch one the other; it is one movement not two and just like cause and effect they cannot be separated. The whole FOP is inseparable, for every cause will bring about an effect/outcome and this will cause the next…and so on, blah blah. But what we know not, and mostly cannot predict, is what exact actions will bring what outcomes. Yes, we can predict some consequences with reasonable accuracy. Smoke and you will be prone to more health problems. Steal, and you will end up in prison, drive too fast and accidents are more likely. One day your husband will smile if you call him a 'fool' and on another day he takes offence. You mortgage the house and invest in shares and make a lot of money, only to lose it years later. You decide to get married and find yourself divorcing later in life. One could go on...but not me, I reckon you intelligent readers got the idea. Bash your children and they won't be happy, don't work and you will be hungry, and so on. So on and on, including not only banal but also the much larger issues. We cannot predict the outcomes of many things that would really count.

Our meaning as persons may be (usually is) sewn up into our currently 'activated' purposes. Often we are stuck in the set-up, and sometimes not very comfortably. What we strive towards will bring meaning...and real meaning has and does in turn provide clearer purposes. Even if at the moment we are just wanting a smaller outcome like a better relationship with someone, or a pay rise.

Your individual features drive what you can do, be, achieve?

Restating: it is clear that nature has a purpose that it carries through biologically. Nature and everything in it is preprogrammed to behave in certain known and unknown but specific ways. Both intuition and the sciences of physics, biology and chemistry have proven to us that we can reliably believe certain rules and laws of nature. 'What goes up must come down' – certain things might happen sometimes in more complex ways, but that expresses what I am trying to say. Some causes have obvious effects/outcomes, and some less so. Most of nature deviates very little from its own imperatives. Evolution and change happen very slowly. Natural outcomes can be not just one, but a range, yet still set within boundaries. That is to say that what goes up must come down, but it can do so at various speeds depending on its weight. And that bigger or smaller cows are born, but never the size of a chicken. That no human being can fly by flapping arms and so on.

Sounds like all is predetermined then

> *IS DETERMINISM A DIRTY WORD? Science and life can at first appear to be rather predetermined. As we said, cows, dogs and roses turn out to be very much within a predetermined range. For people – conscious beings – it is more complex. Determinism does not always go versus freedom of choice. The whole complex question is, you guessed it, not necessary for our work here, but some of it needs investigating.*

I am not a determinist, nor do I believe that we have unlimited free will. Rather, I experience that we have some (seemingly?) free will and many somewhat or entirely determined non-choices. The wars, the good or bad luck, the situations one is born into, and much more, all play a part in both free will and in determinism for me as an individual. It is worthwhile to note that acting intentionally on something facing one is not necessarily the same as being pre- or in any way determined. Note I said 'necessarily' for one cannot be certain even about this. We might be basically determined by our givens, but perhaps we can and do still act with some intent and will. And do so within the (likely) determined boundaries of what is possible for each of us.[16]

We are back to features, many of which are indeed predetermined and built-in, and later perhaps 'constructed' by you and others.

---

16 To explore all that deeply is emphatically not – yet again – needed here.

Folks rush about an awful lot; we study, we learn, we work, we ask questions, we provide answers, we give and take advice. We earnestly believe that there are proper ways of doing things. Sometimes we think that there is some benefit in doing things in better or in different ways. All this is undeniably and very obviously true to anybody who has ever looked at learning to play football, or considered starting a business, or to anyone who has children or indeed to anyone alive who wants to do anything better, for any or no reason at all.

Let's go back for a moment to the plants, stars, animals, cars, pens, money, love, feelings, thoughts. All these things have something in common, an underlying purpose, a reason to be, driven by their features and outcome-benefits.

Consider now that all our individual body parts – organs, eyes, molecules, brain cells, whatever – all have their own individual *features and outcome-benefits,* and therefore can be said to have a major purpose indeed. Plainly, each part of your body has a 'job' to do to keep you well and alive. Your eyes see, but do not do the job of your liver (I hope) and so on. Your brain may tell you to run, but it needs the legs and heart to move, and so on.

When one of our organs plays up, you are said to be ill, unable to operate properly. When things go wrong with our health, we are also affected by psychological fears and worries. The brain/mind/emotional self has its own particular ways of being well or unwell, as everyone knows. The brain/mind, even after great advances, is still perhaps the least known or understood part of being human. Yet, the brain/mind seems to be the most important part of what we abstractly call our 'self', a person.

From here on in, and interchangeably, I will use brain/mind and consciousness to mean much the same thing, for that is all I need. Note that I use brain/mind as a one-off concept, even while I know this is assailable and not entirely correct. However, it will serve us well enough to be thinking of brain/mind and consciousness as the self. And in truth, no brain means no mind.

When the mind is unsettled, the body hungry, when fears attack, or if illness is present, people cannot reach for the best version of themselves. You cannot use your positive features, your mind or body when it is unwell as productively as you can when it is clear and unfettered. I will not go into truly ill minds, schizophrenia or any other psycho or socio pathology, or mechanical body problems, because I aim to discuss the 'norm', average lives and minds (go ahead, laugh at 'normal'). Still, everyone has a reasonable conception of the 'normal/average' term and that will suffice for our dialogues.

I repeat: to get desired outcomes, people use (knowingly or not) their personal givens or features. Although you and I may decide on wanting exactly the same benefit/outcomes (we both want what we think and believe are positive outcomes), the result will be dictated by each of our particular features, i.e. whether our individual features were suitable to achieve the right end results. Let's say we thought you and I had the features needed for a particular outcome. I may in the end find the outcome beneficial and you may find the same outcome not so beneficial after all. Surprise! Even though you said that it was what you wanted. Many people wish to make more money when what they really need is not money but...(fill in as you like).

Alternatively, you have achieved what you wanted, but I did not. You did – and I did not have – the features and givens needed after all. Mistaken beliefs by at least one of us? That is life. For a rather silly example, consider that we both want to fix my leaking toilet, but you are a plumber and I am not. I am not given to handyman jobs; you are not given to book writing. So, the above stands, even if we both had the same plumbing purpose-outcomes in mind. (No smelly puns intended...) Also, either of us may find the result good or bad, or even puzzling, or perhaps uncertain.

Or we both move to the country because that's what we both believe we want. We work hard to achieve this and do it. After a while I say I don't like it, you say you do. 'Oh,' says I, 'I must have moved to the wrong place, that's why'...and so I move to another country place only to find...

Or you want to be a singer, but you have no voice, or you believe that your dissatisfaction is to do with your wife, or you lack of money and fame – look at poor old Robin Williams, rich, famous, well loved. Still, all that was not enough, or not right for him? Don't know.

Or you are doing fine as a salesperson, but think you want to be an artist. You have some talent perhaps, but you don't think you can afford the time or cost to learn. Or you don't believe in your talent, or you have too many other commitments, and so on... What is missing in all these cases is, maybe not only but certainly partly, this:

The appropriate and reasonably accurate self-awareness of one's features and givens.

Our question is always this: what aims, goals or purposes can your features-talents truly build for you? What is really possible for you, and equally, what is not? You can be just about anything at all if you really try? That is and always was idiotic nonsense.

If we are unsure of our purpose(s), and thus features, we might pick goals that bring little more than temporary satisfaction – or misery. Hence, those who chase nothing but wealth can never get enough. We can easily mistake goals and aims for our big P Purpose. 'Category' error. Or we find we simply can't get to our set goals. Or that having achieved our goal, it is after all not so satisfactory. All these are *outcomes* that can happen. Inevitably, mistakes, good and bad luck are what we make and receive on life's rocky roads. Still, they are a sure sign that we are moving, that we are actually doing something. What exactly, and whether it is worthwhile, and whether it can be done, is another story we will consider.

'Socrates said that the unexamined life is not worth living. But what if the examined life turns out to be a clunker as well?' (I think it was Kurt Vonnegut who said this.)

I will be suggesting some ideas and procedures, certain ways of thinking/feeling that will or might be helpful, if and only if you take them on board and actually take action. Meanwhile, a participant in a workshop on communications and relationships once asked me this reasonable question: if you are so smart, why are you not successful, entirely happy and very rich? The question may have occurred to you too. If it has not, perhaps it should have. My cautious answer is that I am OK, I have done what I could in my life and relationships and I am not unsuccessful in either area. I have been, I know now, limited by my own confines, the background I was born into that had to be left behind, and my features, my preprogramming etc. It took me nearly all my life to realise some of the things I might have achieved, if I had comprehended them earlier. Some of that knowledge is too late to put into larger practice now. Others, like writing this book, are just right for timing and for my current available abilities and situation. Am I happy and satisfied then? Not entirely, actually far from it. But I am equally far from the other stinky end as well, and closer to the good end. I am at a stage that is all too human.

The old red herring again: 'money does not make happiness'. Yeah right. But almost everyone wants money. OK, but in the end, often *money may not bring more than a better class of misery*. There are poor people for whom more income would be very helpful, and yet they are happier than many rich ones. There are multimillionaires who give up the high life and go planting trees. There are highly successful academics who eventually change to simpler things, and others who go from simple lives to complex ones. I cannot argue the right way to live and I won't. I was a businessman and nowadays I think I may have been happier as an academic or a writer. Or...?

There is no such a thing as the one and only correct way to live. All human wisdom tells you that and yet religion tells you there is, and that it's all about their particular God. Category error, big time, sorry. Just one question though, and then I shall leave the devout: why do they need to convince others by words, deeds, and why are they (mostly) such hypocrites? And if all of them think theirs is the only right way...and yet only one can be right (according to all of them) then, well, folks, all the others need to be wrong, but which ones?

To find the real questions of life that are important to address, one must start by asking what your particular possibilities/features are! That is the main issue!

The very stuff of life, the purpose of your existence is to find out the purpose of your existence... (which is simple enough and I won't repeat it again). Do it here and now, on the ground, in this world, and living with other people in your society. Why worry about anything else but making the best of your life while you are here. Finding yourself, your features and purposes is the only way to find lasting comfort, emotional equilibrium, and satisfaction for your own life.

※

By the way, researching your features needs you to ask yourself good and productive questions, and to enter what is often a partially closed and hiding mind. When we are digging to unearth our features, goals and end purposes, when we truly explore beliefs and values, or relationships, we need to sincerely look deeply inside of ourselves. And what we are always looking at is **relating** – relationships to everything, to others and to yourself, and how those add the glue to our lives, holding it together in every way.

'*The world is not a number, nor an equation. It is a concrete particular inhabited by physical objects and some of them appear to be causally related to others.*' (Mumford & Anjum 2013) A modest statement that is perhaps too modest, since without it, without being related, no existence appears to be possible.

Getting to know your true features; you already know many of them

Oh dear, here I go again: a feature is whatever brings about a specific or variable outcome. Some features have only a limited range of possible outcomes; others are open and *seemingly* endless. Individuals have several features; some people have more and some even more, or perhaps less. That's just genetics and biology; it can't be helped. You got what you got, right? No and yes, as usual. Things can be improved up to a point.

Exploration – if well done – usually leads to discovery. Research will lead to finding previously perhaps unknown features of yourself. That will show where and what can or might be 'value-added' to your life. For example, my height can't be helped, but lack of education can. I may as well give up wanting to be a jazz singer, or to have a career in politics, or whatever. Then again I find that I can write reasonably good books in English in spite of the fact that it is not my original language. And I have also found that I can actually do...

By finding what features you truly do have, you automatically become more aware of what you in fact don't really have. *Sometimes, when you find you don't have a particular feature, that is all you need to know.* You may need to settle and accept that you don't have certain other features that you always believed you had. That will be a relief and a bit of grief too. Not all of life is within your power to change or direct; you likely cannot make someone love you if they don't, you were born into your society and culture not another, and at this time. You may be a great technician but a rotten picker of the share markets (who isn't) – just for a few examples. Sometimes mere awareness will improve things almost by itself, but usually action is called for. You will never get some things, never be some things. Leave them. Do not spend precious time and energy in the wrong direction. Some stuff is not for you. Some is. You cannot do a number of things, and you've never had certain attributes. Accept it and move on.

Thus you can, once you better know all this, give up some tiresome practical and mental stuff. Some of that may feel sad; one does not easily give up long-held hopes that blah and blah blah. Yet some of it will feel like you are freeing yourself. Usually both. In any case, giving up hopeless stuff and tasks will give you more energy for what you can do.[17]

---

17   It is truly astonishing how many people are work addicts and then complain about the lack of a good intimate relationship. Or trouble with the kids, or loneliness and emptiness or...

By the way, have you heard of the Jewish businessman who sent his partner an email that said, 'Start worrying, details to follow'?

ॐ

For those people who are in business, selling, buying, negotiating, communicating, and for those in personal relationships – so for everyone then – it may be already obvious that features, outcome/benefits and purposes are concepts and actions that may be also characterised as forms of communication. Does this sound surprising? A salesman would call some of what I have offered 'selling techniques', whilst a doctor would call it good therapeutic communication, a psychologist or a philosopher would call it therapy or deeper thinking, or…whatever. No surprise needed when one realises that all a person can and does do is 'communicate' by every action taken, by one's very existence as well as by words and actions.

Therefore:

Your personal features – we keep asserting – also include your belief and value systems, education level, current life situation, hopes, dreams, aims and goals. You were not actually born with any of these in detail, not really. These are of course early and later inputs. They have constructed your thinking-feeling-doing self in an ongoing way. I tease out the concept of 'hope' as a special case. Is hope what we all need to have? Yes and no as usual! Often we have built unrealistic and even idiotic undoable hopes and expectations. We do that to make life better or to act like things are what they are not. People use false 'hope' all too often, sometimes to not see what there truly is, or what there can in fact be. We waste our life, our time waiting – for 'hopeful' things. We think, we hope, that God or someone will be good to us, that life will be fair… Well, maybe, but probably not.

Something like this was said rather audaciously each week in an old Australian TV comedy show: 'Do it to yourself, for no one can do it to you like you can do it to yourself...!' More seriously, consider the quote below, but exclude supernatural intervention or hope:

'Hope is the enduring belief in the attainability of fervent wishes, in spite of the dark urges and rages which mark the beginning of existence. Hope is the ontogenetic basis of faith, and is nourished by the adult faith which pervades patterns of care.' (Eric Erikson 2001)

I worry about 'faith' building in anything other than people and the good earth. Still, faith is needed in something, in you and in life. Way too much, and yet I reckon not enough, has been sanely said about 'hope' over the ages. All this hooks into an earlier discussion. You can only truly hope for something if that is realistic and if you know where you are going, and what you **can** do. If you know what, and how, other people fit in with your hopes, and if you actually have done the work of reaching out towards what you want, then and only then is a hope an attainable, realistic one. Otherwise it is **false** hope; it is just wishing, not wanting to see and face the facts of life. Not much hope you will win the lottery, is there? That is a wish, not a hope, of course, and us silly humans do mistake wish and hope as if they were the same. That I wish I was young again applies to me. I may wish etc., but I know there is no hope at all that I will be young again. How about hope that this book becomes a bestseller? It's a wish that can become a real hope if I do several things to give it a chance and if the book itself is good.

※

Clearly, the concept of FEATURES already has many features. To me, this means that the idea has depth. Plainly, *people are born* with various physical and mental features that might press them towards certain specific goals, aims and purposes that will eventually equal 'life solutions'. Many of these cannot be altered at all; some – like, say, physical fitness – might be improved. But basically, 'you are set like a jelly'.

The features that we often call character, personality, talent or abilities come from and are input by parents and the socio-cultural situation we are born into. A huge input of our features comes from 'learned' input, particularly during the early years of life, and mostly from our parents and schooling. The two inputs, genetic givens and life experience, work together inseparably. Obviously, learning and experiencing goes on till one dies – as does our individual acceptance or rejection of our own features that we experience from time to time.

The positive outcome-benefits, the ones you want and aim for that I spoke of earlier, can only come from having enough of the right sorts of 'givens and learning', that is from your actual features. Benefits are, can only be, the resulting outcomes of whatever **features I have**, and have **activated**. There are 'benefits-outcomes' we may never achieve – I have said it before and say it again – because we simply do not have the right features for them. This brings far more unhappiness than is currently realised. Do not waste time and lives on them.

Some of our features that we are aware of we like, some we do not; thus they can be wanted or not wanted! I am interested in digging up, finding, even building on those of your features that you are unaware of. The unknown features, by the by, operate within you; they are you! Your unknown parts are a bit like the 'car' driving you, rather than you driving the car. I am equally interested in considering the features that I know I have and don't want (like my short fuse, say) as well as those I like and want to use. But it is most important to unearth those features that you may have but are unaware of!

I make the above ideas and suggestions on universal grounds of learning, from my own personal experiences, and from observation and research of myself and of other people. Thirty-two years of facilitating human relationships workshops and of workshops on selling, marketing and the psychology of human behaviour in general has taught me that *much human disappointment and misery happens because we as individuals do not know what features we truly do or do not have.*

Restated: we don't know enough about what real features we have that are working for or against one another (us). I will return to these problems, calling them the causes of our 'inner and outer conflicts', later, from another angle.

The social contract

One factor in life for everyone is the 'social contract' we have tacitly agreed to. We abide by the local laws, and/or agree to do something for someone in exchange for his or her doing something in return for us, either now or in the future. We do this because on some level we believe – and it is possibly true – that the 'exchange' works to our benefit, as it does to the other person's. You scratch my back and I'll scratch yours is an old cliché and a truth...up to a point.

Sometimes we know we are doing this *selling,* doing favours, helping out etc., and yet many other times we do not know we are doing the deed, perhaps mainly for our own, as yet unperceived, below awareness benefit (or supposed benefit). Everything, from family relationships to world economy, rests on the fundamental human behaviour that Rousseau called the

The 'Software' of Your Personality

'social contract'. I am simplifying it but you get the idea. Keep this in mind as we proceed.

For now, let us settle on the notion that you have whatever features you have, whether you are aware of them or not, suspect you have, or believe you do, even though you may not have them. Hark hark. Now, many of your features are not changeable, but some of them are, or may be! It is sometimes sad to see people give themselves too much or not enough credit, or opportunity either. We shake our heads when we see people trying to get a good outcome/benefit without the ability or the materials, the features they need to get that outcome.

Several of the qualities in ourselves that you and I know about, we find surprising or seemingly accidental, while others we have gone out to learn about and improve, early or later in life. Sometimes, we might achieve something surprising; at other times we are sure we could do something and yet find it just too hard or impossible to do. This last movement is likely to be the 'setting yourself up to fail' situation. Do we try to do the best we can for our lives? Perhaps. How can one even know that for sure? How do I know that all I have done in many past years is, or was, the best for my life and givens? The only answer I can honestly give is that in the end I cannot answer that. The point is simple and boringly repeated: unless we know more of what is in us, what our features truly are, we cannot live a positive and purposeful life to our best benefit. I believe that the great majority of human beings live without much, if any, direction, living lives as if by accident.

Let's briefly recap and move on.

In order to do better for ourselves, we proceed by first finding out the what and how of what you do have as features, outcomes, purposes. (Don't worry about the why of it, we don't need it and the past can't be changed.) You need to know more of the 'features of your personality', which are the total of the 'preprogramming', the loaded 'software' and your genetic givens that you are!

Your features drive the possible outcomes, purposes and meaning that you can achieve. Further, one of your features or a whole bunch of them may be such that they won't, indeed cannot 'do', the job you want done! Your features may or may not be appropriate or suited to what needs to be done for the particular beneficial outcome you (have decided to) want. Note that many of your features may operate, as it were, against you! These tend to be the ones we know – or want to know – the least about. We tend to complain about them if we know them, finding them unacceptable without ever investigating them properly. Consider how we try to talk our children out of certain behaviours without really knowing what features drive such performances, and/or whether the features can be reset for better purposes and outcomes.

Most people are familiar in some way with the idea that they have certain patterns of actions. We have belief systems, ethical and moral ideas, and many of these are surprisingly hard to change even if and when you wish to do so. Most of us know that we act or are 'driven' in some ways that have never worked for us all that well. We also have some 'features' that have always worked fairly well. I hasten to add that one can make awesome mistakes; we think we act in some ways that will work for us when in truth they never have. Not really.

Once it is somewhat understood that your very own 'software' structures can work for or against you, then you can consider whether your actual individual FOP makes sense in your total life – or whether you are trying to mix oil with water. Once that assessment is done, you will then get a feeling, a clue, as to what brings negative and what might bring positive results. One way to do this is to look at what is actually beneficial for you and what is not. This will also explain and signpost what outcome/benefits there is no point for you personally to pursue. Reality is after all reality.

One of the silliest ideas our Western society still seems to promote is that 'You can do and be anything you want as long as you really want it!' What nonsense, poppycock and horse manure!

You can certainly achieve a great deal, but unless you get it right, all you are setting yourself up for is failure. Maslow puts this notion forward so well. He uses the word 'potentialities' instead of my word 'features', but it means much the same thing:

> *'One's only rival is one's own potentialities. One's only failure is failing to live up to one's own possibilities...'*
>
> (Abraham Maslow)

Bravo. Wish I said that. To act as the result of just how you are, just the way things worked out, may be good enough moment to moment; it is acceptance for now, and that's a starting point. But it is an empty truism and does not answer many human problems. It shows no movement towards getting more of what you want or need. It does not lead to greater empowerment. What we are looking for and asking is this: can I use any of my particular features that I do have to achieve my purposes and thus live more meaningfully?

At this point, I now want to add to the word 'features' the fuller concept of your learned and existing **'programs'**. You have a number of 'platforms', databases, opinions, beliefs values...they are all *programs*. All of which have features, which you knowingly or otherwise own, or had **installed** into yourself.

Hang on!

Maslow emphatically said that *'It is not easy to know what we really want in life. It is the work of maturation and of deliberate practice to find that.'* Yet it is imperative to find it.

What so-called **benefits** are we looking for?

Start with considering the following:

1. What do you want? No, what do you really want. Is it a decent, honourable want?

2. What do you need to have to get it?

3. You already know your main features; get the digger out and look for gold within.

Once we know what benefit we want, and only then, we can find the right programs that help (or hinder) the wanted benefits. Only then can we make efforts to perhaps **reprogram** within, if we need to. Or else discover that we are better to drop a project, if we do not have the right givens to bring it to life.

Now we time-out this chapter, moving on to choice making and how that works.

Many strong points in this chapter:

- Know your features and know what that truly means.

- Our personal features drive and determine what purpose-benefit we can reach towards.

- You are your main rival, helper, stopper, mover and so on and on.

- Start thinking of your features, wanted outcomes, and so your 'programs' now. Conceptualise them not as good or bad, but just see what there truly is, or is not.

- The very stuff of life, the purpose of your existence, is to find out the purpose of your existence... Yes, and it is possible to do that, but the very stuff of your life is what you actually DO and think/feel.

PSYCHOLOGY, PHILOSOPHY, THERAPY, FEELINGS AND THOUGHTS

'I have reached self-realisation and enlightenment the other morning while shaving! I looked in the mirror and realised that this me is indeed me! Thus I have warned myself to beware of imitations of myself...!'

(Todd 2010)

While I am saying the above tongue in cheek, I actually do mean it up to a point. I don't agree that there is anything whatever out there beyond this life or yourself. Thus if you do have a reasonably good level of awareness of how and who you are, then, friend, you too may have reached what a human being can reach: self-realisation. That is better named as 'self-actualisation', as Mr Maslow said.

In the previous chapter on features we did not ask *why* we have particular features or programs. That sort of inquiry usually finishes in doubtful, unprovable responses. Usually a 'why' exploration does not activate new behaviours or creative actions. You can spend many years looking for answers to 'why' questions, before – if ever – getting any results, and then often doubtful ones. But even if you get an answer, it is usually only a partial and doubtful one and can be a dead end, rather than a call to action. It is when we look to the why questions that we easily get lost in a mind-fucking waste of time. Unfortunately, psychology or psychiatry[18] seems partly to blame for making a lot more dramatic and long work of all this. Yet it is the same psychology and know-how that has also helped people become more aware of *what* and *how* they feel and think. The buzzwords in better areas of psych group work used to be to feel the *'What and How in the Here and Now!'* Good, yes, and yet incomplete, for one reason: because thinking was to be left behind, kind of as the bad brother of feelings.

Indeed, the discovery after years of therapy that your dad had hurt your feelings etc. may be good to know, but I do not think the idea calls you to act on it in a positive sense. And what action exactly could you take now? Still, certainly, to feel your feelings anyway is good and it does free up energies.

An imperfect science and art, the talking cures are, or can be, a dubious affair at times, and yet the aim is to make people maximise their authentic potentials. The increase in personal awareness has been greatly facilitated by psychology over the past 100 years and particularly over the last 40 years. Psychology, in my opinion, has also created some impractical and rather silly beliefs and concepts that many of us poor humans assumed and integrated into ourselves, often in error.[19] The errors were and are many; clients learned a great deal of what was often not much more than the values and thinking of the therapist. The problem lay, I believe, with the methods and even more so with the many not very good therapists. Unfortunately, blame for failure is also

---

18 I have lumped psychology, psychiatry and all kinds of counselling into meaning much the same for our purposes.
19 I too fell for it in practical ways over 30 years ago. In a mistaken understanding about my then current unhappiness I sold my brilliant business to my everlasting regret. I also believed the new programs I was given by therapy, swallowed them whole, garbled them as well. Oh dear.

allocated to the client, and perhaps rightly so, but enough of this side issue. I do acknowledge that psychological counselling can be great and sometimes is a lifesaver.

Wisely, Buddhist and now also various Western styles of psychology are keen to find answers to the 'how and what' of human lives and actions, not the 'why' questions, of what one does, thinks and feels. If the 'what and how' is tackled well, then we are ready to activate better potential lives. Perhaps this is all that **enlightenment** really is: deeply knowing who and how you are and what you do, and how you relate to all else. And of course knowing how to change what is possible for you. The rest, such as caring for others and being kind to yourself and the world, is included and will follow like your puppy on a leash.

Thinking about your feelings? Feelings about your feelings? Feelings about your thoughts... Meta feelings...

Forgive me, reader, but are you truly clear about what a feeling is and how it works and the difference between thoughts and feelings? It is not all so simple. When it comes to it, at times we **think** we **feel** something, not because that is the case, but because we think that we 'should' feel that way. We said earlier that we have 'meta' feelings, which are feelings about feelings. There are only a few basic feelings, such as love, hate, anger, fear, and so on.

Many of our feelings tend to be, as mentioned before, 'meta' feelings; we think/feel something about how we feel, and this is often learned from other situations and people. Have you ever felt or thought something different to what you expected? Or felt and thought the very opposite to what was appropriate in a specific situation? Or felt less than loving at times towards the partner you know you love? To genuinely feel is easy and happens often and may not be always explainable at the time. So we are told. Sometimes we do not even note our feelings, or speedily dismiss them.

Often, we are stuck with meta feelings like, say, feeling bad about feeling bad? Or feeling fears about something we have never been scared by? One must note these meta feelings. Why? Because they are not primary as they rise; they are a learned response and thus possibly not your true response!

Before moving on from the idea of meta feelings, a quick word about something that is often a 'cousin' to it. Once again, I have alluded to this phenomenon earlier, but it is a rather important one. Can they, he or she make us feel good or bad etc.? Can we make others (or ourselves) feel anything? Most of the psych community and my studies of it agree that what I feel is 'mine'; that is in the end true enough. So, no one can make me feel whatever I feel. But, um, hold on, if you tell me that my book is crap, I will feel bad and reason that you have at least 'stimulated' me to feel that way. Yet I also acknowledge that my response, my bad feelings, are mine. You possibly did or did not intend to hurt me, but that is beside the point here; my response of 'feeling bad' or 'I don't care' or 'anger' or whatever is mine. I am the not so pleased owner of bad feelings but love the good ones.

I now think that the idea of 'no one can make me feel anything' attitude has created un-needed stress for many people because it is misunderstood. Some things, words, happenings will make me feel good or bad. For our practical purposes I think that we can indeed make others and ourselves 'feel' some things. Otherwise propaganda, politicians and entertainers would disappear, together with manipulating people. That's as much as we need of the above. There is as usual a hell of a lot more, I am leading further into 'feelings' and 'thinking' in a different direction.

Feelings are learned and programmed into the body/mind/self. Some border and couple with instincts, and these come via our biology. Physical pain, like an upset tummy for a baby, makes them feel bad and cry. No one likes to be yelled at; that feels threatening and thus scary. Some young children appear tactile or cuddly, while others less so. Some of us grow up having tried to be open, to expose our feelings, others keep them to themselves. The environment and socio-cultural and family situation have dictated how 'feelings' are or are not expressed or shared. If repeated tries of expressing feelings are met by hostility at one time or acceptance another time, or sometimes by both, it is confusing. That will reduce one's taking the chance on being emotionally open.

We need to clear up some matters that fit with our overall aims. In any case, feelings come from deep within the psyche that was 'built', 'programmed', constructed, swallowed whole in our early years – as has been said by others and now me too many times. Feelings do not settle at a reliable list, variety or strength, but can and do continually change throughout life.

The whole 'feeling' thing is still a mystery of the brain/mind. As noted earlier, I have decided to connect feeling and thinking into one movement, calling it always feel/think. That has been my personal experience and is agreed on by many thinkers now, at least for practical purposes. Brain science will correctly tell you that I am technically wrong. For us in this book, and for people in their daily lives, the technical correctness does not matter. (Science, please forgive me!)

Thus here is my main point of issue: for us all, our feelings rarely if ever arise without a thought. Thoughts appear more often to rise without a feeling (perhaps). But I think not, it is just that many thoughts, for example rational mind movements, carry less powered and obvious feelings. For us here, suffice it to reiterate that feelings mostly carry thoughts and vice versa.

ಎ

Feelings/thoughts are subject to change, as you know. Things you felt strongly about 20 years ago perhaps are not so important now, while some others are. Newish feelings and thoughts come and go. Maybe you are even more aware of strong feelings about some things of the past now than you ever were – or maybe not. Sometimes we catch thoughts clashing with feelings, because people mostly do not like nor cope well with inner (or outer) conflicts. Which leads us to the next section that looks at your psyche, except I'd rather call it the 'software' of your personality because that simplifies it and makes it imaginable. And that is what we needed – a system of self-understanding and awareness that we could conceptualise without being an expert, a philosopher or a shrink etc.

More will be said about all this in different ways and without the incessant psychobabble like 'how do you feel about that?'

Some important points in this chapter:

- So much has been said about knowing the importance of feelings and that is all good. But some of it was at the expense of thinking well, and that's not so good.

- For most of us, thought and feeling rise together; noting which is which and how one really feels and thinks is a major tool of living well.

- Good thinking, decision making or feeling well – none of these can happen if one is without the others.

THE 'SOFTWARE' OF YOUR PERSONALITY

All the preceding led us to this point of considering the 'software' of your personality. Software that is in fact You. It is you and you are it. We looked at what features/programs we have as individuals. Then we worked on what the purpose of those, our features, was or could be. Now we can better consider the *how and what* of our prerecorded inner 'programs' – our human software. That exploration leads us to better knowledge of what outcomes our being and actions are likely to bring, as things are now. That is, the benefits of positive or negative outcomes that may happen, often surprisingly, to us.

I said earlier that our features-outcomes-purposes (the FOPs) were installed into us in two ways – biologically inherited genetic givens, with the social input. The social input we 'constructed' in answer to all the incoming stimuli of our personal experience as babies, children, adults etc., a process that will never end while we live. The incoming social stimuli may have been small or large, quiet or noisy, insistent and loud. Or, chances are, all of it. Often it was covert, that is for sure, worded or silent, perhaps sneaky and manipulative. Our perceptions are dependent on the combination of our past personal experiences to a great degree, if not entirely. All our programming was always based a priori on what genetic material we inherited. Note that while the same social input affected me in one way, it may not have affected you in the same way. Or it might have. So I re-recapitulate that the primary predispositions (programs-features) and the ones we have 'installed' since were taken on together with and in concert with our biological make-up. What 'software' we 'swallowed' was always somewhat dependent on our individual genetics, on the cultural situation we were born into.

Nature and nurture are always one movement; it is never one or the other, as most scientific approaches now agree, but each affects the other.[20] I am obliged to quote that very wise fellow Maslow yet again:

'Experience is, for me, the highest authority. The touchstone of validity is my own experience. No other person's ideas, and none of my own ideas, are as authoritative as my experience. It is to experience that I must return again and again, to discover a closer approximation to truth as it is in the process of becoming in me. Neither the Bible nor the prophets – neither Freud nor research – neither the revelations of God nor man – can take precedence over my own direct experience.'

Then, importantly, Maslow adds, *'My experience is not authoritative because it is infallible, it is the basis of authority because it can always be checked in new primary ways. In this way its frequent error or fallibility is always open to correction.'* (*On Becoming a Person*, Maslow 1961) I agree almost totally. Allow me to repeat part of what Maslow said because it is so important: *'...My experience is not authoritative because it is infallible...'* rather, because I can check it again and again by thinking, feeling and by consulting others. It is yet indeed my only 'basis of authority' because it can always be checked in new primary ways. In this way errors are still open to corrections. Maslow was clearly a very wise human being, more than I will ever be. That's

---

20 Yet another circular movement and example of cause and effect chasing one the other!

OK though; being able to understand and use his words is good enough for all of us.

Maslow is saying that in the end, all I can rely on is my experience, and yet that is not entirely perfectly reliable because it can be misleading. I can and must check my experiences, reflect on them, and then see in what ways they need adjusting. (If I were not as humble as I am…then I would say that now I am extending Maslow's idea a bit further.) We all know how often we feel, think and are absolutely convinced about something that we have experienced, only to find that our perception this time was wrong.

Life brings continuous further programming, that's obvious, including importantly the input that has been added since the original feature-outcome-purpose-benefit (FOP) was 'installed', read: 'programmed at birth', in the early educative years and every living moment since. Note that just doing what we are doing now, me writing and you reading this, already adds, perhaps even changes,[21] even if only to a small degree, who what and how you and I are at this moment.

We may or may not have freedom of choice…but we are compelled and obligated to make decisions!

That is for certain. As for people having absolute freedom of choice: I believe not, and many, certainly not all, thinkers agree. But we do at least seem to have some ability to consider and make some choices. And it appears to me and to many others that we can enlarge and improve on that ability. All the foregoing in this book and all the rest of it too is in aid of our choice and decision-making processes.

---

21 Writing it has certainly changed me. But that does not mean writing will always bring huge results.

Decisions are what we make once we understand what our choices are... Or should I say, **IF** we truly understand our choices? In any case, we all make decisions knowingly or otherwise 24 hours a day till we die. The making of decisions activates us, our environment, and everyone and all else (cause and effect endlessly) to move in a certain direction. We take action or the opposite, do nothing; it is still cause and effect. Here, we are exploring grounded, real-life, possible decision and thus choice making. Such choice-decisions can be about the trivialities like which movie to see, or bigger things like whether to change jobs, start a business, stop or start a relationship, and so on... (Even about how you actually feel about something.)

If you are clearer about and have a strong concept of your 'software-features-outcomes-purposes-programs', and what and how they do as You, then you will have more and clearer choices leading to easier and more successful decisions. You will be clearer about yourself and your active life. That being the case there will be less agony, and more clarity and speed to seeing the truth of any situation, thought/feeling (or if not the whole truth and all the facts, then at least more of it). Often there is really only one choice and the others are merely what we might call an 'ego trick' (Baggini 2011). Or as Jiddu Krishnamurti said, in truth, we have few if any choices. It is when we can't – or will not – see this fact that we moan 'oh, I am so confused'. (Enough said about yet another large debate we don't need here, yet need to be aware of.)

You and me

When, and if, I can truly explain myself to myself, that's when I am really in touch with my awareness. Then and only then can I *properly explain myself to you, to another.* In that state of putting myself forward, towards you, in that explained-awareness state that I show you, I may change again. You might too; we will change again likely for the better. This happens if, and only if, my explanation and understanding of myself is a reasonably accurate one. Plainly speaking: if I communicate well and clearly. Positive change can happen in that effort because the very explanation of me to me and then to you brings more clarity within, inevitably. Another endless loop, but if all is clear, then a positive one! Or else if all is muddled, then a negative coil, arguments, fights, wars, misery etc. All this may happen not because of what 'you' actually say or think about me. It is much deeper than that sort of triteness. No, just the very process of clear communications and understanding can bring transformation, a something that is new for me and you.

☙

Soon we shall launch into actual processes, methods, techniques that will work and may help to further your potential to be your even better self, to act and flourish as you want to, more positively. The processes may bring you more of what you want materially and internally by helping you to get closer to finding out what you do really want and truly need. Now then, let's move towards several actual processes or methods that will facilitate and bed in true changes that are possible and positive. That's what in fact you are about now: your purposes.

The processes I shall delve into all tend to be figurative, that is analogical and/or metaphoric. The first and most important metaphor/analogy we need as one of our tools is that of your personal computer, be it a desktop, tablet or a laptop. Then we shall move on to other concepts, metaphors all of them, that are entirely unlike the PC idea, and yet exactly the same message is conveyed.

Now I am getting close to branching out using the 'computer that I am' and my internal brain/mind/body as software 'programs'

The 'Software' of Your Personality

and 'databases'. Also the actual internet coupling with the 'internet of my brain/mind' to improve my life. For now, this minute, I am all that I am: hardware consisting of body/brain/mind matter that causes perceptions, feelings and emotions, and the life situation I am in, at my age, in this society in Melbourne, Australia. From this set-up I am aware somewhat at my age that I can do this and not that, and that I may have certain limits, abilities and potentials. Actions I take or leave undone turn out variously positive or negative, the results welcomed, wanted or not wanted.

What can we say about what is a human being? An active consciousness. Yes, and what exactly is that? So just before we go to the metaphors of the PC and such, who and what are you really?

- Features-outcomes-purposes – that is what you are. Don't go looking for it up there or under a rock. You already have what it takes to find and have it all.

- You and another person are yet another 'program'. You affect me and vice versa.

- Life is a continuous 'programming' exercise. Take care: garbage in, garbage out.

We may or may not have freedom of choice...but we must make choices and decisions, or else others will make decisions for you! (Not always a problem, either.)

OK, you do have some choices, not as many and not as few as you think. So?

ONLY IF YOU CAN REMEMBER, IF YOU CAN RECALL MEMORIES, ONLY THEN CAN YOU BE CERTAIN THAT YOU ARE.

YOU AND YOUR CONSCIOUSNESS ARE YOUR MEMORIES AND NARRATIVES

The brain/mind is what I earlier termed as consciousness, and said that such an admittedly relaxed definition shall suffice for our framework. Everyone has a body and within that a brain that is the seat of what we know as consciousness and of awareness, of the 'me' I am familiar with. While there are many similarities, every brain/mind and body differs, sometimes substantially. Without a brain and its consciousness there would be no thoughts or feelings, no being human. Our sensory inputs receive and pass on perceptions and the brain/mind makes sense of them. It also learns, stores, memorises and moment to moment constructs the world around us into a coherent wholeness (or at times, for that matter, into a partial nonsense) we call our life.

Our consciousness and memories are hand in glove and have made sense, or otherwise, of the early input and learning – the programs – we have received and embedded into ourselves. This happened knowingly or unknowingly, but lots of it has happened, far more than we are aware of. If you are reading this, good-o, for then your brain/mind/consciousness is still doing the continuous and appropriate job of sorting, **constructing** and understanding your personal world, and shall go on doing so.

Chip Walter's wonderful book *Last Ape Standing* tells us that *'the purpose of brains generally is to organize the waves of sensory phenomena that nature's cerebrally gifted creatures experience. Their job is to filter the world's chaos effectively enough to avoid, for as long as possible, the disagreeable experience of death. A direct correlation exists between survival and how well a brain maps the world around it.'* (Walter 2013) It certainly does that. In addition, Edward O Wilson's book *On Human Nature* states that *'...culture evolves from and by the instincts and so (from) inborn biases that form our biological nature.'* (Wilson 1978) Another round trip, as we learn socio-cultural input and yet we shape it as well.

To spell it out: the brain sorts input not only to avoid death, but to avoid all the evils of mental disorders, bodily dangers, commonplace or serious confusions, emotional traumas, feelings and thoughts. And to maximise the life it is. The brain does this at some cost to us because it will rely rather too often on what it already knows, and that can bring from us responses that are not always the best possible choices after all, given all the available solutions.

As for our genetic dispositions, the *'"structural genome" – each of us inherits in fifty-fifty doses from our parents resolutely continue[s] the construction of our own* **wetware***, and its underlying neuronal infrastructure, complete with our specific talents and predispositions. Just as some of us may inherit stocky bodies and others long, slim ones, our parents can also issue brains that incline us to be gregarious or shy, a leader more than a follower, mathematically, musically, or verbally predisposed. This part of us is a genetic crapshoot, and we have no control over it.'* (Walter 2013) He says 'wetware', but I prefer to call it 'software' – much the same, I believe. So, are we poor human blobs set like a jelly?

Genetic directives do not add up to total destiny. Nature is greatly affected by nurture, cultivation and experience. The experiences and environments we find ourselves in affect outcomes of who and how we turn out to be. Fortunately, this means that we are a somewhat, although never entirely, **'editable' life form**. I said never entirely because an editor cannot rewrite a book, only edit it for clarity. This 'editing' idea (a metaphor) harks backwards and forwards in this book using several other metaphors or analogies. The most obvious idea here is that, for example, a counsellor or therapist can be said to be **'editing'** people when there is a therapeutic intervention. That usually happens when the psyche is somewhat disturbed, but it can also happen if people simply wish to explore deeper into their awareness. (That is what this book is mainly about.) You are also your own 'editor' and just thinking of it that way means that you better get a good read of your material (you)!

You are a narrative and the narrative is you.

There is, so it seems (I agree with many thinkers), no underlying essence of people, no soul, no before- and after-life. Our lives, our mental mind-stuff, psychological and physical elements rise and cease and are interdependent with the world around us. Human life can be said to be a 'narrative' – a story of sorts that we form and recall. This recalling of yourself as a story is what provides your continuity and recognisability as you (Fivush & Neisser 1994). It is narratives that play over and over in the mind, and are forgotten or recalled – perhaps not unlike trains pulling out of the station one after another. Some stories, 'journeys', are longer and more complicated than others. Some stories are simple but all lives are narratives.

We are a **'narrative'**, and can be a short or long story, each of us individually and also as groups large and small. As a rule, narratives, stories, often need 'editing'. We are absolutely the product of Mum and Dad's genetic donations, but we are 'editable', by others and by ourselves, and even by, say, education and by our own ongoing experiences. Our experiences as they actually happen are sort of on automatic editing; they tend to be chewed over, checked, 'proofread'...sometimes without our explicit consent or awareness. So we are a story we recall.

Memory? Oh yes, I remind myself...

All my internal software programs are contained within what we call our memory. These memorised, well-known and exercised programs make me myself. My personality, character traits, features, programs and so on, by whatever name we call them, have serious and important loadings. I strongly concur with many thinkers that this memory of ours is the vital integrated issue of our identity. ***Our memories are us. There are no other us. We are, the individual self is, equal to memory*** (Neisser, Fivush, Bruner, Dennett and others). Try and think of something about yourself that is not memory. Impossible. In fact, even thinking/feeling about oneself is obviously memory already. The here and now of our experience is turned into a narrative the moment it happens. This can be an aware but is mostly an unaware process. Perhaps there are additional factors that make up identity and thus our consciousness; I need not debate that here.

I suggest then that identity is not much more or less than memory, and my memories were created as responses to my life experiences. That is the entire external-internal endless loop that a human life is. Sounds too simple?[22] Such movements are constantly fuelled by input from out there, and by interpretations from in here, from your 'software'. Now, it follows that I am, and you are, indeed a complex affair, but one that can be understood if – and only if – there is a framework that is accessible to me, so that I can then make that accessible to you – if I wish to do so; that is relating. That framework, as said before, has to be *flexible*

---

22 Yes and no, depending on the level of our investigating.

enough, meaning that no framework ought to be too solid, never again to be changed or challenged.

So, sorry, I have to repeat that we know some of our predispositions and we do not know others. Just the same about the memories that are Me or You. We tend to behave as usual, on autopilot, as is familiar to us. This can be, as Robert Anton Wilson (1983) described it, 'robotic behaviour'! Additionally, things can happen to us for which we have no immediate response, or we are temporarily stumped for one. I am talking about things that matter, not odd one-liners addressed to us by a stranger, or a brick falling on your foot. Sometimes we cannot instantly and necessarily know whether we actually have a predisposition or not when something happens to us. For example, the first time you go overseas and cannot understand a language, or you fall in love, or the first time you fail or succeed at something, or whatever. Immediately you look for the appropriate response in your appropriate 'program files' (memories), and often you finish up by reacting as you were told to, that is programmed.

We have seen that new or unusual situations particularly are usually answered by old preprogrammed responses. Ordinary everyday situations are also often instantly addressed by what we know. Fair enough at one time and not good enough at another. This is how everyone is, and this is how and why old pains, emotional hurts, values, beliefs, etc., many of which are inappropriate to a new situation, may well drive our responses more than we know. I doubt that anyone who has explored this idea would disagree.

Recall, remember, wakey-wakey...

What rises for each of us when we awaken is always memory of sorts. That's not strong enough; what rises when we wake is more, it is the 'me' and it rises as my memory bank. Then the 'me' that suddenly reappears is a continuing story. It is not a whole actual completed story but what is needed from the programmed files in our minds right now, in order to make what is happening 'sensible'! Memory is more than the twin brother of thought/feeling; memory is it. And it is what we do or do not remember on command.

Again: **memories are us**! (Sounds like one of those dodgy carpet adverts.) The memories we do not recall at all we term unconscious – if they are in existence at all. Others we know as 'my' oft known memories, still others are perhaps only suspected to be memories or are there but dormant, waiting for me to say: 'oh yes, this tree reminds me of...' Memories are curiously changeable in their details, and yet fixed as an absolute in their meaning as a rule. Memories are set up with rules as they happen, feelings and thoughts all mixed in with them. Often the details become flexible and at each telling we might change them slightly (Neisser & Fivush 1994). Ah yes, almost inevitably we change or colour a little our memories at each telling. So, if our memories are mainly bad, then living a constantly nice life is that much harder, and vice versa.

If you can experience one of your preset programs, if you get very familiar with it and watch it move and act as if by itself, then you have that program pretty well under control. All it takes is one honest catch; you will never forget it! You can then observe it and separate it from your total self, see it as a program that you can have access to, if you wish. (It's all memory, right?) Now you can do a bit of what Krishnamurti, Buddha, contemporary psychology and various other schools of thought nominate as an 'uncritical observation' of what you have in there. Only then can you 'transcend' it, change it, use it, delete it, see it for what it may be positively used for – or for what it does to you. Or simply see whether it is what you want or not.

But, is non-judgemental and non-critical possible?

I worried, in the chapter about 'Krishnamurti', about whether people can actually be non-critical. I confess I do not think that it is possible to be entirely non-critical and non-judgemental. And I believe that is just as well for we need to have a 'discriminating' ability. So then, if you have your 'Critic' and his/her software running, you cannot be non-critical, clearly. Still, if you are aware, if you can see that you have an installed 'critical' program running, then perhaps you can lessen its power. You do this by the simple observation of it and by 'switching on' another idea: that it is OK to be, or not to be, critical. (Thanks, Shakespeare.) How to not be critical about your criticalness is a curly and frustrating proposition. Let me recommend it for now anyway. To reduce the nasty effects of your inner 'Critic' (again, a memory) sabotaging your thinking and actions is a must. I have already done so but will offer some more suggestions on how to do that later. Again, all this happens with the memory bank offering up what it can by way of thought/feeling.

The next two chapters unpack more of this business of 'narratives', the stories we actually are, and how they affect our lives – *are* our lives! Our narratives are our memories and they are 'us'. These chapters are partly taken from my doctoral thesis and thus they are somewhat more formal and academic. All of which in plain English means that it might be a harder read, but an immensely important one. Please persevere because there are several ideas that hook in with all else presented before and after.

One major, major point from this chapter:

- Your memories are you. There is, it seems, no other you. So what are memories made of? Narratives.

NARRATIVES

'We are born into a universe of stories.'

(Parry 1991)

In this key section (partly taken from my PhD exegesis 2013), I will look deeper at what narratives are and how they affect and indeed probably are the mysterious 'self' we are always looking for or at. Our narratives have a powerful effect in human affairs socially and personally. Appreciating this aspect of being human would – I believe – lead to an enhancement of anyone's life.

Writers and commentators use various expressions for what are wide, socio-cultural narratives, such as: Master, Meta, Universal, or Grand narratives. I see no substantive difference between these and shall use the term MASTER NARRATIVE from here on. The term refers to pre-existent socio-cultural forms of interpretation and institutions; these are the mores and norms of a society (Bamberg 2004). *'The principal way in which our minds, our "realities" get shaped to the patterns of daily cultural life is through the stories we tell, listen to, and read – true or fictional.'* (Bruner 2006)

I will distinguish the 'master' from the 'personal' narrative later in this section, and this differentiation will be shown to be very important. To clarify quickly: the 'personal narrative' is that which we individually construct from the early and ongoing input of the social/master narratives, plus the genetic and physical givens, and abilities. I will examine the impact, effect and meaning of master and personal narratives and the potential conflict between them. Such conflicts are what we usually think of as psychological tensions and they are a whole of life occurrence.

I mean to look at narratives as a concept, in a wider sense than simply 'narrative equals a story'. In this, my broader sense, I use the term 'narrative' to include story, propaganda, socio-cultural imperatives, the arts, body language, life story, experience and more. I think of 'narratives' for this exploration as the plot and story of life/consciousness. The work of writers such as Bruner (1986), Eakin (1999), Ochs and Capps (1996), Lyotard (1995), McAdams (1993), Polkinghorne (1988), Richardson (2009), Wyle and Pare (2001), and many others appear to agree that narratives at large include, and are, the general socio-cultural inputs via myths, laws, rules, norms and ethics of a given society.

Narratives powerfully fill the idea of lives

We know our local culture implicitly, perhaps like fish might know water, that is without knowing they know it. People are inevitably immersed all their lives in the situation of society and culture.

Narratives are 'us', the 'me' I know and show to others. *'If you want to know me, then you must know my story, for my story defines who I am.'* (McAdams 1993) Psychologist and thinker Jerome Bruner said that human beings understand the world in one of two ways: in a paradigmatic or in a narrative mode. It is in the narrative mode that we understand and live personal lives, and deal with the *'vicissitudes of human intention organized in time'*. (McAdams 1993) I agree and add that it is never one but always both paradigmatic and narrative. What we use and how we use it to make sense of things is what drives the whole deal.

In this way, via our own and others' narratives, we see '*a representation of causally related series of events.*' (Richardson 1997) Ample evidence is offered by all the thinkers mentioned that we are our narratives and the narratives are us. Two good examples are the books *The Stories We Live By* (McAdams 1993), which explores the master and personal 'myths' we are and act out, and *How Our Lives Become Stories* (Eakin 1999) which states that our realities are shaped by and to the pattern of the stories we hear and see, tell and formulate. Bruner adds an important rider: that it is largely narrative interventions that achieve cultural and social cohesion.

There is no suggestion that all master narratives are good or bad, but caution and insight are needed when examining our master and/or personal narratives. Our culturally shaped preconceptions depend not only on language, but also on sharing our thoughts and the business of the 'exchange' of life (Bruner 1986).

I intensify the idea by adding that not only cohesion, but also coercions are done mainly by the development of certain master narratives of a given society.

Notable and of much weight it is that some of these master or personal directives are 'tacit', while others are overwhelmingly explicit. Some are banal, others larger in impact, '*in fact, we easily and often eagerly embrace the banalities of our cultural setting and even object if critics attack them.*' (Bruner 2006) And do so even when we ourselves might be opposing such, I mean, who accepts all that life dishes up entirely? However, master narratives are not 'natural': they are not like the laws of nature. Rather, they are what society constructs (Hutcheon 1988). Further, '*The grand (master) narrative has lost its credibility.*' (Lyotard 2006, p. 83) (I wonder whether it has just changed to another version as a matter of its own principle.) '*The decline, perhaps the ruin of the universal idea, can free thought and life from totalizing obsessions.*'

The 'Software' of Your Personality

So offered Lyotard (1993), who called for a replacement of the grand nonsense master narratives by 'mini narratives' – what I now offer as 'personal narratives' that include some forms of lesser powered master narratives. In very ordinary words: no absolutism, no dogma, no bullshit.

Much as I wish that master narratives were diminishing, in my experience, opinion and research this does not seem to be the case. We mostly replace one with another. The point is to be extra careful what master narratives one adapts and then develops into one's own personal narratives.

In summary, master narratives pervade lives and thinking, and are dynamic and ever-changing. At times, a particular master narrative is obviously dropped, usually only to be replaced by another. Sigmund Freud replaced the narrative of repressed sexuality with a new one, which is still a master affair in its tone and content. Similarly, some outdated religious narratives have been replaced (at least for some people) by perhaps an atheistic one, for example as regards to morals, and much else.

Master narratives rather than mini ones – to use Lyotard's concept – tend to uphold certain dogmatic views of history, human action and thought. Such are biblical stories, isms, the obeying of laws, morals and ethics in a given civilisation, as the ideals everyone *must* follow. The master narratives, as already mentioned, construct and form the personal narratives we each hold and identify with. An example is the old global master narrative of the Ten Commandments: the 'no killing' rule is usually accepted by most people as also their personal narrative. (The immediate master to personal narrative clash is obvious if you are a soldier, or if you are attacked. I will explore such conflicts in more detail later.)

How we build and embed master and personal narratives; how they become our 'programs'

Charlotte Linde looks at 'narratives and social **tacit** knowledge'. (Linde 2001) 'Tacit knowledge' as opposed to explicit. Linde's work refers to unconscious social knowledge about interactions in society, practices that are not at the foreground of conscious thinking. Although tacit (or unconscious), this know-how is necessary to make one's way in the world. Tacit know-how is conveyed via master narratives and *'Narrative induction is the process by which newcomers to a group take on the story as their own.'* (Linde 2001) It is partly from these tacit master stories, as well as from the explicit ones, that we construct our personal narratives in our early years. This happens with or often without the awareness of having built them. It is as if initially our personal narratives are hidden from us by the overwhelming nature of the master narratives. True enough. Yet from the beginning we make space for our individual voices and connect our personal and group narratives. This is also the bridge between *'the tacit and the explicit'* and it is made by our smaller, personal narratives, what Linde and others also call our autoethnographies (Linde 2001).

Clearly, our knowledge of the world is picked up by simply participating in everyday life as we gain the (often tacit) *'cultural toolkits'*, the made-up models of the world patterned to the local set of rules (Bruner 1985 and in various of his writings). I want to point out that such 'tacit' automatic acceptance of some master narratives by populations (the Holocaust or the Chinese Mao's 'cultural' revolution, etc.) can be disastrous. The issue is even more worrying given that it is language that carries the master narratives, and language may be the most tacit form of tacit knowledge. One knows how to speak or hear without thinking about it. Tragedy shapes talk, as Ruth Wajnryb observed (2001). And I say that talk shapes tragedy! The problem is that much of our identity and personal history emanates from our tacit knowledge. Linde goes on to draw a parallel regarding how groups accept specific tacit and implied, and explicit input. Nazism built the 'master race' idea as the useful (for them) master narrative. The victims had to rebuild their master narratives after the Holocaust, often 'sanitising' their stories, for to tell it all as it happened was too much: *'I was afraid of giving it more validity... more power by telling it all...'* (Wajnryb 2001)

All stories are personal, and yet they are also group stories, as Ulric Neisser (1994) suggested. His is a 'constructivist' understanding of both the self and of the lives and stories we 'construct'. Society is fabricated by individuals, and the individual builds society (Neisser & Fivush 1994). And it's all based on narratives, mere stories of how events were interpreted and passed on. This is my stance, and it is by now an idea I have embedded in my own psyche, thinking and actions. It is part, a large part, of my master and indeed my personal narratives.

The Perceived Self and **The Remembering Self** (Neisser & Fivush 1994; Neisser 1994) are books of essays that had a great impact on understanding what I finally did or did not allow into this work in both a personal way and in a wider frame. Our known narratives, master and personal, are at once what we might term as our 'remembered self'. I note that not only society and parents, but also the *'reading books of fiction'* and art in general construct the self, and the *'power of fiction...'* affects and *'transforms the reader's self'*. (Doring 2006)

It is rather obvious that if we are unfamiliar with locally shared cultural stories, the prevailing master narratives, then we will be outsiders. As a migrant I experienced the Australian master narrative of 1957 somewhat as shown in the movie *They're a Weird Mob* (directed by John O'Grady 1957). As I learned the then current local master narrative, I had to reconstruct my personal ones, for example, cherished ideas about how to keep safe from communists...or policemen. Or that one could say virtually anything without fear. Or that there were laws to protect everyone, not only the main group.

❧

Each time we tell a story – it pays to note – whenever we narrate, we do so always with the 'hearer or reader' in mind and thus we 'tailor' the telling to what we think will suit (Linde 2001). During work on this book I became keenly aware that with one ear I was listening to myself, with another ear to what the reader might think about my writing, and with my third ear (?) to what an academic might think about this work. Are there – can there be – stories that do not include the influence of master narratives? I believe not. Henry James said that stories happen to those who know how to tell them (Eakin 2004). Yes, but they also happen to those who are not good at telling them, or hearing them (it is just that you won't hear much from this second source). This is part of the so-called silent majority in some ways. The story 'telling' always involves mainly one's own version, and that version is part of one's personal narratives, the ones that were (to this day) constructed. The input of society and culture shapes our cognitive processes constantly. This guides our storytelling so powerfully that eventually we both believe and become the 'narratives' we have told as our lives (Bruner 2004).

I do not want to state that people are nothing but narrative, though it appears hard to say what else one is other than this language-narrative based identity and meaning that equals the 'remembered self' (Bamberg & Andrews 2004; Bruner 2004; Eakin 1999; Neisser 1994).

❧

My suggested model of the hierarchy of Master Narratives that lead to the construction of Personal Narratives.

Now I turn to adding something I think of as more practical to the above academic material. The thought of master and personal narratives is a large one. I believe breaking it down into smaller segments will help our understanding of the whole idea.

My proposal is a kind of hierarchy that serves to break up and illustrate the rather too wide-open and all-encompassing term of 'narratives' into further detail. This may assist in the further understanding of the power and the conflicts inherent in both the master and personal narratives. The confusion narratives can create in an individual's life is the very stuff of writing fictional narratives, by the way; this is shown clearly in literature and all the arts. 'Real lives' carry stories and dramas and conflicts in just the same way, and are caused – I suggest – by the conflicts inherent between our master and personal narratives.

Excuse the following whimsy:

In the beginning there was the word (the master narrative) and, as children, we saw that it was good (or believed it) and acted very much within the framework set by it and the Gods (Mum and Dad etc.). Later (as we grew up), we began to have experience and developed curiosity towards the 'trees of knowledge'. As that progressed we built our individual narratives, weighing these against the master narratives, that of God and society, and trouble started.

That God threw us out of the fabled garden may also be a good metaphor for the individuation separation process of children from their parents, and for the developing of awareness about the hypocrisy of society's narratives. Questions, conflicts, agreements and debates arose as 'master' and 'personal' narratives, and began to show one the other as less than consistent or perfect (Horney 1999; Neisser & Fivush 1994; Yalom 2002; Todd 2013).

ঔ

I was researching autoethnography, the works of Anderson 2006, Bochner & Ellis 2003, Bullough & Pinnegar 2001, and these had (partly) led me to offer here an admittedly subjective view of how the many and various master narratives may build upon one another and yet conflict with one another. As said earlier, I felt the need to break down what seemed like an all too solid block called master narratives into smaller segments. In my thinking I have found that there appeared to be a kind of vertical structure, a progression flowing from global master narratives down to personal narratives. (Perhaps imagine a pyramid?)

The base of the mountain: global master narratives.

Meta, Master, Grand or Universal narratives by any name are the global socio-cultural mores and norms. These incorporate and publish ideas such as the Ten Commandments, accepted history, being nice to guests, not cheating/lying, global trading laws, cultural admonitions and recommendations, morality and ethics and much more. I refer mostly to the European/Western narratives that drive a similar enough worldwide view about how humans 'should' live (Bamberg & Andrews 2004; Kessel, Cole & Johnson 1992; Lyotard 1995). However, many of these global master narratives appear throughout the world. Example: for the Hungarian Jews in the 1940s, anti-Semitism was part of their global and local master narratives, but the actual Holocaust was not – how could it have been? It was unimaginable (Popkin 2003). That adultery is not acceptable, stealing is bad, and so on, are all globally accepted master narratives. (Even though much of it is highly hypocritical and lied about.)

Looking up towards the peak in all directions

There are huge and obvious differences between the master narratives of various societies and cultures, while some of the global ones are more or less accepted by all. However, several of these global narratives are already in conflict. For example, Western morals, ethics and ideals often conflict with Eastern ones, even while cooperating, at least regarding commercial trading laws. 'Our Western culture with its "individualistic orientation" gives rise to a sharply demarcated sense of self' (Lutz 1995, p.68), as opposed to say the Muslims of Java whose focus is on the soul as different to the individualistic orientation (Cox & Stromquist 1998; Lutz 1995).

On the way up, there are, for example, religious narratives: Christian, Muslim, Jewish, Buddhist and many more.

I see the power of underlying religious narratives as possibly the greatest force for most people on earth. They encompass ethics and morality, sexuality, accurate or not history, gender roles, and even affect commercial matters, and a lot more. Religious belief has had a huge input on many master (and personal) narratives. One can almost say that the basics of master narratives come from, in one way or another, various God belief-laden formulations.

The actual or practical narratives, rules and modes may vary between religions, but most share some of the global ideas about, say, monotheism, morality and ethical ways. There are master narrative conflicts even within the same religions. Sadly, that very fact, and its attendant tragedies, escapes many of their leaders and participants. Secular laws, behaviours and ethics have often grown from such mainly outdated narratives. Wisdom and science handed down over the ages is subject to change like all else.

Old master narratives are sometimes thrown out or outdate themselves. For example, the rules about meat eating on Friday for Catholics, the ordination of women or gay people for Anglicans, female Rabbis, changes in birth control and so on (Bamberg & Andrews 2004; Kessel, Cole & Johnson 1992). In the past such actions or ways of living were outlawed, ignoring the rules was sometimes even dangerous, but now they are more sanctioned and desirable. There are some confusing master narratives from our Muslim brothers to this day; on one hand they are pressed to change all people to Islam, and yet on the other hand many know the impossibility of such a narrative. Even solidly Jewish people realise that eating pork is not an act against anyone or anything (other than the poor pig). Many other examples are sometimes sad, hilarious or downright dangerous.

Country or regional narratives

These are around the middle of the hill climb and incorporate many of the above, but not all. There are great variations between, say, Egypt and England, or America North and South, and even between countries next to each other, language being one obvious and major variant (Pinker 1994). There are various historical, traditional, cultural and nationalistic master narratives that each country tends to support and use to instruct their inhabitants. The American identity is obviously different – it makes powerful claims on its members and does so differently to, say, the Japanese or Chinese or Nigerian etc. ethos.

Local narratives: city, town, village, neighbourhood

All the above may be included, or at least some, but they are additions that belong to a specific area. Melbourne, Australia, for example, includes not only the global, Western, Christian, capitalist and Australian modes, but also some extra ones – some rather commonplace ones like football, or more important ones, like the narrative of multiculturalism. Members of the public constantly debate about what shared values should underpin Australian multiculturalism (Cox & Stromquist 1998; Feldman 2006; Kerkyasharian 1998). Now we are at home up the top of the pyramid, yes? No, not entirely. By necessity I have kept all these descriptions very short. Now we are near the top looking at and getting close to 'personal narratives'. But there are always some buts, aren't there?

Gender based master narratives; are they obvious?

Master narratives also break down, inevitably, into the male-female variation. In a TV interview with Moyers, writer Toni Morrison quotes the protagonist of her book *The Bluest Eye* (Morrison 1970):

'Morrison: She has surrendered completely to the so-called Master Narrative, the whole notion of what is ugliness, what is worthlessness. She got it from her family; she got it from school; she got it from the movies; she got it from everywhere.

'Moyers: The Master Narrative...what is...that's life.

'Morrison: No. It's white male life. The Master Narrative is whatever ideological script is being imposed by the people in authority on everybody else: The Master Fiction.' (Moyers 1989)

Clearly Morrison is correct. Just about all of the master narratives were initiated, written and enforced by males and this appears to be true of the great majority of the world right up to this day. However, it is changing in some cultures at least. As I type this, I heard that Saudi Arabia has for the first time allowed women to stand for at least local elections. A small but potentially huge change in the master narrative.

Although both genders have a great deal in common, there is also the obvious fact that gender distinctions mean that a male can never have some of the female experience/narrative and vice versa. Thus there are some separate female and male master narratives even within the more global ones. One rather obvious example is the sneaky acceptance of younger males playing around sexually, while the same actions have been frowned upon (or worse) for young women. Have most master narratives been authored by male dominated societies? It sure seems so. I reckon The 'Hero's journey' (Campbell 1993), for example, salient as it is, might have been also called the 'Heroine's journey'.

Another side of the mountain, partly out of sight: the science and technology narratives/paradigms.

Science and technology certainly drive many master (and personal) narratives. Usually there can be conflicts taking place between any and all of the above narratives, due to the input and constant changes in science and technology. Paradigm-breaking scientific narratives can, and usually do, greatly change many master and personal narratives. For example, the birth control pill facilitated change and brought stress to global, local, religious and certainly personal narratives. The pill helped further the cause of women's liberation, giving more power to new feminist narratives, gay liberation, etc. It changed sexual behaviour, social, moral and cultural rules (Djerassi 1992, 2001; Kotz 2010). Other examples can be seen in education, psychology, electronic communications, the arts and literature.

Narratives at all levels change from time to time (Kuhn 1970; Todd 2013). An even further breakdown of the master narratives concept is no doubt possible, and perhaps desirable, but this much will suffice for our purposes. The point is, yet again, to form a concept of your large, even huge, master narratives from which you have constructed your smaller personal narratives. When I say 'smaller', that is not to say that your personal narratives are less important; simply they are mostly just yours rather than applicable to everyone. A mistake us faulty people tend to make is to think that we people all have the same master and personal narratives. Yes, there are many similar ones, and no, not entirely or necessarily so.

The story moves on...

Herewith a few samples of the Hungarian narratives of my youth, 1941–1956, taken on board at first as the commands of God, communism, Jewishness, and the prevailing Hungarian socio-cultural master narrative to live by. These huge major narratives and many others were what I developed into my early personal narratives. The not so tacit 'demand' inherent in my list below was that these narratives of the Hungarian Stalinist regime community of the 1950s were to be accepted as the only way to live. To me they were confusing, often scary, at times clearly hypocritical, or else nonsensical. Here is a brief list:

Keep the law of the land, but never admit that you are Jewish or that you are not a communist.

We were always short of money, but we were definitely not the 'proletariat'. Heavens no, just hungry and worried! A personal narrative I knew well.

Marriage is between two people and for keeps, but I knew Mum had a hopeless alcoholic second husband and a boyfriend... How to react to all this personally? What to make of it?

The Hungarian police represented and enforced the law, but we needed to bribe them and/or stay away from them. This was a well-known master narrative about authorities that engendered fear.

The nice man below us used to be a Nazi; he is now a communist.

The Nazis might come back to finish the job.

Grandmothers are like mine, very nice – but one of mine would not feed us when starving.

And, why can't we have chewing gum and listen to English jazz on the radio?

I'll briefly dig into a bit of all this. I voraciously read books, often way beyond my comprehension, where the heroes were upright, noble, kind, brilliant people – the authors were venerated as great men and Hungarian heroes...except when it came to Jews. Lots of confusion and worry about this last one: I mean, if even my heroes hate Jews... It is not hard to see how one, particularly a younger person, might build his or her identity out of the master narratives of the day.

Because this chapter is a fairly busy and heavier one, I won't nominate too many points as important, but just a couple.

'The principal way in which our minds, our "realities" get shaped to the patterns of daily cultural life is through the stories we tell, listen to, and read – true or fictional.' (Bruner 2006, p. 14)

'Narrative induction is the process by which newcomers to a group take on the story as their own.' (Linde 2001, p. 3)

The 'Software' of Your Personality

Knowing and comprehending your main master and personal narratives is a powerful way to be. It also works for the best results for those around you and for all of humanity.

NARRATIVE, MEANING, PERSONAL IDENTITY AND NARRATIVE CONFLICT

> 'Narrative is international, trans-historical, trans-cultural: it is simply there, like life itself.'
>
> (Barthes 2000)

Writers and theorists of narrative enquiry, such as Bruner (2004, 2006), Eakin (1999, 2004), Herman (2003), McAdams (2008) and Polkinghorne (1988), appear to agree that the self, personal identity and meaning are constructed from and by our narratives. It is hard to imagine human life or a self without its inherent narratives. David Herman says that an essential part of our mental lives is a narratively organised system of signs, which are 'socially constituted and propagated, being embedded in social groups and constructed in social encounters', and represented by way of narratives. Human intelligence and action comes from narrative ways of knowledge and interaction (Herman 2009, pp. 7–12). This speaks of the nature of human existence and of the structures of mind, and refers to master narratives (Cox & Stromquist 1998; McAdams 2008).

On the other hand, Cameron Lee (1996) argues for the rightness of religious beliefs and master narratives thereof, saying that these MNs should not be thrown out with the postmodern idea of getting rid of all master narratives. Much as I disagree, and see most, if not all, God or religion based MNs as a disaster for humanity, some of what Lee argues is salient to establishing the need for and value of narratives – but I think personal and master narratives. My disagreement with Lee is only about **which** MNs are good for humanity (yes, in my opinion). Lee quotes narrative therapists Jill Freedman and Gene Coombs (1996) whose stance also defines that reality is socially constructed through language use, and is maintained and organised via narratives. Lee also firmly notes, and I totally agree, that understanding of ourselves and others is set in narrative mode. Lee is particularly cautious about the loss of religious narratives whilst I would especially like to lose some of those, particularly the 'orthodox' made and held views.

Personal meaning can only be thought of as a narrative of sorts

So said Jerome Bruner writing about meaning-centred psychology. Humans must organise their individual and social world through the use of narrative and language structures. This is done by participation in the symbolic systems of a given culture. The narratives have an intrinsically teleological structure. We speak of stories from the past, and propose possible narrative futures, for our personal selves and for the society around us (Bruner 1990, pp. 42–45).

Individuals are **tangled** up in stories before they even realise it (Ricoeur 1991). Narrating stories outwardly may or may not happen, but narrating them inside one's skull happens inevitably and nonstop. As in literature, so it also happens in real life that significant events are not always immediately seen by characters. This is clear in many well-written novels such as *The Unbearable Lightness of Being* (Kundera 1984), *The World According to*

Garp (Irving 1988) or in *The Reader* (Schlink 1995). The main characters are shown to have a past and a projected (or at least reader-imagined) future. Real life imitates art, art imitates real lives, both are done through narrated stories.

Narrative clashes

Not only do master narratives clash, but also conflict can occur at all levels, particularly at the personal level. Then also personal narratives sometimes contradict the master story, or move against it. There are banal examples: I recall the first time I got on a motorcycle. It was not possible not to somewhat copy and feel like a biker from the movie 'Easy Rider' or like Marlon Brando. That trite enough narrative, of how one is or looks like on a motorcycle, was embedded into me. As a migrant, I thought I was stuck in the working class mode: bottle-washer, chair-maker, rubber-cutter and grape-picker. The model stuck with me and needed a conscious effort (and some luck) to break it. We make our worlds within what is available, yes, but world making is always and can only be a remaking, given the world is *'already on hand'* (Herman 2009).

Personal and emotional narratives

Now we have arrived at what I mainly wanted to explore, but that was not possible without the concept of master narratives understood. Here I explore, among others, some propositions by Elinor Ochs and Lisa Capps: *'Narrative is simultaneously born out of experience and gives shape to experience. Narrative activity provides tellers with an opportunity to impose order on otherwise disconnected events, and to create continuity between past, present, and imagined worlds.'* (Ochs & Capps 1996) It means that we make sense of our internal and external lives and actions by 'telling' ourselves our experiences, our 'story' in a way that makes sense. This is done via all the filters of the master and personal narratives that prevail in us.

I said previously that personal and master narratives, while always interactive, were also often contradictory. *'Personal narrative simultaneously is born out of experience and gives shape to experience. In this sense, narrative and self are inseparable.'* (Ochs & Capps 1996) Narrative and self are inseparable as many commentators have agreed, and as it is – I think – obvious. So that *'personal narratives reveal multiple and conflicting self-expressions.'* (McAdams 2008) That struggle is likely to be inevitable if you are a human being.

All narratives are a memory; all memory is a story of sorts

Now I want and need to link up the all-important function of memory as part of, or even all of, the me I call the 'self'. A part of the struggle and conflict mentioned refers inevitably to one's memory, to what writer Milan Kundera calls a paradoxical relationship between remembering and forgetting. While warning us that *'the struggle of man against power is the struggle of memory against forgetting'*, Kundera (1988) despairs that memory never captures authentic experience. *'We immediately transform the present moment into its abstraction. We need only recount an episode we experienced a few hours ago: the dialogue contracts to a brief summary, the setting to a few general features... Remembering is not the negative of forgetting. Remembering is a form of forgetting.'* (Kundera 1988) This is hugely important! I believe Kundera means that we might forget the many facts as they truly were. But did we ever really know, can we be sure of what the 'facts' were? Does the dialogue always contract to a brief summary? It seems so. And mainly, in my opinion, memory, which is instantly a story, is always filtered through our preset master and personal narratives. Meaning that the new or old story is fitted and incorporated into our preset programs.

Interesting and telling it is that even though survivors of traumatic events sometimes wish to 'sanitise' their stories, trauma is often not contractible (Wajnryb 2001). Conflict and trauma often facilitate the start of story-making, be it in real life or in fiction, books, movies or the arts. Kundera (1988) notes that one important challenge we all face is to recognise that our life stories are the pasts we tell and retell to ourselves.

To summarise so far:

Individuals build personal narratives from the global master narratives and attribute such to others in order to make sense, explain and understand them – and to be an active member of society (Bruner 1990, 1985; Eakin 1999; Herman 2009, 2003; Polkinghorne 1988). This is because, as George Lakoff and Mark Johnson are quoted by Eakin, *'all experience is cultural through and through...experience, meaning and identity all take from... cultural presuppositions.'* (Eakin 1999, p. 35) And this is where the power of cultural master narratives comes from. Note that 'presuppositions' are what I call simply 'programs'.

ॐ

Kessel, Cole and Johnson, in a paper titled **'The Self as a Center of Narrative Gravity'**, say that *'we are self-enhanced by an illusion of greater unity.'* (1992) This important idea I understand as one coming from both the personal and master narratives that have built the individual personality. Further, they suggest a lack of self as a unity. That I write this book from my research and presuppositions (and as a unity of sorts, illusion or not), may be because *'we are all virtuoso novelists'*, and *'we try to make our material cohere into a single good story.'* (Kessel, Cole & Johnson

1992) The situation is the same whether I am writing this serious piece or a novel or telling myself a story about something that took or did not take place (memory).

Famous fiction academic writer and one of the great thinkers of our times, Umberto Eco, cautions one to look closely at what narratives we have swallowed and are living by. He states that though words define, they may also lie, leading always through a distortion to both tragedy and comedy. *'The world as we represent it to ourselves is an effect of interpretation.'* (Eco 1997) The stories that energise life and emotional trauma do so via the incoherence of the lies that were defined as truth, but were hypocrisy and lies just the same, and part of the 'story plot' we surfaced with in order to make sense of our individual world. We are trained to think in the narrative mode from day one; indeed, how else could we be trained?

As life came at me by way of the master narratives, I began to hide many things, quickly becoming aware of the fact that bucking the master narrative and *'not participating in the "proper" brought with it usually absolutely no punishment...'* (Lem 1983) unless you were found out, and that in Stalinist Hungary in 1956 could be deadly.

༄

I consider that both personal and master narratives form and then act via certain kinds of 'plots', though I am not suggesting an entirely preset deterministic plot, far from it. We see a 'plot' only when examining and understanding our lives (Kundera 2000). Thus all our narratives might form the life plot(s) we hold but do not rule out that there may have been alternative plots. But, dear reader, a plot is usually a completed story, a book a movie... whatever. A fictional plot has a start and an ending. A plot can be productive and positive or else the opposite, or even some of both. In all ways, a plot is laden with programs, presuppositions, features, opinions, beliefs, and on and on. Just as actual life and people happen to be.

☙

I have shown that **we are inevitably our narratives**. What we have 'written' into our individual lives is like the food we eat, and what we do eat, it 'walks and talks and acts' as the 'me' and my life – so to speak.

The self and the conflict of narratives.

Now we are at another tangent, starting to consider whether there is really only one unified absolute self that we can call ME. Neuroscientist Michael Gazzaniga offered that the *'mind is not beautifully unified, but a problematic yoked-together bundle of partly autonomous systems.'* (in Kessel, Cole & Johnson 1992) A wonderful phrase and image 'yoked-together'! Bruner says that *'Incommensurability of individuality on one hand and the cultural identity on the other...has not been resolved.'* (Bruner 2006) And I wonder if it can be 'resolved' or whether it is just simply the human condition. Yet I want to differentiate three versions of this incommensurability:

A. Between master narratives themselves out in the world.

B. Between society's master and the individual's personal narratives.

C. The clash of personal narratives within the individual.

In 2015 I published a novel ***A Doubtful Inheritance*** (available from Amazon and others). I called it an 'autobiofiction' that demonstrates the narrative of how we are our remembered narrated selves, as Neisser (1994) and many others proposed. A

The 'Software' of Your Personality

'self' is not an entity, but an abstraction (Barclay 1994; Bruner 1986; Herman 2009; MacIntyre 1984; Neisser 2006). *'An account of the self as substantial is problematic because the concept of the self does not have an ontological referent – it is not a thing, substance, organisation, or further fact.'* (McCarthy 2007)

While a mother is 'sharing' memories via narratives, the child soaks them up, as if they were also his (Neisser 1994). Then the memory can morph, alter in some way, or one finds that Mum's story was incorrect. In later adult life, after much research into self and others, I began to appreciate that shared stories were indeed **relation-building or destroying**. The lack of inherited narratives, memories, and what one does with all that, can be problematic. So many of my master and personal narratives clash, as do yours, reader, when you consider it all.

Herewith an example of some obvious clashes. It is relevant to note that Dailey and Corey write from a gay male point of view. They refer to the clash of homosexual and heterosexual master narratives which is a strong example of conflict. Medical science, for example, used to refer to homosexuality as a disease, '... *perversion, deviance, unnatural acts.*' (Dailey & Corey 1998) Religion added the concept of sin to both being gay and to heterosexuality.

In my novel *A Doubtful Inheritance*, I offer a story of how 'Father Stalin' saved the Jews and then how, overnight, he was declared a mass murderer by Mr Khrushchev. This chapter happened to be a story from my own young life. The 'Stalin our Father and saviour' story was a master narrative swallowed whole by me at the time as part of my security system. Russians were godly, Germans were deadly, full stop. Yet I already knew that communism was a bloody affair and all was not well in Hungary, and that we were not 'free' – whatever that meant at the time. I ingested that Father Stalin and the heroic Russians saved particularly us,

Jews. The story tells how shaken I was when Stalin was deposed, which was – in any case – after he died. My personal and master narratives, and therefore my security system, were destroyed in a few minutes.

Another, if trivial, example of an inherited master narrative that became a personal one for me: *'Mum used to watch me turn around to look at a sexy looking female when I was perhaps 14. She'd say, "Why are you looking at that 'cheap' woman?"'* A conflict between 'her' and 'our' master narrative and my 'personal one'; what I thought of as sexy was merely 'cheap'. Ouch.

Therapy and narratives

All the preceding about 'narratives' shows a viable, even an obvious relationship between narratives and psychological therapies. I include all 'talking cures' that seek to help people via the telling-hearing, and the **resetting** of their stories under the banner of therapy.[23]

'Narrative Therapy', for example, is a specific style of therapy that explicitly states that: *Emotional problems are not to be mistaken for the totality of their owner. It is the problem that is the problem.* Such separation of problem and its owner is important because it refers to the 'storied' component of a person, the narratives they live by (Morgan 2000). Most therapies seek to 'read' the stories people live by, and work to enable clarification, deletion, or rewriting of the stories, sometimes by actual writing. Narrative therapists speak of the effects of 'dominant' (master) narrative-stories that are the broad social and the personal ones (Morgan 2000) that are constructed one from the other in an endless loop.

---

[23] Please note that I do not recommend any particular therapy. They all have various benefits and at times drawbacks. It is as hard to be a great therapist as it is difficult to find one!

Basically, as people 'separate from their narratives' they develop a stronger sense of personal agency and an enhanced capacity to direct their own lives. Individuals need to look critically and analytically at, and perhaps separate out from, the master/social narratives they have accepted as the only way to live (White & Epston 1990). Our personal narratives, I remind the reader, were always constructed from our learned master narratives. Much is said about repression in psychological therapies. I think of repressions as 'bad chapters' written into the psyche. They can be roadblocks to free expression and to a generally creative and satisfactory life.

When identification with the past ends

That is when a newer, freer, clearer, and more user-friendly version can be built? Hopefully, yes, but caution is required, for many of us have often replaced good or bad master narratives with other useless, and sometimes tragic ones.

I suggest that the reader finds the main points of this chapter in a more personal way.

Now we change tack in this story, tackling some different ways to see and read our lives. The following is one of several practical ways to reconceptualise and then reset life and your feelings, thoughts and actions.

THE BRAIN/MIND AS A PREPROGRAMMED PC (COMPUTER) IS HARDWARE AND SOFTWARE

What follows, what I intended throughout this book, is meant to bring a notion, a conception and action-activation of the brain/mind, bringing its behaviours and problems onto an easily imagined foundation – one that we can better navigate and use on a daily basis. Yo ho ho, what follows is one such concept.

The PC analogy

Whether my linking of the PC (computer) with human thought and actions is technically accurate or not is not the point of this chapter or book. Again, I paraphrase what Einstein and other scientists have said: *that which you cannot conceptualise, you cannot know or further investigate.*

Computers are limited in their abilities, and have no consciousness. Yet they can do huge amounts of calculations and work beyond the best of human ability in some areas. The PC is made to a certain fixed recipe. Perhaps we can add more hard drive and RAM to it, within certain limits. We can certainly delete or install preloaded programs to suit what we wish to do.

The 'Software' of Your Personality

There are confines to this, since new software needs so much more memory and ability. Also, beware, if you delete the basic operating system, or the 'windows' etc., then that is akin to (technological) 'suicide' for most users of the PC. So we keep the PC's basic set-up as it comes from its 'maker' – the factory – and then add whatever new programs we think will best suit what we want to achieve. Just so with ourselves: we keep some of what we got from Mum, Dad, family and society, since there is no choice in that and we need some of it anyway. Then we add learning, and various other inputs and actual life experiences. Some inputs are physical and some are mental inputs; many are both.

At times we find that our old PC won't do this or that. All one can do then is to chuck out the old machine and get a new one. This, of course, is where my PC analogy cracks a touch, because you cannot throw away your own personal in-your-head 'hard drive', as that is your self – body/brain and mind.

See important footnote [24] below.

People are made of 'hardware and software'. The combination of those makes me Ted Todd, ex Tibor Toth, ex Tibor Weisz – the three names I have had in my life. (And, oh dear, I reckon I am also familiar with several 'selves' within me, each of which belongs to the various names and times, somewhat...)

I understand myself somewhat, a bit like – but hopefully better than – I understand how my computer works. Some people understand their computer better than they understand themselves. Or they can use the PC better than their own mind. I

---

24 That 'throwing away' of 'hardware' that is a person – perhaps this is what happens when someone sadly and mistakenly, so to speak, commits suicide; the old machine is seen as just so bad that the owner, in a scrambled state of mind, throws it away, not entirely realising the finality of it.

know very little actually of how my PC works in a technical way. I just accept it, having researched what sort of a machine I needed to write books, play games, and surf the net. The salespeople told me the Apple had this much power and that much process ability, storage and so on, and ease of use. I accepted what I heard. The salesperson and I agreed that indeed this machine would also do some other jobs I need to do.

I have some small understanding that my PC has a hard drive that has limited memory and is capable of storing only so much information and no more. Same as my head. My Random Access Memory (RAM) is the part that allows me quicker access to certain files or programs that I had previously installed into my PC. It also allows me to access any of the many software programs that I may need for different jobs. I also know, having learned by trial and error and from advice from other PC users, that I cannot write these pages with a spreadsheet program or with a drawing program. What else do I know? Various bits and pieces about how diverse software packages work, what actions I need to take if I do want to draw, play games or do my accounts with the accounting software.

I discovered a few other things in my amateurish way: don't go to bed with the PC, it isn't cuddly. Don't drop it – it is fragile. There are things called chips and diodes or something, which are not food. All this I barely comprehend, but I don't need to. In fact, now that I think about it, the whole idea of computers is practically magic; I haven't much of a clue how they work! Is this sounding like a description of much of human life and of human beings? Do we not pretend that we know more about ourselves than we do? Does it happen to you at times that an aspect, a feeling, a thought rises from you that is a surprise?

Well, well, well, so good to say it thrice, for I confess the humble TV is still a total mystery to me. No, even the radio is amazing.

The 'Software' of Your Personality

Now, the only reason I wish to impress the fact that I am not a technological genius is to point out that I do not need to know **why** or even how tech things actually work. *I just need to know how to best use them* – which button to push on my hi-fi to get sweet music (which is what I need right now).

So perhaps **I need not know exactly why or how all my human parts operate** either. That is a relief, particularly since no one knows the whole thing about human beings anyway. But again, as long as I know **which of my very human buttons to push**, where, so to speak, to put my mental 'cursor', and which of my set software programs to switch on for the issue at hand...then I can action things to happen the way I want. I will have more control.

So, I do have to know which 'button to push and where to put the cursor' etc. I do have to know how to get on the 'internet' of my 'brain/mind' to search for the appropriate information I need. And I do have to know how to do that search properly – to call up thoughts and feelings, say – and then to focus the energy on the subject at hand. I do have to know what 'programs' are in there in my body/brain/mind. Otherwise, I may get millions of junk pages, or nothing useful. A jumbled mind reveals little that's useful. A much jumbled one, when people simply cannot focus it, is what we call troubled, or worse, traumatic and perhaps pathologically ill. Just like a PC that has been 'corrupted'.

So while there is much to find out and learn about me, body/brain/mind, I need not know exactly how my spleen operates, or why my toenails grow, or the colour of my brain cells. And much of what I do need to know about me is fairly easily accessible, if I make a conscious effort to pursue and learn the basics.[25]

---

25 By any words this is the process of life: a continuous quest for more awareness.

The PC of me

What follows here is a simplified (even a touch playful) version of conceptualising the PC as an analogy/metaphor for the human (emotional and thinking) world. It is not a matter of whether my explanations of the PC features or buzzwords are technically correct or not, I am certain they could be improved. What really matters is that my list allows a sort of reconceptualising of a great deal of our day-to-day human self and operation. Other PC word-concepts may be added as long as you can clearly translate them into how 'you operate'.

Here are a few useful associations and parallels:

The Computer, let's say, is the whole you. It is, you are, the hardware and the loaded programs.

Windows, the basic operating system: Your basic underlying view of your universe and self. It is also your particular view that you have right now of yourself and the world, the whole of your vision that you use in most circumstances.

Hard drive: You have extensive, and yet limited, ability and time. Just as you can't use a computer without some knowledge about how to use it best, make sure you are using the 'machinery' (yourself and body) to best advantage. Take active care of your physical and mental hard drive.

Gigabytes, hard drive memory capacity, random access memory: Your brain and intelligence capacity. Some have more, some less. This can be improved and it was enhanced as you grew, by education, for example. Also think of this notion as the one for holding memory long and short term. Just as you can overload a computer, you can also overload your brain/mind/emotions etc. **Memory** is the capacity to hold and keep information, knowing where you filed it (into which file/role)... This memory capacity

The 'Software' of Your Personality

is limited in your PC, less so in you, and it can even be extended somewhat. Particularly, your RAM (random access memory) is limited. Here is some hope that one can change and improve on nature, for you can install extra RAM into yourself: education, body care and health etc. are such. For you, 'random access is something you might recall; some memories you don't or cannot now recall, but know or suspect they are there. And remember that the memories you know and cherish or hate, or whatever... are also all part of the total and they work in the background.

Desktop: The immediate visible things or self. The daily business of living, tasks you need to do, the most important or most used items in the now are in front of you on the desktop of your mind and imagination.

Software programs: The big thing! Your preprogrammed features (selves), and note the plural! Roles, personality traits, features etc. all come from 'preprogramming', both from your given biology – genetics – and the original accidental or deliberate 'installations' of new programs since your birth. You have biologically installed programs that came with your body-hardware-computer. Then parents, culture and society installed many other features-software-programs into you. Some of those were or are necessary, but many may be well 'outdated' and work against your best interests now.

Folders and files: They contain certain specific 'jobs' to be done, situations, and even the 'roles' of your selves. Many older ideas, feelings and choices, beliefs and values are in these files stored away. You can run out of 'file' space, just as your PC can. But you cannot buy a new hard drive for your head. Take care about 'overloading'.

Edit and insert: This is what you are doing by reading this book, for example, because as you explore, you are inserting-editing, perhaps 'rewriting' feelings and thoughts. Rewrite? We have the ability to consider and recraft a better or clearer 'narrative' of what has or may have (even should have) happened in our lives. This is where you can also delete, insert and correct words and sentences, even feelings. Or add more or less to what is 'written'.

Delete, trash: A hugely important function! This is what we use to get rid of outdated files and outdated, useless programs. Particularly those programs that we discover to be clashing with one another. Or are contaminated by a 'virus' (bad ideas). Delete old useless 'files' that are no longer applicable or needed. Lighten up your 'hard drive': yourself. Get rid of old notions, feelings, ideas, hurts, blames, claims...that do not serve you well now. Trash outdated data and programs.

Save file? Back up: You keep useful files when you are working within a program. But be aware that whenever you 'save' something in your head, you are saving it as a whole, the good and the less so. Do save, and **back yourself up** to another 'hard drive'. Such other 'hard drives' may actually be a piece of paper, diaries, other written stuff like your stories and ideas, computer files, pictures, recordings and so on. Taking yourself genuinely seriously needs a bit of organising. Whatever is most salient to your many selves, career and your relationships ought to be 'backed up'. Don't leave it to chance. Having a good outside backup system of many things will free up your energies, head and creativity.

Open a file or document: This is focusing on what you are doing now. Know what or who you are dealing with right now and why, and focus on it. Leave other files closed for the time being. For example, while you are reading this, let go of your criticism of it, don't worry about what the car mechanic said yesterday or what your boss is like. Concentration is what even a cheap PC does perfectly. It's much harder for people. So focus and leave other matters alone. **If you do open a file, act on it**, do something with it; do it now and handle it just once, don't just rename or shift it from one place to another.

Internet: Represents the world out there, and in your head. The entire universe perhaps. It is mind-boggling, huge and messy. Go searching and surfing by all means, try things, but take care of how far you divert yourself. There is information and entertainment out there that is often positive and helpful, or rubbish, or not entirely true. Don't believe everything you see, hear or read on the news, or from experts or from society; question it, test it yourself.

Help: You can get help easily on your PC and you can get help just as easily for yourself, providing you are not too proud or silly to ask for it. Asking for help makes friends and brings much satisfaction and better relationships. However, ask the right 'help desks', the appropriate ones, and remember what one of my daughters has on her card: *'If you think professionals are expensive, then just try an amateur!'*

Home page: Your daily core self, the one you have learned to rely on as the basis for almost anything. Don't clutter it. Check from time to time whether any of it needs a refresh, deletion or addition. Build a good, clear, not overly complicated 'home page' – this is where your daily, solid practical life is, after all. Consider who else has access to your home page and why. Not everything you are has to be on your open home page. Be discriminatory as to what you put out on public view.

Social media: Too obvious! We are all in it, I mean, in the real socio-cultural world. Some of what is called social media is intruding into your head. Be careful out there, but not risk averse. Going too far here is as bad as not being in it at all. You need not be on every channel. Use what you can. Explore what you are getting involved with before you join it.

☙

When I switch on my computer, I first get the windows environment. Let me use a bit of whimsy and say that this is a bit like when after sleeping we wake up: we see programs, actions, jobs to be done, mail coming in and out, we recall things like the footy game etc. On my PC I choose a program, word processing, say. Now I may bring certain tools or abilities of this program into play. I open a saved file – something I have been working on. (This last statement needs to be added to by saying that the 'saved file' is mine, it is in a sense me, and yet it is not the totality of ME, but put that aside for a moment.) I enter into the 'saved' file and it flicks onto my screen. This is like how a 'thought or memory' rises within me, when I want to think or act on something: it is my internal information processing system; it flicks onto the screen of my awareness.

Of course, you know all the usable programs your machine has, but your psyche has both known and unknown programs (and files). All my programs will automatically respond to incoming perceptions. My mind will respond consciously or subconsciously, or even unconsciously, but there will be responses of sorts. When I am working, I think about the work at hand. Like, ah…wait, a friend is coming to meet me soon… So I have already 'switched' on that program (friends) – or it switched itself on – even while the 'work' program is still running, although it is now running at a less focused or frantic pace.

Your genetic givens, IQ and input learning may be great but are not unlimited. As you can with your PC, so you can add to your self by education, exploration and interactions if done in a focused way. You are limited by your genes, but you are never

The 'Software' of Your Personality

ever near your maximum potential. Not that you have to be. On the other hand, do not kid yourself about your infinite ability either. You can't fool your PC, which is a good thing, but you can and do fool yourself all the time. A shame, but entirely human and true enough for most of us.

ಏ

There are many more computer word-concepts one could usefully employ but the above will do for our purposes. People are in some ways more and in other ways much less limited than a PC – not as much as we think we are, and yet perhaps more than we know.

We have our personal individual contents some of which are much the same as any other human, and yet always somewhat different. Our hardware and software – body and mind and installed programs – are partly shared by everyone. Some are not. Inherited genes are both hardware and software potentially. Learned software is what we mostly seem to employ in our lives and it is limited and sometimes way too entrenched. Both inherited and installed software are unique to each of us and both carry our limitations and our potentials. We also have these things that make us human called emotions, a rather large and important component of us. Our emotions are affected by and interact with our thoughts inseparably. Thoughts, feelings and attached memories interact and direct in some sense much, I think likely all, we do; thought/feelings are in fact what and who we are and what we do.

You already knew some of this.

In some ways we can always explore, and most of us have, our inner and more obvious 'operating systems and programs'. We sort of know a lot about many of our features, ideas, feelings/

thoughts etc.; we have always done some internal exploration of ourselves to a degree. This too is part of our nature, as it is to be curious and to question things, but we tend to stop shorter than might be desirable. Many people hold education in high esteem, yet various socio-cultural values limit even that. Individuals are born into a huge variety of cultural modes, not all of which welcome universal education and make it available for all.[26]

That the PC idea is generally acceptable is not that surprising, given the PC was somewhat modelled on how the human brain/mind operates. There are several other metaphors or analogies that could also be used. As long as they are clear and need no expertise to conceptualise your self (or selves), that is fine.

Before we move on, let's bed some of this in:

Some software programs are too large for a computer with a small capacity. So it is also with people. Some computer hard disks fill up and can take no more input of programs or files. The same can happen with people. Also, if you try to do something with a PC program that the particular program is not designed for, it will soon tell you that it cannot do that. Same for people? Not necessarily so. Sometimes your mind will indicate or even yell/tell you that something is not on, and sometimes you will totally stress out and even 'break down'. If one tries to merge two unlike PC programs, it usually does not work. The very same can apply to people. You cannot be a greenie and sell cigarettes at the same time... Well, you can, but it ain't good.

---

26 Generally speaking, our current Western socio-cultural values and ideals are probably better than they have been in previous times. I am slightly optimistic. The main thing holding back the expansion of more minds and human endeavour are the ridiculously outdated religious belief systems of the world! I won't pursue this line of thought further, but do consider the blockages religious ideology has created in thought and deed.

To free up space by deleting old files and programs that you no longer need or use takes a different sort of effort to the PC. More later, but we have already covered some ways and means.

The good news

You have done all this, all this sort of program manipulating and deleting from your mind, all your life! You believed in Santa only for so long and then you deleted the idea as a fact, or updated it to a quaint cultural idea, but no longer accepted it as fact. Same with many other issues. You have realised that your parents were a bit hypocritical about the no lying rule, you have discovered that not everyone is trustworthy, you have discovered adult love and feelings that replaced some of the innocent childish ones and so on. So you have already, and often, done deleting, and updated and sorted programs, mostly on autopilot, but at times on purpose. You have installed new programs and written new files etc., like being a parent, building a profession or career, overcoming fears, etc.

Updating your own inner programs, deleting outdated data, and so on, happens all the time for all of us. Mostly it is all done automatically, seems to just happen. All you need to add now is to do some more of this fully focused and **purposefully and resolutely!** The capacity is already built into the marvellous machine we call a human being. In a PC you might need a new piece of software to be rid of old ones. People also may need some new input ('mental' software), in order to get rid of old ideas, bad or outdated programs, or less than productive features that bring no joy. Indeed, to get rid of many of your old programs that have created bad habits takes an effort. Hoping and praying won't do it, friends! Actions of the right sort will help.

My ideas about the tooth fairy, women, men, God, communism and capitalism, and so on, my own beliefs and programmed narratives were one thing when I was 10 years old, another at 20 and still another at 40. By now they are all very much updated by many more years of experience and often by my own conscious efforts. Many times I needed new software input for my head, in order to make proper sense of it all. I used education, therapy, reading and research, and talking to others as my 'deleting' and 'reprogramming' tools.

By the way, even the outward presentation of you to another person can be improved by a new piece of software, like for example a new understanding of your body language, or a new piece of learning. Instead of throwing away an old relationship, perhaps that also needs new input-software (or even, who knows, hardware...?). Or maybe it does have to go! But please, not before a proper investigation. The buzz word in business circles is that there is a need for constant 'reinvention' of the business. The same is true for you and relationships, work etc., and it is an effort, but it can be most satisfactory doing it and great outcomes are possible. All it needs most of the time is some new 'software' that becomes new thinking/feeling.

You might know that not all initial installation of software is perfect, or you may find that you do not have the right software for what you wanted to achieve. Not all new programs, packages, data, ideas out there are good for everyone. Or even necessary. Far from it, so do not go confusing yourself by the choices and by overloading. Don't go and buy 10 self-help books immediately. Chew on one for some time. Resist the temptation to 'buy' without research and discrimination, which means doing a lot of thinking/feeling. There are experts you can refer to about your PC, just as there are about yourself. (But be careful. Many 'experts' are not so good at it either.)

If the right electrical connection, modem, router settings are not made, whatever, then your PC won't work well. Neither will you

The 'Software' of Your Personality

operate that well if you eat badly, don't exercise, drink or take drugs...you are just making bad brain/mind connections worse.

I said before that adding to the 'files' within you happens automatically and often – as does reducing or deleting the information contained within. Worse luck, the PC recalls anything with one click and usually perfectly. The human memory is far less reliable...so watch it and ask whether your memory of significant past events is entirely correct. What is a significant past event? Anything you readily recall, be it big and ugly or small and lovely. And perhaps some you can't actually entirely recall. If you can remember it, it certainly means something. Ask yourself always: is your interpretation of a memory correct? Is it the only possible understanding of it, or are there other ways to see it.

ॐ

It would be easier for people who need access to update, delete or change the files in their heads and bodies, if we knew what damned original files were programmed into our hard drive (memory bank) – but we do not know. And if we knew exactly what programs we are running that we know of – or are unaware of. It's a silly fact that no one is totally aware of it all. Far from it. Then again, people are often aware with a partial comprehension. We have certain memories, beliefs, value systems, dos and don'ts, imperatives, musts. We were programmed by the great programmers (no, not God) from day one or from even earlier. The great programmer? Oh yes: the great programmers were your parents, nature and nurture, society, culture etc.

All these agendas, programs, drivers, plans, by whatever name you prefer, they have formed and are now potentially with you as memories. They come from, originated – we might say – when time began, billions of years ago. Only nature and evolution have changed them, taking eons of time. The good news is that now we humans might be at a time in our evolution when we can effect more positive changes on ourselves more speedily and with intention. We might just be at a stage when we can understand enough, be aware of enough to know what it really is that an individual and a society can be like. Things do not look well in the world; in fact, it seems it is a mess in many ways. Yet my optimistic mind says that our consciousness has never been higher than today. I hope I am correct. Here then is a most important point: psychology and philosophy have usually asked for awareness of how you feel and think. That is as it should be and I too recommend it. Yet it has all been not so easy and not so successful either. These days we are pushing the boundaries. We need easy tools, like when earlier I added an additional and easily investigable enquiry. That was to explore what **features** you actually possess here and now, and even more importantly, to ask what features you may have **in potential**, ones that you may be able to use to positively maximise your life. All this is hidden or perhaps readily available to you; it is all in your memory bank.

Surprisingly little attention has been paid to the aspect of knowing your actual features, and yet it is, in every way, a most important and salient question. People are doers. We do things and need to do so. Thus, whether you are searching for a better job, a better life, a new or old relationship, or spiritual endeavours, self-awareness of who-how you are right now is the issue. Alas, it is right here where people get stuck and rarely pass through stage one. I think this happens because if we just navel gaze, it is easy to get lost in the beauty and the dirt, the pain and the highs of an inner self drama-dialogue. But once the exploration of your actual features takes place, there are some new qualities that enter the picture. Some facts that are undeniable will surface, as do some that are wobbly and soft and are in need of investigating and doing something about. When exploring anything, from a recipe to a murder story, new information and facts, new byways and highways soon come into the picture.

It really is a vital concern to know what features I have now and what I may have as potential ones waiting to be brought out into actuality!

Now, I must reiterate the important and tricky issue that during this exploration you will find several of your 'features' are kind of hazy, hidden, or sort of vague. Some, or even most of these, are not, may not be, your features at all. There are features you believe you do have, would have liked to have had, Mum would have liked you to have, the party or the religion would have liked you to have...and so on and on...but most likely you don't, never did and possibly never will have them. Give up on all that sloshy wishful thinking.

Or else the situation may be the opposite to what I have just outlined. No way to know which, until you really consider and check them out. Dig your brains not the garden for a while. Here is an obvious example: almost everyone believes they are good listeners. But most people will tell you that most people are bad listeners...Aha. Well, which one? Cannot be both. In my experience of facilitating workshops for sales and marketing, or for human relationships, or counselling sessions, I am convinced that most people are terrible listeners. Sorry about that, folks. Some look like they are listening, but are unable to 'hear' well. (No hearing aid will cure that.)

Like in any proper exploration of anything, there will be lost and found parts, clusters, feelings, thoughts... There will be sadness and laughter, highs and lows, potential creative excitement and perhaps even feelings of shame for having fooled yourself. There is no need for shame or any other negative emotion to linger. Upon finding them, if any, let them slip into the garbage can of the mind; use your 'delete these files' button. Have no regrets; it is just the way things have been and now, as the ex Australian Prime Minister Julia Gillard and most other pollies often say, 'Let's move forward...'

Oh, by the way, it is not that easy to have no regrets. It is not so simple to just delete unwanted data. (Yes, I have said this many times before.) True, but if you conceptualise what you want to delete, and then imagine deleting it...and use your 'tools', some of which may be what I suggest in this book or else what others have offered, then it will get easier and easier to do it. For now, do what you can and feel no sorrow about what you can't do. I am not dead against having some regrets either, by the way. Sometimes you can indeed learn a lot from recalling them, but I am dead against using regrets to freeze the future.

I'd feel blameworthy if I did not say something about guilt and fear

However, I shall only touch these large and very human emotions and feelings. There are volumes written about it all, much of it rubbish. Fear is at the base of so many other feelings that it is at times barely, if at all, recognised for what it is: abject fear. Fear underlies anger, lies, violence, and more. Guilt too has a big element of fear.

Fear spells out and has these components: **F**alse **E**vidence **A**ppears **R**eal. Wonderful stuff and I know I am borrowing it from someone, but I cannot recall from whom (sorry author). However cute, it is not entirely true either, for fear can be not false but real evidence and if it is then we need to recognise and address it properly rather than reverting to anger, stupid ideas like dogma, violence etc. The often denigrated idea of guilt is part of our total scheme. I recognise how hard it is to give up regrets and even harder to let guilt go. The emotion called 'guilt' seems part of all of us, to various degrees. Contrary to some others, I do not think that guilt is entirely useless, but rather that there are positive and negative sides to it.

It is clearly odd to feel that you are a 'sinner' given that you did not ask to be born, and you became what every human being has, a person who has been at least partly and unavoidably programmed. It is dreadful that so many feel like sinners, or guilty about that area of human life.

It is, however, not at all crazy to feel bad about hurting another person, or about doing harm to the good earth even. The problem is how one handles it. You can and indeed should feel guilty about some things, but the feeling ought to be more like an awareness that you must not do something again or anymore. Guilt is, or can be, debilitating, and when it is, it's a killer and will make you 'write bad cheques'... It will twist your life out of shape; it will force you to make silly choices and actions. At some deeper level that often happens to fanatics of religion or political persuasions or whatever, guilt can transform into a form of self-righteous actual killer.

Unless you catch guilt and see the obvious, which is that what has gone is gone, you cannot be rid of it or use its energy to better ends. You can do something about your feelings of guilt, but you cannot change past actions. You certainly can work towards not doing them again. The next two quotes tell the crux of what is to be done other than carrying guilt for all your life. Maslow has made many and various important points in his writings, but two stand out for me specially. You can feel guilty, worried, or whatever about your past – or future – however you can only take action in the present, the now moment. To act in the now is a major sign of mental wellness. And equally important, and this is the crux of what I am about in this book: unless you reach out, and use, go for whatever talents you have and clearly employ them to good ends, you will never feel fulfilled and happy. (I have paraphrased Mr Maslow.)

A great deal of existential angst comes from this last one, a sort of feeling of guilt that one has not done what one might have. And now, as Bugs Bunny would say, there is no more on this subject. I move on now towards what may seem as a side issue, but trust me, it is totally integrated with sane and successful lives.

Keep in mind:

- That yes, you already do know a lot more about this and less about that, but usually not as much as you need to know about you. Even though we tend to think we know ourselves.

- Of course you are not a computer; you are much more than that…only you are not as good at doing some things that a $1000 PC can do. But hey, that's fine. Don't get hung up on what is an analogy, a metaphor that is aimed to help understanding.

- Fear and guilt can be real or false. They can be productive or debilitating.

- I believe that we feel major and correct guilt in our lives – which we cover up – when we do not do the best we can for ourselves and others.

THE WORLD AND YOU.

'You are the world, and the world is you' (Krishnamurti) is an idea of enormous importance worth exploring a little before we trek further. We must add, factor into all I've said so far, the rest of the world! That is to say that **the world as we know it is relationships**.

You are also already in a relationship within, with yourself. Within yourselves there are opinions, conflicts, needs, wants. (I hope this sounds very familiar and rings a bell.) You are already an entire world all by yourself.

No one would argue that we are in constant, never-ending relationships with others and everything, with all there is. We are in relationships with people close to us and far, animals, trees, the universe, and we constantly relate to ideas, thoughts and feelings. As John Donne said many years ago 'no man is an island'. One might then wonder why it is that some people do a lot of swimming to get to islands that are not that brilliant and have next to nothing growing on them... (I love metaphors.)

Everyone, even everything that exists is always in relationship to all else. Your own thoughts, feelings, ideas and actions are also in relationship with one another – and with all else within and out there. Yet some of our common, individual 'relating programs' may be by now out of date as has been suggested earlier. Some are or were not good programs, not the best ones that you could have input... Some people have relating programs that are better and faster than yours, others less so. That's the way it is.

The humble PC itself sits silent, waiting for its relationship with a human being. It is nothing until it is switched on, someone's fingers activate it. This is a significant example of intentionality and relationship. Once again, not one or the other, but the two; you and the PC create what can be. (Of course 'two' is in fact countless if you think about it.) Yes, citizens, your computer is inert matter, plastic, glass and metals, a heap of junk – until it comes into relationship with someone! Phew!

Interact with a machine or with other people and magic might happen. What transpires then is partly, yes only partly, up to you, and up to the ability of the man-made machine, or the person you are relating to. By now, I trust you know that each time I say 'machine' you could replace that with Tom, Dick or Helen…(not that your relating is the same with a person as with a machine).

We do this interacting-relating with people incessantly, even in our sleep! In fact, there is and can be nothing else for humans but to relate. Humans? Not only – all life is related to many other strands.

Life is relationships, relationships are lives

All our memories, which I said previously are in fact the ME I know, are a story of relating to someone or something, or to ourselves. Every memory then is in a sense an US… The internal-external relating loop touches us inevitably and unceasingly, and also touches the rest of the world. Actually, 'touches' is an understatement for it is the very fabric of the world and us.

What the out there 'world' brings to you is often, perhaps even mostly, a random happening. I said before that my view of you overtly or covertly could affect your view and even your 'software' – and that in turn, me and mine. Round and round it goes, another endless circle that we call relating-communicating.

The 'Software' of Your Personality

Relating and relationships are tantamount to communicating; no relating can be done without a form of communication. That, friends, is one reason why things can and do go wrong in the world, for to communicate really well is not an easy task. You were born with the potential to communicate, but not with the ability to do it well. That is more of a learned thing, alas, often badly explained and demonstrated by adults to children. Or should I say not at all explained? For most children basically just follow example.

So then, my particular way of 'being', and of communicating in this book will – or at least might – 'switch' on, or off, parts of your programs even as you read! Or it may not do anything. I said earlier that change and how it happens comes with the 'aha' experience of understanding. That 'aha' might come because you agree, or disagree, like or otherwise, what is being communicated to you.

Now come a couple of cute, fun ideas, but how true they are!

Where and what do people 'bank'?

Many people favour the well-known banks, such as the CBA or the ANZ and the like, and yet most people also have *secret* accounts in other banks. Sometimes they don't even know that they have banked and have an account in:

The Bank of Resentment (Copyright Dr Ted Todd 2010)

In this bank you put in a little something and eventually you get a lot back...sometimes even when you were not going to make a withdrawal. Your small investment always brings a huge interest, and the Bank of Resentment loves to pay you out. In fact, they will pay out several times, no worries. You can visit them day after day and they will pay out again and again, probably increasing the interest as well.

Ah yes, there are several other wonderful and well paying banks out there that most of us use. Big payouts are available from the Bank of Meanness, the Bank of Anger, the Bank of Hate...just to mention a few. They all compete to give you a big payback on even a small deposit. Curiously enough though, even the Bank of Love will return to you a huge payout on just a smallish deposit. Where do you bank mainly?

Then there is yet another bank that is so terribly important: **The Bank of Time.**

Imagine that a bank credits $86,400 to your account every morning. But it does not carry over the balance from day to day, so the unused portion of the money disappears. So what you need to do is to draw out every cent every day!

Each of us has this bank called **The Bank of Time**. Every morning it credits you with 86,400 seconds, and every night it writes off whatever part you have failed to call on, to have invested to a good purpose. Again, it carries over no balance. There is no overdraft, and if you have failed to use the day's deposit, it is your problem and yours alone. Bad as it is, there is no drawing against tomorrow's or yesterday's deposit; you can only live on today's deposit today. So take care and invest each moment so as to get the best possible results, success, happiness, love, health... whatever, for the clock is running. Make the most of today.

Main points:

- *Yesterday is History, Tomorrow is Mystery. Today is the Present, and a Present is a Gift!* (Someone sent me this great little thing by email.)

- Take care where you bank...

- You really is de world, man.

WHAT CAN BE LEARNED? WHAT IS THE 'NEW'?

Particularly in difficult situations we tend to be '**doing more and more of what had never worked all that well**'. This is a sort of doing it 'as if'... The question was and still is how to get away from these old dispositions and preprogramming? How to see what's happening now as a new situation, not the same as past others?

Hold on, you say; you might not want to, or need to, find new responses. You might throw up just the right old responses...yes? Oh all right, that can be the case, but in challenging situations we often get lost and finish up not as well as we might have. This happens lots in business and often in personal relating, or even when you want to organise the kids to do well in school. Or in your own head, as you mull over what or where you should take action next.

As for your old or new responses – how does one know whether it will be a positive one for you? All we can note is the strength of our responses; the stronger, the more dogmatically one holds a view, the more likely you are a 'robotic personality' acting from your old, perhaps outdated programs in what is now a new situation.

Actually all situations are always new

They are not the same as yesterday's, or last year's or whatever. Every moment is actually brand new; they just look like the same old. They are eggs made to look like chickens...to trick your ego mind into taking the easiest ways out.

Every moment is new.

The opposite to one being heavy and dogmatic seems to be having wishy-washy opinions and responses. Actually, that is not the opposite at all, because someone who has no views or convictions and is open to all and any input is not a free nor a robotic character, but rather, as we know, an unformed personality.

We are likely to instantly squeeze whatever situation or problem we come to into a formula we think works, and so answer from the old dearly held material. If we have the tools, we can change and learn, but it ain't as simple – or as difficult – as people usually think. Right responses at times are likely to be different (perhaps) to what you thought until now. The issue centres – as I keep saying – on the ability to conceptualise what you have, what you want and what you can do to get it (I am endlessly repeating this because it is so necessary to the whole of the argument).

I do not mean learning just new information or simple new skills here. There is lots of that coming in and needs to be learned simply by living. Learning information can be relatively easy. The real question is whether we can learn something **anew** about ourselves inner and outer, about our thoughts, feelings and relating/communicating. And then, about our outgoing responses. That is, learning something new about our emotional and actioned lives, without immediately painting every situation with our own (old) coloured brush.

Seeing anew needs solid perceptions of awareness of our preprograms without instantly and often unknowingly 'filing' the new into the old 'archives'. You know how this works: I happen on a new situation – and every moment and situation is always new, strictly speaking – and immediately I reflect 'ah, this is like such and such'. I don't necessarily 'think' all this consciously, but the mind relates to it in this way, automatically reacting in a fashion that comes out of me as if this new situation is exactly the same as...

In other words, we make what might be newish immediately the old. We do that for the sake of comfort and because our pre-recording allows little else. Unless, that is, the pre-recording is affected by an incoming new program, one that directs that anything new, each moment, needs to be seen and considered as such: *new*. That's hard to take on board, but it is doable if you persevere. It is more or less what the Buddhists call mindfulness. We do not need all hocus-pocus-focus on anything else beyond being here and being mindful!

It is not actually our subject matter here to go too far into consciousness beyond stating that the process of predispositions admits mostly what the consciousness is comfortable with. Our consciousness holds all our predispositions or preprograms as deep memories. Note that you can recall some of your memories, and that you also have other memories that you are not aware of, don't know, but something might make them surface unintentionally. That's when we say oh...aha, wow... All this can happen when we are faced with another human being or with a new situation, or even if we just suddenly stumble upon a secluded feeling/thought.

When it comes to people, a new or an old friend, a family member, your spouse, or even yourself, how could you possibly see them as new each time? You do and don't have to do that, but must keep an eye on your predispositions perceiving what (you think) you have seen and heard before... To listen well, seems an easy program, and yet it appears hard for people to do. Curiously, everyone believes that they are good listeners, but good hearers are rare. Yet, we all know someone we think of in that way, and many others we think of as bad listeners, right? There is something special about good hearers; they are well liked and trusted. When I meet my wife later today, I need to hear and see what she is telling me, what there is actually now, rather than the usual.

We know clearer communications between people are a good thing, but how about (how about, indeed) clear communications between me and myself? For until that happens there will be limits to my relationships with others and with all ideas and actions. And I will keep doing more and more of what has (perhaps) not worked!

All I have said so far begs the question: can you really change and to what degree? And when I asked if one is able to learn anything fresh, I did not mean just new information; there is lots of that and it's relatively easy to do it. You can 'install' newly learned info and get no results beyond a temporary buzz that you got that degree, or cooked a new dish or fixed the car. Not that all these are not worthwhile – they certainly are!

ॐ

The question I am asking is deeper, the one that the genius knower of human behaviour, Jiddu Krishnamurti (and many others) has asked. To make it absolutely clear again: can one experience-learn-see-understand something anew? That is, without immediately painting it with our own coloured brush, using our existing filtering system, the one that is already in there? Can we see things as new? That would also mean the understanding that today is today, not a day past, similar to… Can we receive input without instantly probing which existing file to put it in, thinking it is the same as the…? Is it possible to not bring to a new event the old experiences that immediately sort what genre, size, program etc. it belongs to? Oh dear, all that happens and does so automatically, does it not?

It is how the brain operates, it seems. We do that also for the sake of comfort and because of the enormous amounts of material we all need to cope with in daily lives. Thus, some of the way we operate can't be helped; indeed, there is nothing else we can do. The brain/mind can only hold and see so much at a time. Our brain/mind has defences and automatic moves that are necessary. We do need to recognise rules, laws, the nature of everyday life in the society you live in. We do need to be sorting and relating one experience to another at least to some degree. And so we do need some of the stock standard programs we have been loaded with. Unavoidable, yes, and yet there are some people who escape the 'robotic personality' mode at times, just now and then. They are outstanding creative, notable people. Not necessarily famous or even well known, though some are.

The point is to have a reasonably good grasp of the whole idea at a level where you actually recognise when something 'new' or newish arises, something that matters. And what 'matters' is in fact usually new. And it is a potentially new learning or understanding of something that one has not known or fully understood before. This whole movement, by the way, is responsible for why we might learn a new skill, say, and yet not retain it. To clarify, we learn a new skill and not having bedded it in as such, as 'new', sufficiently, we do not retain it. Children learn lots of things fast because their brain/minds are fresh and available to, shall we say, see and hear incoming learning as new. Children have fewer programs running and insisting on fitting things into old frames.

The 'Software' of Your Personality

This learning of the new is vitally important when you are exploring yourself or others in the world out there. Just imagine your own movement in this regard. When you explore your thoughts and feelings one often does not do much more than tiring and even boring 'mind-fucking'. That is because we tend to repeat think/feel what we always did, what has never helped. We are endlessly stuck in repeating and comparing the same sort of things to one another – the feelings and experiences, the thoughts and the actions. Yet, and again, this too is necessary.

> *Sometimes, even often, people try to do more and more of what has never truly worked for them.*

And that happens because it is not easy to see and hear something new that is coming from out there, let alone to hear the 'new' coming from your own self! All this is a skill that has to be consciously learned. You were born with the potential for it, but not the skill.

In a practical sense, consider what happens when you formally study a new subject, say, if you have gone back to university. Even then, your mind will want to shuffle the material into old 'files' because it is easier to do that. Yet when you can and do see newness, you rejoice and enjoy it, don't you? It is exciting. Rarely boring. But it can also be threatening. So beware when you are learning things in a formal way, just as you should be cautious when you are investigating yourself. Look for the 'new' without necessarily framing it with the old.

'Learning' new 'people', relearning the ones you know, and relating to others and yourself.

Let's now briefly focus on what happens between only two people, that being a relatively simple (ha ha?) interaction. I said simple and smirk in recognition that we are talking about two of the most complex entities (or information processing systems) we know. Possibly abler and more complex than perhaps we will ever know! So how do I face up to this new piece of learning, in this case to this new person I have just met – or even to an already well-known individual? How do I respond and comprehend an exchange without coming from (entirely) the old framework? Is it possible for me to consider this person and situation new each time? Can I hear and see what there is **now, today** actually?

Clear communications between people, indeed clear communications between me and myself, is what all this is leading to. When I talk to Sharon, we have two complex systems trying to communicate in order to arrive at some sort of outcome. Good communication with Sharon will lead us both to a result that hopefully we both find satisfactory enough. The analogy I am building here is this: I need to **be a good, or better still great, communicator with my very own self (or selves)** in order to hear and learn something new from all of my communications with others. Good communications with Sharon and with myself can and will only happen if we check and cross-check with one another as to what we think each of us has heard and understood.

When it comes to communicating with myself, a further complication is that in some ways I am more likely to 'misunderstand' one of my own answers or 'voices', motivations and feelings. This happens precisely because I cannot cross-check as I can with Sharon, that is, with someone outside of myself for a variation in my internal perceptions. That, by the way, is why therapists, counsellors and friends are and can be very important in helping with this project, precisely because they are not part of you. (They can also be a calamity.)

This chapter is as usual, part of a much larger thought. No further tripping into this subject is needed for our purposes here.

The main points in this chapter were:

- Be aware of how hard it is to 'see' the 'new', and that there are times when it is important to see things and people and events as 'new'.

- No, it can't be done entirely and 24 hours a day, but some aware focus will get very good outcomes.

- Relating is communicating, and vice versa.

Sometimes, even often, people try to do more and more of what has never truly worked for them.

REPROGRAMMING YOUR SELF IS POSSIBLE

Sometimes you can free up space on your PC by deleting old files and programs that you no longer need or use. Just so with people, I suggested, but it takes a different effort to delete 'files' and your often strongly held but outdated programs. PC files can be saved, updated, deleted, and easily altered. The preset programs in a PC are limited and mostly cannot be changed. The 'presets' in your head are actually more flexible and change friendly than the computer's, but take various and often subtle efforts to change them.

Good news, yet again, already, and repeatedly

I have mentioned already that you have done all this before; all this sort of program changing from your mind, and your life! You have always done it, whether you knew you were doing it or not: deleted, renewed, updated programs. All you need now is to do some of this purposefully and resolutely! Hoping and praying won't do it, friends! (God helps those who help themselves…)

By the way, even the outward presentation of you to another person can be improved by a new piece of software, like for example a new understanding of your body language, or a new piece of learning (even a new jumper may do it?). Instead of throwing away an old relationship, perhaps that also needs new input-software (or even, who knows, hardware?) The buzzword

The 'Software' of Your Personality

in business circles is that there is a need for constant 'reinvention' of the business. It is the same for relationships, and it is an effort, but it can be most satisfactory doing the work, and it may bring a great outcome. All it needs most of the time is some 'new software', fresh thinking/feeling.

You already know that not all initial installation of software into you was necessarily the best. You may have found already that you do not have the right piece of software for some things. Beware though. Not all new programs out there are necessary for everyone. Far from it, so do not go confusing yourself by overloading. Don't go and buy 10 self-help books immediately. Chew on one for some time. Mine, says I. Resist the temptation to 'buy' without research and discrimination, which means thinking/feeling. There are experts you can refer to about your PC, and also about yourself. If the right electrical connections, modem, router settings are not made, your PC won't work well. Neither will you operate that well if you eat badly, don't exercise, drink or take drugs...you are just making bad connections worse.

I've said already that adding to the 'files' within you has happened at times automatically, and so has the deleting of files and programs within. Worse luck, but the PC recalls anything that is in it with one click and usually perfectly. The human memory is far less reliable...but far more flexible and capable. So watch your memories and narratives carefully and ask whether your explanations are the only possible understanding of them, or are there other ways to see it.

It would be easier for people who need to update, delete, change files in their heads, if we knew exactly what damned original files were programmed into our hard drive (and memory bank). If we knew all the programs we are running or are unaware of! No one is totally aware of it all. That is not possible or even necessary. Then again, if we are aware with only partial comprehension, that is certainly tricky. We have certain memories, beliefs, value systems, dos and don'ts and imperatives. We were programmed by the great programmers (no, not God) from day one or from even earlier. Who? The great programmer? Oh yes, the great programmers were your parents, nature and nurture, society, culture etc.

All these agendas, programs, drivers, plans, and so on, they formed and are now potentially with you. No, they are You! They come from since time began, billions of years ago. Only nature and evolution has changed them, taking eons of time. The good news is that now we humans might be at a time in our evolution when we can effect changes on ourselves speedily with resolve and intention. We might just be at a stage where we can understand enough, be aware of enough to know what an individual and society is like and can be like.

Here then is a most important point: psychology and philosophy have usually asked for awareness of how you feel and think. That is as it should be and I too recommend that method. Earlier I have added an additional and easily investigable enquiry: and that is to explore what **features** you actually possess here and now. Even more importantly, to ask what features you may have **in potential**, ones that you may be able to use to positively maximise your life.

Surprisingly little attention has been paid to the research of one's actual features, and yet it is, in a practical sense, a most important and salient question. It's only in the last few years that some more attention is being paid to this point. People are doers. We do things and need to do so. Thus, whether you are searching for a better job, a better life, a new or old relationship, or spiritual endeavours, self-awareness of who-how you are right now is the <u>only</u> issue. Alas, it is right here where people get stuck and rarely pass through stage one. I think this happens because if we just navel gaze, it is easy to get lost in the beauty and the dirt, the pain and the highs of an inner self drama-dialogue. But once the exploration of your actual features takes place, there are some new qualities that might enter the picture. Some facts that are undeniable may surface, as do some that are wobbly and soft and are in need of investigating and doing something about. When exploring anything, from a recipe to a murder story, new information and facts, new byways and highways will come into the picture!

It is vital to know what features you have and employ now and what you might have as potential ones waiting to be brought out into actuality!

I must mention another important and tricky issue. During your exploration you will find several of your 'features' that are kind of hazy, hidden, or sort of vague. Some or even most of these may not be your features at all; they are features you would have liked to have had, but most likely never did and possibly never will have. Or else the opposite to what I have just said. No way to know which, until you really consider and check them out. One obvious example, a prior one about how everyone seems to think they are good listeners. But most people will tell you that most people they know are bad listeners…Aha. Well, which one? Through my experience of facilitating workshops for sales and marketing or for human relationships, or counselling sessions, I am convinced that most people are terrible listeners. Sorry about that.

Like in any proper exploration of anything, there will be lost and found parts, and feelings, thoughts, sadness and laughter, highs and lows, potential creative excitement and perhaps feelings of shame for having fooled yourself. There is no need for shame or any other negative emotion to linger. Upon finding them, if any, let them slip into the garbage can of the mind; use your mental 'delete these files' button. Have no regrets; it is just the way things have been and now, as the ex Australian Prime Minister Julia Gillard and most other pollies tell you all too often, 'Let's move forward...'

Oh, by the way, it is not that easy to have no regrets. It is not so simple to just delete outdated, unwanted data. True, but if you conceptualise what you want to delete, and then imagine deleting it...and use your 'tools', then it will get easier and easier to do it. For now, do what you can and feel no sorrow about what you can't. I am not dead against having regrets. Sometimes you can indeed learn a lot from them. But I am dead against using regrets to freeze your future.

By now I feel sure you realise that all our predispositions are somewhat biologically directed plus preprogrammed, at least in the childhood and early adult years. Your genetic givens affect what you are offered and can accept from the socio-cultural input – to a large degree, if not entirely. The circumstances of the times and situation you were born into, how and where you had experienced your formative years all count. Adults are usually aware of some of their preprograms and know little or nothing about, or deny, others. Each of us is familiar with our physical limits, and yet we will know or at least suspect some other attributes that we (possibly) seem to have. For it is not until the early adult years that one begins to ponder some often trite and/or big questions about many things.

You have by now made certain 'decisions'. Some of that was done automatically, without you consciously making a 'choice'; the decision was made by one of your programs. For example,

The 'Software' of Your Personality

your religion, nationality, politics, language and world views early on are likely to almost entirely reflect those of your parents and culture/society. Later, you might change this, even go to opposite views, but in any case you have taken on manners, convictions, moral precepts, ethics, belief systems and so on. I hasten to add that this is not entirely a bad thing; in fact, it is a necessary condition of being in the world.

Even now, not everything you hold strongly (or weakly) can be totally relied on as the solution for all that will happen to you, certainly not every time. For example, I think that capital punishment is not right; however, I do not know (cannot know) how I would feel about it if one of my friends were blown up. I am not sure, indeed can never be certain, that I even have a predisposition to this or to certain other things that may happen to me, or affect my life in a big or small way, such as a war. That I was born Jewish is, it seems, forever held against me by many people. I abhor that they feel this way, and I am also puzzled; it actually and honestly makes no sense to me. Yet, evidently, my feelings make no sense to those who hold anti-Jewish feelings. Given that many bigots and racists have never even met or been harmed by a Jew or a Muslim or a black person, it is all the more puzzling. The obvious question to ask is if those who hold such prejudices have made what they were told into some sort of sense of their own, a faulty sense (nonsense) though it is?

An old cliché appears to offer much wisdom: *A folly even if the outcome succeeds, still is and always was irrational.*

There is broad agreement by most psychologists and thinkers that a great deal of what we might term as major 'programming' takes place for a human child in the first three years. Training, teaching, guiding children is incoming experience and thus learning, making sense of experiences; the teaching may be verbally given or otherwise, and receiving all that is coming is a necessary feature of being a child. Although this training/programming never stops, it has peak times other than early years. For example, it gains a kind of new strength again at puberty and into the teenage and early (and later) adult years. Then again, it also gains force at various other later ages and at major life events. The continuous 'reconstruction' (Neisser & Fivush 1994) of what I call the 'Software of Your Personality', our programming, might slow down in later years, but still, it never ends. It cannot end because humans are always a product of what has gone before, plus what is happening now. We are what we have 'deposited' in our memory banks, feeling/thought banks, and action patterns. These are, after all, the factors that make us humans, intelligent beyond, it seems, animals or veggies, at least in some sense. Let's just say that we are more conscious, mobile and more choice making than any other life form on earth. That will suffice for our exploration anyway.[27] So all this is a heavy brew: we have a set of rules, roles, programs, we behave in a fairly fixed and predictable manner (mostly) and then suddenly life comes at us with its freewheeling, sometimes surprising inputs.

The point is that we are and always will be preprogrammed to greater or lesser extent and this is not something you can, should, or need to get rid of entirely. What you do need, what will be helpful, is greater awareness and conceptualisation of the software of your very own personality. Meaning that you need to know who and how you are, AND how you might use what you have and are. Then, perhaps, you might make better, conscious decisions to choose what you do on a clearer basis. I said and

---

[27] Choice making is another long and tricky subject. As I see it, there is some small amount of free will we can and do exercise. However, I do not believe in the totality of free will, as it is usually understood. One thing for certain is that one cannot ever prove actions taken were 'free willed'.

repeat that we are programmed and that this needs to be the case. It is actually the people who are not well enough programmed, whose 'wires' and systems are jumbled, that tend to make life difficult for themselves and for others. We all need an amount of programming, an amount of appropriate 'software' in our heads to live in our society. But 'appropriate' is not always so easy or simple. And it can be even dangerous.

Your mind paths

Use it or lose it is common parlance usually in reference to the body and also to the brain. What we do not use tends to get weaker and wither away: *'The more often the path is walked the more grooved it becomes. Paths may even become, metaphorically, paved or built into interstate highways, autobahns of thought and experience, because they are travelled so often. The highways remain for life, but in time, if the dirt paths and the back roads aren't travelled much, they disappear from lack of use. Only the well-travelled roads survive.'* (Walter 2013)

Yes, but I see that these paths – not only the highways – can and need to be retained and even refurbished, or like any real road they can lead to places we did not want to go. So what choices do we truly have? Have you ever really considered this?

A few more points from this chapter:

- Whether you are searching for a better job, a better life, a new or old relationship, or spiritual endeavours, self-awareness of who-how you are right now is the only issue.

- We are preprogrammed and that is necessary. YOU can reprogram yourself to a degree. You already know how to do that to a degree so one must simply take more charge of it and do more of it on purpose.

- Use it or lose it. Do not give in to losses too easily when it comes to your body or mind.

CHOICE VS. DETERMINISM (YET ANOTHER LOOK)

We are preconditioned for certain, yet that does not mean that everything about our lives is predetermined. Let's accept that we are always predisposed to act and react in certain ways – a statement in need of deeper digging. I have argued that on one hand, we can never prove that a decision we have made was not somewhat predetermined. Yet also, we can in no way prove that we actually have full freedom of choice either. So we are neither making free choices nor is everything predetermined – this is what I believe and that is indeed my personal experience.

When I say predetermined, I do not mean that everything in life may be 'predetermined' in the 'it is written' sense. That's utterly ridiculous and irrational. I do mean that my responses to an event come from a limited, perhaps large or maybe small range of reactions possible for me. My potential reactions are limited. Within this perhaps huge but incomplete range, conceivably I may have some choices, or perhaps not! There is much disagreement on this problem. Science says that there is no way to prove full freedom of choice. They don't say that all is predetermined. Then again, we can see the bleedingly obvious, that some things are absolutely determined, such as the laws of nature. Still, even then there is a range of outcomes. The laws of nature are set, even if we don't know or are unable to understand them. The laws of people include some laws of nature plus...all the huge variety of things that self-conscious beings bring to it.

Some philosophers argue for and others against free will and choices. Religious systems say that life does not make sense without full freedom of choice. I am making sense of my life without ever thinking I have total free choice. However, neither proposition, we must admit, can be entirely proven nor disproven. And for me there is no need to labour on this problem any further, for this discussion has gone on for thousands of years unsolved – and we don't need to resolve it here. What we do need is simply to see that life works in certain reliable and unreliable ways.

Life is not an already written story

I say that I do not have total freedom to choose, and yet I also said that my life is not entirely predetermined. It is still being 'written'. Mostly by me (?) but not entirely. I can see all that. And this has repercussions all through what this book is about, what I call the 'software of our personality' and how that operates, constructs, reconstructs and writes our lives.

What we do have, what we act from and with – as above stated – is a limited, but partly preprogrammed range of dispositions. From these we act in answer to incoming stimuli. To make my argument clearer, allow me to propose that I can never have or employ the 'I am not Jewish' range of possible responses or choices in certain situations. That's so even though I do not practise that or any religion, and I am a declared atheist. An Australian Christian or Muslim, or black or Chinese or whatever person will never have my possible and potential Hungarian Jewish choice range either. Nor the exact same range of either determined or chosen outcomes. There may be certain overlaps in some but not all areas of our human experiences. (I am referring to the entire cultural, geological, ethical and situational backgrounds.)

This will hold true about many other situations, be they large or trite events. My responses will always be those of a middle-sized body, rather than a tall person's, one who is a migrant, not one born here, an older male with a divorce, an educated fellow, not a labourer, not a woman, not a…etc. Now I repeat that some of these predispositions were genetically given and some were absorbed as software programs, learned agendas, a combination of both genetic and learned. Nature plus nurture. The genetics will have affected the possible potential range of software programs my early situation has accepted, i.e. 'loaded' into me. I was never going to be a chemist, say, and having left my native country young, I now carry two partial cultural inputs, plus whatever I have picked up from my travels and life.

Thus, having developed from all my predispositions, there are some strong programs that I now have embedded within me as Me. It is all there, even though, as stated previously, I may not actually **know** all my programs. In fact, it is impossible to be aware of all one's programs. It would be too much for the poor human brain, it seems, to be constantly aware of everything. The brain/mind is very clever and looks after me, for as Walter said, *'The purpose of brains generally is to organize the waves of sensory phenomena that nature's cerebrally gifted creatures experience. Their job is to filter the world's chaos effectively enough to avoid, for as long as possible, the disagreeable experience of death. A direct correlation exists between survival and how well a brain maps the world around it.'* (Walter 2013)

I suggested that you consider that we have very limited truly free choices. Yet what we appear to 'choose' decides what happens to us. We are not predetermined in the old idiotic sense, but we are determined within the range of possibilities we have and are in.

If, and only if, we want to reprogram our brain/mind/body

To reprogram ourselves for a more positive and successful and fulfilling life, we need to rethink/feel and act on a number of things:

1. Your features are part of your programs but not necessarily all of it.

2. Become aware of your major active and dormant 'software', your 'preprograms' and their features, positive and/or negative.

3. Become aware of how your features use, aid and abet your programs and how the software you have has constructed and reconstructed some of your features. This is always a two-way movement!

4. See if a currently operating and often dearly held program is still as useful to you or not. That is, does it bring you what you (properly) want?

5. Make a broad and firm decision (at first) about which of your program(s) you wish to keep, alter, delete or update. Pick a particular program or two, but no more, to act on.

6. Find a way to update, alter, or erase the programs in need of change (more about how to do this later).

7. Find those characteristics within your body and mind that might help in all this endeavour. Such characteristics/features may be part of one or several of your larger programs. This can be tricky. It often needs an outside person to help you to explore it (more about how to do it and with whom later).

8. Load new special 'programs' – such as this book.

When loading new special 'programs', watch out for outdated material, fear of change, anxiety about anything new or anything that is negative. Take care of what you do select. Check and see if a new program is working for you by activating it and testing the results. Interestingly, some of this is easier to do than one might think. As already said, we all do some of this anyway. Like the Santa belief, or that the world owes you, or that love fixes it all, or that if only you had money, or that if you lived more simply… and so on, then things would be better, or that if you had a boat… etc.

We have erased much of various other heavy beliefs about many things already. For example, Mum and Dad, communism, capitalism, religion, etc. So the good news is that we already 'sort of know' how to do 'erasing-deleting' and changing-updating. However, we tend to do it by accident or when we are pushed to do it. Sometimes we do not properly 'delete' some of our old outdated programs; thus, sometimes we find ourselves falling back into and repeating useless old behaviours, and even feel surprised!

We can, do and must make decisions on dedicated purpose

We do make decisions about small and large things, don't we? I won't bother exploring choice making on the really simple level of which film to see or whether to buy a red or white couch. If something substantial needs extensive change in us, or in our lives, it is done by an exercise of will. Done by 'will' plus the ability to make the needed/wanted change. This ability you might or might not have. Such bigger issues might be a separation from a partner or changing to a new career, getting married, having children, just to name a few. We make bigger decisions, so we like to think, after much free thought and feeling. Yes, maybe so – and no, maybe not so free. We vacillate, or make no decision, or do so too late, same story.

What is notable is that substantial changes are about changing some things outside and also inside of ourselves. The outside, let's say practical, changes usually bring further changes within us anyway, or might. The popular conception is that large dramatic changes that affect us will change our lives. True enough, but caution is offered: the changes are not necessarily always for the better. Outcomes may well be brilliant or negatively mistaken ones. Our aims may have been 'wrong' in some ways. Or we chose something we had little ability to achieve. Or simply: that's life, bad luck.

It is the human condition, after all, that:

- There are no guarantees about anything we decide to do.
- The universe owes us nothing.
- Other people owe you nothing either.
- Life is not necessarily fair.
- Living is more like a 'chaos theory' that we try to organise as best we can.

Still, the point is that we can actually do something about (almost) anything. Hmm, I think as I write this. That 'almost anything' may be going too far. Let me reduce it to this: we can do something about many more things than we think.

Let's say we were programmed into thinking we are dumb or clever, beautiful or ordinary, too short...whatever. Or that you believe in God, or you do not, or you believe in labor or in right-

The 'Software' of Your Personality

wing politics, or you hold any other major life belief (program) positions. You know by now that as your life has unfolded so far, you have changed some of your beliefs/programs, just because your life experience turned out to be different from what was prescribed by other people and society. Well, at least I hope that's what you have found, for those who have dogmatically stuck with all the programs installed into them by others...are unlikely to be reading this sort of a book.

We have all experienced many changes consciously made, and also changes that have just happened, whether we wanted them or not. What we are about now is to take more control of change than we had before. By finding and focusing on some of our major programs/beliefs, we shall develop tools with which to effect positive changes we do want. Many new programs can be input by education, yet I am using the concept 'education' broadly, not necessarily as a back to school thing.

Identify what best features and programs you have.

> *'Every creature, human, animal and even the plant world has an evolved talent for identifying what is surprising or out of the ordinary for one simple reason: it's central to survival. Those that fail to tune in to the change around them, those that aren't sensitive to surprise, soon join the legions of species no longer with us.'*
>
> (Walter 2013, 1998)

Why is a nurse unlikely to become a real estate salesperson or vice versa? Why would a rich finance person give it all up and move to grow vegies? If we were loaded too heavily with a specific program that dictated our first chosen profession, later we may well discover that it does not suit our true features/programs or our now more developed programs, belief systems. And the same story applies – or it can – to our choice of marriage partners, and many other things, particularly when we were younger, starting out as 'inexperienced' adults into the world.

There are several clashing programs in there within us, and that is for certain; our inner conflicts rule much of us. If you have had, say, a divorce, that will stir up old guilty or inadequacy programs, or your inner 'Critic', judge etc.[28] People usually think something like if you had loved them enough it would not have happened… Or that because you love the other, he or she will reciprocate. Or that you have taken great care of your partner and now… Nice if things do work out, but it is only bad luck if it did not.

Still, how many of you older than 40 recall various of your choices in your early twenties and either laugh or regret them? How many of us consciously and knowingly chose their partners at the age of 20+? What criteria did we use? Oh yes, the criterion was that we 'fell in love'. That's beaut and it is human, but had we really considered 'compatibility', for example? Did we honestly tell each other what we had in mind about life? Did we even know any of that really? ('Fell in love' by the way usually means fell in lust, more likely.)

Marital break-up? It is usually nobody's fault, and yet everyone feels bad. Oh, is that right, is the break-up no one's fault? Well, yes, 'no blame, no claim' would be a good ideal. Do, however, consider that the choices you and another person made were made from and within your programs: that is your ideals, morality, ethics, sense of security, fears…whatever else. Picking an intimate partner is, I think I can safely say, something of a lottery even when you are more mature. We put a lot of emphasis on sexual attraction. I agree with that up to a point, only in as

---

28 More about these role labels and their job in your life in a later chapter.

much that if it is not there, then more is unlikely to develop. But it might, so it should not be the only criterion. Far from it. Some American psychologist with a worldwide fame once told me that if I entered a room full of people and my eyes locked onto a beautiful woman's eyes across the room, and I felt sweat and blood rise...then turn around and run away... I got what he meant, but...

Contemplate another silly thought we often hear about marital splits: that you should have known better, and now no one can be trusted...etc. How could you have known what you did not? So don't spend energy on these usually muddled one-liners that you hear and repeat between friends and relatives endlessly. Just move on ASAP. And many people can be trusted, but perhaps not in the same ways.

According to the stats, just about as many second marriages break up as first ones. Precisely because people have not changed, erased or altered faulty, outdated programs, the ones that picked a partner badly in the first place – your program that did not want to see what now seems bloody obvious. Yet there is nothing like a major drama to activate positive change in people; that is obvious. And it would be nice to view a marital break-up as an 'opportunity to change', tough as it is while you are entirely grief stricken. This is a big ask, but a sane one. Except, you need to go about it differently. You need to chuck out the 'blame-claim' program first and with it any venom. That it was your fault or his/her fault really does not now matter. Also forget, delete, the bits that say you or he/she should have done this or that. It's all gone, brothers and sisters. Ya all done what you did – the past is gone and even if never forgotten, put it into a file and lock it away, or throw it in the trash can. It is an old, outdated, faulty program file now, that's for sure. You have the proof: it did not work out. So don't use that program again. But so many do: we take our patterns, features, programs and offer it all up again, set ourselves up again just as before.

I repeat: if as many second marriages break up as first ones, then that points to the fact that **'people do more and more of what did not work so well'!** So, if you choose a new partner, say, without changing anything within your thinking/feeling programs, then you are still using the old, perhaps unknown, programs and criteria that drove your first selection.

Thus, your next move forward needs to come from different, updated software programs that you have chosen and decide to activate. And all this will hold true about relationship problems, careers, or your golf stroke…(or writing a book) or improving the relationship with the kids, forming a political party or opening a pastry shop.

In summary: we have often made and make choices, or so it seems. One can never prove that we made a 'free choice'. Fine, so what? In any case, a choice ought to be made on a well-researched and informed basis. The new job, the new relationship may look very different today, but your internal feelings, outward actions, limited choices were and are still at the bottom off your decision-making process. If that's so, you are likely to repeat past unsatisfactory situations. I repeat without apology that if you do not know what is driving you, what your predisposed programs are, then 'they', the programs/beliefs you are not familiar with, will 'control' you. This is so even if you do have the illusion that you are controlling things and making new choices.

A few chapter points:

- Your features are part of your programs but not necessarily all of it. You may have features that are hard to find in your program groupings.

The 'Software' of Your Personality

- You are predetermined, indeed programmed, to have to make choices all your life and that is just as well.

- You make your choices from what you perceive is available.

- It is rare that it is easy to see what choices one does or does not actually have.

- We take choices from and via our existing programs – it is hard to step outside of powerful programs and truly see what there is, or is not.

- So, you better be as aware of your 'set-up' as possible.

IF YOU DON'T KNOW WHERE YOU ARE GOING THEN YOU ARE LIABLE TO END UP NOWHERE

And that, friends, is another old cliché (academics and critics will get me for it), but it is an old favourite one-liner, possibly a Chinese saying. The point is:

- You cannot know where you are going except to the degree that you know yourself.

- Unless we have a good grasp on that, we cannot activate and actualise our full potential.

- In order to use our best potentials – our positive features, abilities – we first need to find out what these, our 'contents', are.

Forgive me, I have said all this before several times, but please do commit it to mind as a mini software program in itself. So, let's say that you are now more familiar with your actual software. That can never be fully done, since every moment of life, experience or research, both inside and outside of me, affects the process. There is always the new (at least potentially) coming at us; there is never a still point to arrive at. Nonstop perceptions are incoming all our lives. Our very busy, nonstop 24 hours brain/

The 'Software' of Your Personality

mind and physical activity never cease. The awareness process continues from birth to death. Let's use it and enjoy it!

Earlier, I asked if it was possible to learn anything new about ourselves and others.

To really master the use of a new program in your computer you do a number of things:

- Decide what you need to do and acquire the correct program for the task.

- You load it into your hard drive so it is up and running at call.

- You learn how to use the program, what it does, what its limitations are etc. and you focus on which major features of this program may be helpful in achieving what you set out to accomplish.

- You know that you cannot change or pollute this program with another or it will quit on you. You also know that you must not overload your program or your hard drive (yourself).

Much the same goes for human brain/minds. The human mind is far more complex and more capable, but needs different ways of access. More complex means more potential for good results – and more possible problems too. The human mind is a 'changeable' computer; yet to call the mind a computer is of course oversimplifying (but we need the model). The brain/mind is able to synthesise unlike and unlikely things, to add words, numbers, pictures, ideas and translate them all into a response that is sometimes brilliantly correct, or else painfully otherwise. Emotional integrity and intelligence is tricky. Your emotions and intelligence mix with memories, and so sometimes with 'ghosts' you never knew you had – memories that were perhaps never entirely accurate. The outcomes can range from silly to dangerous, or simply not useful, working for or against your best interest. This is how most of us live, by a kind of meandering, accidental, seemingly self-organised minor or large chaos, where life just happens.

You have decided to research yourself with a specific aim

You intend to change something in your life. Let's look at the main issues in that process again in some more detail:

Decide what you need to do and find the correct program to do it.

Ah, now here is a tricky statement! Let's say that we want to stop a relationship or change our career. Big decisions, these two, but equally, the same process applies to smaller issues also. If we are asking if it is easy to make the important decisions, then we must say yes and no, depending on your current programs/beliefs. Watch out for fooling yourself at this point, for it is a common thing to do and to an extent, we all do it, opt for the (seemingly) easiest way. We do it because the current software program acts wanting the fastest and easiest answers; it is in itself a partially inherited (and necessary) genetic and biological defence program. It is the 'job description' your 'defence ministry' runs on (just like the PC has its protocols). Then again, some people get bogged down in overcomplications as well. That is their load and defence, to take too much time and detail and procrastinate and overcomplicate. The desired idea is to know well where you are 'coming from' – and to be aware of what you have and what you want and can do.

The 'Software' of Your Personality

We'll say that you have made a decision about what outcome you want. All right, it's all clear, yes, you know exactly what you want? I urge much caution even now, before proceeding to action. What you want may be a smokescreen – it could be a positive move, or the exact opposite. The fact is that it is just so damn easy to fool the human self. It happens for many different reasons, emotional, philosophical, biological – but mainly because there really is a program 'let me see what I want to see', and it kicks in (defence system). We don't want change; it is threatening and hard work, or so it seems. Yet we all learned to say that we must have and like change. Hmm, and I think not.

We will at times do anything rather than understand the current *reality that is possible* for us as a way of life or situation. This sort of self 'sabotage' is hardwired in there in each of us. But even 'possible reality' may be a bridge too far to contemplate anyway – any sort of reality that we do not want to see or be aware of will be twisted around by the dear old defensive brain/mind. And this is the same mind that is serving you and wants the best for you! Does it not? Your ego/mind/defence wants to squeeze things back into the box, into what suits, what's easier, what seems attractive and so on.

That, friends, is the nature of the brain/mind: the easier solution, the already known solutions, that's where the brain/mind will likely lead us. Who knows how many relationships break up for all the wrong reasons; and some keep going for all the wrong – or for the right – reasons? Who knows how many people work at something unsatisfactory that they are unhappy with anyway and are badly (or even well) paid? How many unhappy rich people would be happier digging the ground? How many poor people believe totally that it is money they need to solve everything? (Yes, it would help.) Who knows how many people believe this or that, and whether they do so for the right or the wrong reasons? Then again, never mind these last few mind-fucking questions. Once aware of them, bypass them all. There are generally no definitive answers to many of the above, and if there are, you still need to find your own. And how to do that is what this book is about.

Suffice to say that we all do mind/knee-jerk reactions to our brain/mind/emotions. More often than not, they turn out to be not the best decisions. A few people sit down and evaluate what went wrong, and when they do, they tend to do it on their own; it's a closed circuit, often leading us around in circles, within circles, or spirals within spirals. (I am not allowed to quote that song from many years ago about spirals and wheels but if you are old enough you might recall it.)

Deeper exploration about all this later, and in a different to the usual way, in the chapters dealing with voice dialogue. There, we will consider working on our various programs/beliefs/selves (by any word, it's all the same to me), and on our memories that we hold, consciously or otherwise. And we sure do hold some 'memories' unconsciously, but they surface now and then. Digging some up purposely will also aid our main project, which is simple, as you recall:

TO BECOME THE BEST POSSIBLE VERSION OF YOU.

ॐ

But where do you get 'garden-fresh' software for your brain/mind?

Let's say that we have decided, after some wild or boring living, some elephant or chicken-shit tears and laughter and great and crappy decisions, that serious research into our selves and our features needs to be considered. This book has convinced us (maybe, or you are smart and lucky enough to have got there by whatever means) that whatever we think, however things are now, it may well be that we can do something EVEN more satisfactory. Indeed, we must do so, since the making of the best you possible is the purpose and meaning of human lives.

So here we are, having seriously considered our life arrangements and having made as certain as we could that we are not embarking on a wild bull chase created by our devious ego/mind. You have also decided – after much agonising – on specific outcomes you'd really like. From here on we shall tackle more of the 'how and where' do you get the new software programs that will achieve what we want. And thus the vexed question of how to better exercise those of your own existing features that suit where you want to go.

I said that we get new input programs from education of various sorts, therapy, friends, reading good material, and even from our own past experiences, although beware, these can be either valuable or else the opposite. Do not be like the politicians or the police department, evaluating and checking on itself.

When we reach for a new software program, we can be and often are easily fooled into 'buying' into the wrong one, and sometimes we need more than one to achieve the positive results we want. Now let's assume we have covered all this as best as possible, earnestly and honestly and with the help of outside agencies to make sure that we are not fooling our dear old selves.

Ground control to Major You, OK and activating?

Taking action becomes a must after the thinking/feeling is done. Decisions must be made. Some well-considered risks must be taken too. Action is needed to actually apply the new input/programs and integrate them with your features.

Beep... Beep... Warning.

The danger now is that we will slip into using our **new programs** as you used the old ones. For example, I wrote this book with the latest Microsoft Word program. I know how to use it, yes, partly because it is so similar to the previous version. I also know that I am not using its full potential. I have not learned enough about it at this stage. Just so with your body/mind and new programs. It is so easy to just use the major elements that you are familiar with, instead of the more productive, fresher bits that take some deeper effort.

I want this new program of mine that took some effort to obtain (I call it 'Author') to help to achieve what I wanted: writing this and several other books. That is the clear sharp benefit/outcome I am seeking. I want a successful, well-read and regarded, and helpful work that people find useful.

Writing this book is what I wanted to do; therefore, I needed to know my features in that direction: Do I have the ability to write at all, let alone this sort of philosophical-psychological thing? Do I have the experience and the knowledge? Do I have the perseverance needed for writing a book, researching facts and so on? Do I have the imagination, and enough information to synthesise many varied ideas and knowledge into such a book as this? If I miss out on any of the above, then I will not do a good job of it. So, if my answer is no to some of the above questions (and to several others that I did ask of myself), then back to the formula I recommended: get new input, programs, check them out, and look at what you do have in the reservoir of your mind. All this sounds like more heavy work than it needs to be. In fact, some people procrastinate too long, and find themselves on tangents they wanted to avoid.

I needed to know the features of the new PC program (such as my MS Word program) and the newly acquired emotional/ intellectual programs I have or will need to load into my brain

The 'Software' of Your Personality

box which is far more complex than the PC. That is a good and a bad thing. I need to be very careful that I do not pollute new programs in my head by some other older ones, such as dearly held old memories, facts, beliefs, knowledge and (perhaps) outdated opinions. Note this last one 'opinions'.[29]

What I intended to offer in this book is something newish, a different way to see yourself and your actions, abilities and possibilities. Some, even many, of my old ideas, opinions, knowledge and experiences may well be correct and usable. Others, I cautioned, will need a look and careful consideration. I may need to study the latest research on several varied topics for this book. Then, I also need to consider my 'Inner Critic program' the one we all have for it is part of human biology and circumstance. The 'Critic' whispers that I simply am not a good writer or thinker etc. Or another of my innate preprograms: the 'doer program'. This is the one that pushes me saying I should have finished the book by now, that I don't do enough work (yeah, I am a bit slow). That I must read and research more etc. And so I need to be vigilant that I do not overload myself (my hard drive = body/mind) and sacrifice all my other living for what would amount to an obsession if taken too far. Overload, in any case, will cause shutdown of my computer or my head. When it is very severe, put boldly, we call it a nervous breakdown; in truth there is nothing that breaks in one's head. We can get overloaded with work, wrong concepts, emotional pain, sadness, confusion, too much meat, wine or potatoes...and too much self-criticism and the like. One leads to the other.

---

29 Most opinions emanate from belief systems; to put it simply, they are programs that have formed your opinions as they were given to you. These are the features I call me and mine.

Important: I am emphatically again *not* saying that all your old preprograms/beliefs/features or aims are, or were, wrong. They are and can be useful; they got you this far and you are still alive and reading. (Possibly getting bored with this chapter?) All you are at this moment is most useful as a step towards something even better. I am also not advocating whether you need MORE, or LESS. I don't know exactly what you need – it could be more or it might be less.

Some issues in this chapter:

- Decide what you want to consider, improve, get rid of, etc.

- Take purposeful, researched and focused action.

- Take considered, sensible risks, yes, but...

- You have already done programming all your life!

- Be careful you don't fool yourself when working on the self that is you.

- There is no need to allow the 'Critic', yours or one from outside, to bomb you.

- Deciding to change nothing is fine, providing you have done the work and you are not kidding yourself.

ARE YOU NO MORE OR LESS THAN YOUR 'EDITABLE' MEMORIES?

This chapter is a small step back towards a previous chapter, enhancing our ability to comprehend more deeply what we are considering in this book.

Writer Milan Kundera draws attention to a paradoxical relationship between remembering and forgetting and I paraphrase him: people struggle against power and forget outcomes we should recall. Kundera despairs that memory never captures authentic experience. *'We immediately transform the present moment into its abstraction. We need only recount an episode we experienced a few hours ago: the dialogue contracts to a brief summary, the setting to a few general features... Remembering is not the negative of forgetting. Remembering is a form of forgetting.'* (Kundera 1988) Kundera means that we forget many of the facts as they truly were. But did we ever really know, can we be sure of what all the 'facts' were? I doubt that, but agree with Kundera; memory is at least also a form of forgetting.

To my mind, and to other greater minds, this is an interesting screwdriver thrown into the mind's works: all we are, each of us individually and as a greater group, may well be nothing more or less than a **story**! (Neisser & Fivush 1994) Think about memory and stories for a moment. *All memories are stories.* Without these stories and the continuance of yourself as a 'story', a narrative, you would not be entirely sane or rational. You would not know you! I rather doubt there would be an actual you at all. Since you use, and are, a metaphor, which is in fact a story (or narrative), you are then also a ***plot*** that likely includes both fact and fiction!

I am not suggesting that a person is nothing else than a narrative. I dare not at this stage. But, people, it looks as if one is nothing else. But what else are we? What is an 'ego' but a bunch of recallable stories? (No, I need no soul or an out there hypothesis, not even remotely; I see no use for one, other than perhaps for some false comfort.) This is a big idea that I have no space to pursue too far. But it is a big idea every human being ought to know and consider. And so should every family group, city, country and so on. Let's move a little more into all this.

Life experiences, actually living your life, can be said to be a 'narrative' a continuing story we all constantly '**edit**'…almost as if we were literary editors who are, after all, also much like psychotherapists. Both search to understand and perhaps change the '**story**' that you had 'written' knowingly or otherwise as the 'self-life' that you know as you.

It is generally accepted that there may be two types of memory styles, the autobiographical and the episodic. These are memorising movements that our minds employ to make sense of our world as individuals. In a book she co-edited, *Autobiographical Memory and the Construction of a Narrative Self: Developmental and Cultural Perspectives*, Catherine Haden states that '*each of us creates a life narrative embedded in sociocultural frameworks that define what is appropriate to remember, how to remember it, and what it means to be a self with an autobiographical past.*' (Fivush & Haden 2003)

Our identity is always couched in and as a story of sorts, but our various and many selves form it. Stories are always full of characters, scenes and events that happen. Just so is the only way I can identify myself, via my own stories. (McAdams 1996, 1993, 1985).

I have now sufficiently introduced the fairly well accepted theory that in some ways a person, an identity, is like a narrative of sorts. I added that such a story is a kind of metaphor for the self. And that it is editable. Pressing on, please note our problem is simply complex: your story/identity is open to whatever 'interpretation' is brought to it by yourself or by others. And then by a mixed up version of the two: your and others' interpretations. Such interpretations should always be cautiously limited, as Umberto Eco suggested about reading fictional literature (Eco 2006). A story, let's say a 'whodunnit', is hopefully never interpreted as a love story, for example. That wonderful, if tired, old fairy tale, the Bible, is seen by some as an instruction book, by some as a tale, by others as history, or whatever (plenty of metaphors in the Bible, God knows what they all mean, or are meant to mean).

The important issue is to discern that our 'autobiographical selves' are continuously in the making and remaking, constantly constructed, as we said earlier. Much of this is done by relationships with and in the world, and by the metaphors received and used and the like. Jerome Bruner posed some critical questions about identity and how changeable the self might be. He asked whether selves – note the plural – were constructed through our lived narratives. These days many thinkers would say yes to that question. Do narratives convey an existing deep sense of self? I believe, with Bruner, that it is an ongoing 'construction'[30] of the self, and that there is also a deeper sense of self added to and given by our biology. Once again, there is no need for the God metaphor. A deep sense of self is not a soul. It is more like the engine, a part built into a car; it is our biological body/mind.

---

30 There is a whole school of thought called 'constructionist' when it comes to all the above.

Then, as life goes on, we construct what we can as we go, based on our experiences. We 'write' them into our self (which is memory) as a way of conveying who we are to both ourselves and to others. The movement is dynamic and it replays, reconstructs itself, depending on what responses we get back from our environment. Lots of this happens automatically without us even noticing it, but not all of it. The problem is that we often partially misinterpret what we 'read'. And so do 'they'.

The deep self comes from and gives out our version of our built narratives. Perhaps this is the only big self, the only sort of underlying self there is. A sort of body/mental self; in my sense the only sort of 'spiritual' or, if you must have one, a 'greater' self. I personally, intuitively and through my education and experiences, do believe all the above. I now wish to change my words 'I believe' to 'I know' – in relation to the constructing and reconstructing of our selves and life as we go, and the existence of a deep underlying potential self. Let us repeat now that such self and/or selves are built and known from our own stories. However, it is all one movement, the total of which is a person. Contemplate then the following quote:

'However there is another amazing question to consider: do selves exist as independent entities or only in relation to and as a reflection of others? These are questions that are both enduring and unanswerable, as reality must lie in the tension between these alternatives.' (McAdams 2008)

Must it lie in and as the tension? Much as I admire and agree with McAdams, I am puzzled at the remark that the question is not answerable. I even rather think he had answered the problem. Clearly human lives are always in relationships with other humans and with all else there is on earth. Therefore, there appears no evidence that self or selves exist or could do so as independent entities... And even if they did...independent of what exactly?

I am sorry if I digressed a touch. Back to the main game, I say sternly to myself. Um, to myself? Well, to that 'part' of me that is writing this, and that part is a distinctly different...more later.

ॐ

Many problems arise from the fact that we have both remembered and non-remembered memory

This, of course, is one of the big differences between people and computers. People knowingly or otherwise process information coming in, and then react in some way that has been – usually – preset by all that has gone before. Another difficulty is that at times we store memories that are barely more than pure feeling states. These are the so-called nonverbal or pre-verbal feelings/memories. As such, these are vague at best, and completely un-conceptualised by the very young, and mostly unremembered by the older, except perhaps as dim feelings. Further problems for the poor human being rise due to the immense capacity of our nonstop systems which are capable of, and insist on, considering and synthesising various pieces of information, amalgamating all the input into a coherence of sorts.

Your brain/mind simply has to do this. If it does not, then there are ill mental states. It has to sort it all into some sort of coherence, even if that coherence is irrational – or else we may well go 'crazy' or get very stressed. What a wonder the brain/mind is, and what potential treason it can bring, exactly because it is so vastly capable – and what wonders of art, science and goodness as well.

Right here is what might be the main problem for people. For the coherences we tend to surface with, the way we decide on what is or is not meaningful or of importance to each of us, the way we receive perceptions is often partly or entirely wrong. Amigos, the stories we interpret in some ways because we must do that!

I have said it before and it is so important that it has to be said again: what rises in me, all that rises in me, is emphatically based on memories and carried by memories, known or otherwise. As soon as we can be said to be able to think, we make unavoidable mistakes in processing incoming information and therefore we jointly make mistakes about processing our own thoughts and feelings.

We also take in external material sometimes not the way it was intended. We may have misperceived, misread, misunderstood it. We feel pain or joy and easily hang it on this or that – sometimes incorrectly. Or if it was correctly understood, then we may have translated the deeper meaning in error, once again, in order to 'fit it all' into our already existing framework of thinking/feeling our story.

Caution about deciphering, analysing, explaining and comprehending incoming material. Interpretation can be fun or not so

We cannot change the contents of a book, or of the computer program, or the patterns and colour of trees, or the facts of science merely by interpreting them to ourselves in any way we please. Yet we often do exactly that. Outrageous, you say... Not me...you say. Well, good on you.

The 'Software' of Your Personality

We interpret incoming material (in short, 'communications'), we guess at things and people, use our faculties to judge things. Sometimes to our benefit, or else rather mistakenly. That happens particularly when dealing face to face with other people. We tend to jump in often too quickly and use what we already know and hold as an 'ah, this is like...'[31] There are limits to the meaning of our interpretations of the world out there or in here. But those limits at times might be far wider than we think. Or narrower! Interpreting, deducing, translating incoming material is what happens all the time. It happens with or without us necessarily knowing that we are 'receiving' and 'translating'. What effect we have on one another and on ourselves, and in what way, is not always instantly obvious or knowable. We like or clash with each other. Or nothing much, no interest. Or...type in whatever you want here. What happens between people may be, I think it is, directed because my 'program' may or may not 'fit' or respond well to yours – at least right now. For example, I am into writing this, I'm focused and active; my productive and thinking program has been activated for the last two hours. It is running well when my wife interrupts with a story that is of some weight to her (say). I don't respond well, showing impatience and little care. Hmm, you see what might happen? (A trite example, but consider it on a larger, even on a global scale etc.)

Indeed, you and I are two identities forever linked as a sort of 'network' – if and when we have anything to do with one another. We can be that way because of our common 'human programs' – the ones that were installed at the Mum-baby 'factory'. However, as is obvious, such programs are extremely varied by socio-cultural, parental and educational inputs. One problem in this connection is that everyone is all too ready to act the **'as if'**. **As if** we knew exactly what we were doing or saying. 'As if' everything

---

31 *A man was found drowned in his bowl of cereal. It seems a large currant grabbed hold of him.* Yes, sir and ma'am, this was a joke, and like all of them, jokes are made right at the border of tragedy, reality and our ability to cope with life.

was a simple matter of obvious cause and simple effects. 'As if' what went up had to come down. Sometimes this can be near enough to accurate, while at other times, and I think more often, it is far from being accurate or clear. And it all happens on both the small, trite, personal scale and on a larger one. Another issue follows what's above.

Consciousness is like reading a book?

If we ask what actually is a book, it is immediately obvious that a book is not the sum of its paper and mechanical quality, or just the contents. Rather, it is both the physical entity of a book as well as its contents. Consciousness works just that way for people, and it is not just housed in the body, **it is** the body/mind.

A book when you read it has the same contents as when I read it. The book has the same contents, yes, the same typed words, but you might read and translate it to yourself differently to how I did. (That's what people argue in book clubs.) Fortunately, we are likely to be at least in the same swimming pool mostly, but not always. What is good or even funny to me in this culture is an offence to someone in another culture. A novel that describes sex, love, anger and so on can be interpreted by individuals rather similarly and yet very differently. One reader loves book 'A' and another hates it, and another can't be bothered with it. This is rather like 'reading people'. The book does not change its letters and story, its paragraph or pages, or the chronology of its happenings. The difference is in the **way you read** it from your mostly preset, preprogrammed brain/mind. The book's message and even style is then judged from each of our 'predisposed' positions.

The point I am strongly selling here is that the individual is predisposed to what 'contents' he holds, and that affects the

The 'Software' of Your Personality

way he translates and understands a story. And, folks, oh dear, remember: all one is, is a narrative **memory**!

All that has gone into me and has been interpreted (or not), amalgamated with other pieces of information, or not, is now recalled from my known memory or at times even from the (perhaps) forgotten 'files'. All this means that one is always prerecorded, programmed, predisposed…and therefore 'prejudiced'. That is the human condition and it is not avoidable. This, all of this, is also what we usually speak of as our memory. All my **memories are prejudiced stories** of sorts written with much 'assistance' from others. Or were they actually mainly written by others and little authored by myself??? Yes, and yes a thousand times.

One more important point follows. Each of us can bring a different view when interpreting the preset contents of a storybook without the actual book changing. Not so when dealing with another human being. Dealing with myself or with another ego/self is likely to affect the so-called contents of both myself and the other. (It may not, of course.) The curly issue is to note that my view of you, or of myself for that matter, overtly or covertly may affect, shake up, activate, change my and your actual 'contents'. Which in turn may affect the story I hold as memory. And on and on. Hey, that's OK; it is human life with all its glory, drama and fun.

- Read your consciousness like a book, but be aware that interpretations are tricky.

- Allow yourself the fact that you may make incorrect decisions and interpretations of your own memories, of yourself and very much so of others.

PRESENT PASTS? CONFUSION, DISCRIMINATION, DECISIONS AND REVISIONS...

The past is always present, or at least some of it is. The present becomes the past real fast; some of it we retain and want to, some we wish to forget. Whatever the case, we might or might not know which bit of our past is having influence on us right now. Indeed, we cannot fully know that, yet the more we are aware of, the better our choice making becomes. It gets worse and better: what I call a piece of past that I know partly operates in me could be a faulty interpretation of my own. Yet another time I may be dead accurate. Often some of each! This is a worrisome fact. Much of what I've said to start this chapter will seem obvious to many who have considered the human situation. Yet the problems remain:

- My interpretations of events.

- What I do or do not actively recall.

- Memory is forgetting much of it, as per previous chapter.

None of the past stays entirely static either. That is to say that my teenage interpretations, feelings, thoughts about Mum or migration, or my first broken heart are now viewed very differently. Let's dig in a bit more.

What rises within now as a response to life are thoughts and feelings and they always have much to do with all that has happened before. Thoughts and feelings are therefore always a 'present past' (Morris 1996). Included in what rises within are previous dispositions, experiences, evaluations, actions and, of course, feelings/thoughts. I have argued a while ago, that what rises by necessity and/or habit is always likely to be an old response. This may be nearly inevitable, and having some ready responses is necessary. But what automatically rises as a reaction is not necessarily the best or most useful response each time. Our first immediate response then is likely to be one that is, shall we say, safe. The safe one is interested in further perpetuating the status quo. It is all the brain/mind can do, because for most of us it was all it was ever programmed to do: to respond and do the already known, what I am comfortable with, or convinced of, and to do all that kind of automatically. (I already said that there is nothing necessarily wrong with this; or right...for that matter.)

One problem can be that what rises as if by magic when looking for a new response may even look as if it were new. It can honestly fool us. And not only when I am perceiving something actually new. All the time, in fact, since every new moment is new, it is new even if it is or looks, sounds, and smells the same as yesterday's brew. Every moment is of course brand new! We need not pursue that too far, but it is important to comprehend. Everything that looks old, or as if you knew it, a gesture of your wife or child, the smell of fresh bread, the colour of your red roses, they are all – in truth – new each time you perceive them. When it comes to more complex matters, to feelings and decision making, to needing to act in some new way, we might suddenly find that 'phew, I feel confused'... What's that about?

Confusion? It is clear enough...

Jiddu Krishnamurti, yes, that old Indian man of huge wisdom again, said somewhat dryly that we need a state of non-critical awareness in order to properly, clearly 'hear' what is going on within us. That, by the way, is the true meditative state, said he. Being non-critical is a big ask for most people, a huge idea most of us never even think about. I must say that much as it is a wonderful idea that I utterly agree with, I doubt that it is entirely possible to do it. Still, aiming at being less critical of self and others is obviously a good thing (most of the time).

Now we are at a kind of crossroads though. Non-critical, non-judgemental would also mean – I believe – the letting go of the idea of totally free human choices. Krishnamurti goes on to say that only when we *think* that we have many choices, only then do we get confused. To clarify: whenever I think that there are choices, whenever I believe there are at least two possible ones to pick from, a potential for confusion can arise. This need to choose situation rises often in lives. For a simple example: will I buy this Canon camera or an Olympus brand? That may be a touch unclear, but a bit of exploration will solve it.

The above example is not the sort of bewilderment Krishnamurti had in mind, and with what he had in mind I do agree. What he explained was that we often think and believe that we have various choices when in truth we do not really have any. We simply do not want to see and comprehend the one and only actuality of the matter. Instead we do this 'as if' choosing pretence. Why? Because we simply do not want to face the fact that there is only one choice; we like to think and believe we have absolute freedom and power. Well, yes, we have some of each, not as much and not as little as many often think. So I am not as absolute here as the old man who was undoubtedly one of the greatest minds of the 20th century.

Unlike Krishnamurti, who applied all the above to human thought, feelings and actions, I don't think that there always has to be confusion when there is a choice. There can indeed be times when one is faced with a limited number, two or three possible choices one could take. For example, you are offered two jobs. This is not so confusing if you explore the issues and your own heart and mind properly. Emotional/thinking confusion is more of what Krishnamurti spoke of. I agree with him that often there simply is no choice here, and if we refuse to see that, for whatever reason, then we can obfuscate and say 'oh, I am so confused'. Worse luck, but everyone is likely to be familiar with the fact that when we feel emotional confusion, doubt, fear or procrastination, usually this is not a good time for good decision making. I am all for being well in touch with how one feels/thinks.

Some of the above, the business of choice making, again remains an unsolved discussion. I agree to the idea of sometimes choice-less-ness intuitively, and based on my experience and studies. But please do recognise that one would have to know and be aware of **all the facts** to recognise the only possible right choice to be made. And this, being aware of ALL the facts, is impossible as a rule. To go further in this direction is an entire other book, and we need not go there for our purposes. What's to be done then? Use discrimination and always ask yourself whether you have done so.

Discrimination

To make good choices, we need to explore issues with a great deal of 'discrimination'. Discrimination is a synonym for discernment, acumen, judgement and more. Meaning that we need to be properly informed about potential situations and about the possible choices (if any) hanging off them. Now, Krishnamurti made some disparaging remarks about the human propensity not to want to see the obvious, but to rather consider imaginary, or pretended possible choices. He is correct. We love to fool ourselves. I add that often we feel confused because we are not well enough informed. If emotions are involved, there is, as oft stated, even more difficulty. Then, maybe because it is painful, comes the 'we might not want to see that we have no choice' or 'that we don't like the only choice we have'. No choice always feels kind of weak for us. And oh sorry, people, for the bleatingly obvious I am about to say, but having no choice is NOT a choice, it just is a fact...maybe.

Another issue, one already tackled before in other chapters, is that our brain/mind 'interprets' all incoming information and does it well or badly. Thus we need to be vigilant and discriminative before we make a decision. Hesitating forever is a life wasted. Commitment is a must once a choice is made, unless along the way we are clearly proven wrong about our decisions. This is all common enough sense, is it not? Yet so many people and organisations, even governments, don't follow it. Accepting that there is No Choice is often a simple must. Think for example of the Israeli–Palestinian conflict: is it not utterly obvious that both parties must settle? There is no choice whatever. Or if you are a battered spouse: no choice, leave now. She does not love you anymore? She said so: move on. And so on and on with, of course, some situations being not this easy and clear. But do not obfuscate, mystify, bugger around forever and kid yourself about it. Consider properly and decide to see what, if any, choices there are. Then take action.

Allow me to go a touch further in this direction. Krishnamurti offered that where there is 'true clarity', there is nothing to choose, and there can be no confusion. Clarity means the clear ability to see or hear what there truly is, rather than the confusing mess of endless questioning what this or that means. A state of clarity is certainly always somewhat pleasing. Hmm, yes, it would be, but it ain't so easy to get it. I experience things as pleasant at times, or else otherwise. If it is pleasant, we tend to accept it as it is, but if it is not agreeable, then we tend to look for so-called other choices, for ways out of displeasure, as if such were readily and simply available. 'Oh, I'm so confused'? I trust you are not saying that about this brief chapter. Yet, I fear we poor humans are rarely able to follow it all so easily, if at all. Some of the reasons for that follow.

Can thought see itself and communicate with it?

Is it possible for the mind to be non-judgemental and non-critical, choiceless, and so clear on any issue or thought? Can thought catch and see itself? Can consciousness be aware of itself? Krishnamurti and many others through the ages have asked all these questions. I have pursued them (and similar ideas) all my life, often with some alarm at the damned seeming absoluteness of it all. Still, just thinking about what Krishnamurti suggested is a great way to clarify one's life and self. For me it has been, and still is, kind of fun to ponder on these quests, exactly because they tend to bring something newish to my mind. 'New' is rarely boring; the old can be.

The only problems, as I see it, with Krishnamurti, Buddhism and other similar Eastern or Western philosophical thought systems is that they all tend to ask for total commitment and results. Humans are not well programmed to do either 'total' or 'complete'. We can but strive in such directions...

Hey, wait a minute...

We are back to striving to be the best possible version of ourselves... That is our end purpose, meaning and reason for living!

Therefore, don't worry too much about the absoluteness of the great asks; just do what you can in the right direction. Do not do what most people do: throw away the baby with the wine just because it all sounds too big and complex.

'Do what you can' means to:

Live your life as an unfinished draft of a book, rather than cheat yourself by polishing and waiting for that final perfection you will never achieve.

How far can the mind know its motivations and sources (predispositions and the ensuing resulting programs) and thus its reality? That's a big question, but the degree to which you can know your own self/mind will be exactly the degree to which you will be able to know all other minds. If the mind cannot comprehend even its owner, or if it can do so only marginally, then understanding others and life will be a shallower affair. If the mind can catch and comprehend its own programs, it will then understand a great deal about many things and many other people. That must culminate in truly making better decisions because one will be choosing from a 'discriminating', and therefore from a much better informed base. Much as I love the non-mystical, earth-grounded teachings of Krishnamurti, there is no need to explore them any deeper here. Yet tackling them even briefly has allowed me and you to perhaps add to a renewal of the way we understand ourselves and our interconnected world.

THE 'SOFTWARE OF OUR PERSONALITY' IS NECESSARY, USEFUL, UNAVOIDABLE, BEAUTIFUL, MARVELLOUS…AND CAN BE A PROBLEM

Oh dear, we have touched on this several times already. Yet, we need to see it all from another perspective and also to reinforce it even further. For this is very much what this work is about.

Respect and love your brain/mind/body and current software for that is the only unique you there is. Mum and Dad made it; you got what you have. I reiterate that although acceptance of yourself, of what there is, may be hard, it is the first step to changing aspects of yourself and of your active life. I am not even suggesting absolute acceptance, just a minimal intake of breath and relaxing into saying 'ah, this me is Me'. Someone much wiser than me said 'choose your own life'. Wow, yes indeed, but that is not always easy. (I find that I have managed to choose just over half of mine and can be still rebellious against the rest. That leaves me as a searcher and at times still struggling with…me mainly.)

'No one knowingly does themselves harm'...so said Socrates and many other great thinkers. A huge statement, for often we do seem to knowingly do ourselves harm. But we meant to do ourselves some good actually, yes? It is just that what we see, believe or convince ourselves of as a good move, alas it was a bad one. Every human being has done this! There is no devil in or outside of you. Even terrorists, in fact particularly terrorists, firmly believe that what they are doing is the right thing for themselves and others.

What I just said means that we cannot always entirely rely on our self/mind for doing the best for us. That is a disturbing but fairly obvious fact. Hmm, now that's a worry. Yet that is how life seems to be. Biologically our brain/mind, the mess of jelly substance, is on your side. It is preprogrammed by your genes to survive, thrive and reproduce. Nonetheless, it receives inputs once you are born into this world, 'programs' from out there, since day one, and then uses those as best as it can. When the programs are not so good and work too far against you (or if you were born with some faulty genes), we can be said to become ill, neurotic, or worse, psychotic.

The incoming programs after birth can even damage the actual physical brain/mind, and certainly the emotional part of the psyche/mind. Perhaps, and I am convinced of it, no one knowingly sets out to do themselves harm (unless there are mental disturbances of some sorts). Everyone believes they are doing good for themselves and even for others. Putty we are, so easily fooled by our own and the world's complexities that come into play inside our brain/bodies. When we get ill, psychologically depressed or confused, or sad, that would be a bit akin to when your computer says 'no good, you have committed a fatal error, the system will be shut down'. What happens in life and why has a great deal to do with feelings and thoughts.

Meta feeling/thinking

We spoke about it earlier. When you think about how you think about yourself, you are experiencing what psychologists call meta-consciousness, the ability to be aware that you are aware. Meta, yes, but I rather believe that thoughts and feeling are not separable (not for our purposes). Conversing as we do with ourselves makes me wonder what many people must have asked before me: if **I am** doing the talking, then to whom am I talking? And when I hear **myself listening**, then who is actually talking? Am I then two persons or even more? And that 'voice' we call 'thought/feeling' comes from where? How, and what 'voices' got into my head?

*Note: I shall use 'voices' and 'programs' interchangeably from here on.

Interconnected; no person is an island

All this is part of the awareness process explored yet again. Now allow me to add '...*we can't think about whiteness, or light, or etc. without it being attached to something*' (*The God Problem: How a Godless Cosmos Creates* by Howard Bloom). We can't think or feel about ourselves without everyone and all else also being attached to our thoughts. So, although I don't know you, reader, you have been somewhat taken into consideration already. Just as people I have read or learned from have been. So has the wife, the kids and my past retail business and the idiot estate agent I dealt with just the other day. In a way, what rises within, the content (the story) and the feeling/thoughts, is always everything we are and entirely attached to all else. I won't go too far with this.

When we get angry it is not just anger, but perhaps frustration, fear, feeling misunderstood or a myriad other thoughts and feelings. When a stone falls into the water it makes waves that stop at the side of the pool, but we cannot see how far the wave may have travelled in the ocean. The interconnectedness of all, of each of us to each other and to all else including nature, the rest of the world, the universe and simply everything, are heady philosophical thoughts. There is no separate or separable self out there that we can consider. We can only sense, feel, or think about our selves within the world! Only as part of the world. In a sense there really is no 'duality', no them and me as separate things. This makes things seemingly complex, but in fact it is a simplex, once you see it. (We can fortunately sidestep going deeper into such hard issues any further, yet it is worth keeping it in mind.)

I have said earlier that all systems and isms are a kind of defence. You do need protection and defensive moves at times, that is agreed. But not perhaps as often or as heavily as they come into play. And not in a way that they are driving you. For usually the defence system just springs up without giving one the chance to say whether or not, or how far it is wanted. One is then in danger of becoming dogmatic, defensive, blocking and so on. The defensive usually rises automatically exactly because it is a piece of preprogrammed personality software! It is switched on, triggered, by certain happenings that you might be aware of – or barely so, or not at all. Now some of that, once again, is both necessary and useful.

No freedom of thought can happen in automatic defensive situations. No actual seeing-hearing can happen once the defensive programs are activated. All that can happen are the old responses, at times papered over, directed by past messages of memory making up what might look like good responses to the current perceived stimulation.

For thought to see itself as itself rising is a tall order – we spoke of it recently – and a seemingly impossible one. We need not go too far in this direction either, but we can and do observe movement within ourselves and out there as it rises every day, every moment. That operation is in-built, instinctive and interactive. Emotions are one of the more obvious things we do notice; if we take the time, we observe them. Such are pain, confusions, anger, joy and so on. We also notice and observe thoughts rational and otherwise passing through. We do have some dispositions and ability to see and note what we feel and think, obviously. The problem often is that we simply don't take enough time to observe and consider our feelings/thoughts. So we can do it, we do do it, but many people – I think most of us – are not really good at it. We can greatly improve. (Some people will say they don't have the time... Now that is really silly.)

I have asserted right through this book the good news that we do have the ability to do the job of living well, potentially. The bad news is that we don't tend to follow the steps needed to find out what the 'good' life **for you** might be. Or that you look for it out there or even worse, up there...

Up there the sky is blue or cloudy, no God, simply natural phenomena just as all of us are. Out there everyone wants to have a good life. Some do, many don't. Injustices, no opportunities, greedy other people, etc. etc., I won't sermonise this, you all know it. There is but one aim, meaning and purpose in life and that is to have a good one, a truly good life that harms no others. Self-actualisation means what it says. See the next chapter.

This chapter served to bring together various issues explored in earlier chapters and to add a little more to each of them. Again, I leave to the reader to tease out the many main points. Not because I am lazy (I protest) but because I do think that if you have come this far it is a great way to bed in the knowledge that applies to your particular situation and personality.

SELF-ACTUALISATION

Self-actualisation is no mystery; it is done here and now, by you, with a little help from others. Maslow, often quoted throughout this book, was a great, if perhaps a lesser known, post-Freudian psychologist and thinker. I have already mentioned some of his ideas and I repeat an important one paraphrased: 'What you can be – achieve, you must.' Your purpose, even 'mission' in life, is this thing in itself, to fulfil your purpose, which is to become the best potential you that is possible. I know I have written here a sort of circular argument, and I meant to.

The above is the fuel for your energy because it is the very meaning/reason for your existence. And recognition of this is all one needs to begin with. Well almost all; it is certainly a big step towards realisation of your self and actualisation. In this endeavour there is no need for higher powers, no mysterious other worlds, no gods, no need to starve yourself or mumble mantras for 50 years. You can even eat meat and drink wine.

Maslow coined the term of 'self-actualisation'. His ideas, with additions from others (and now me too), shall be briefly regurgitated, reformulated below. Self-actualisation is not the same sort of thing as, say, the ideas of self-realisation, or nirvana, nor is it any sort of directly spiritual, mystical, out of this world idea. It is the focus – a meaning/reason – for one's life and actions. All of which, if properly pursued, become an end in themselves, actually becoming one's reason and purpose in living. I say it again, friends, not much more is needed except your commitment and comprehension of the idea. No, this should not be a mere belief, but proven experience by and to yourself. Your life happens now, and this reaching out for the best sort of you is your only (dare I say) salvation.

An easy task it is not, nor a very hard one. It is a clear and simple offering; hey, you can even eat pork and make love or stay at home, or go out with the children. You can work, rise in your career, change your mind, and so on. You can even earn and spend money! (Reasonably.) All this is simply...well, all too simply human (as Nietzsche said), and that's what it is.

Self-actualisation is a process; it is a 'doing-being' that is never-ending. It is a way of travelling rather than arriving at a destination. All stops, all stations along the way are the process and goal.

The process IS the product

I wish I knew who said that first. It is something you do actively, rather than just dream, think or meditate about. Action taken, thought and felt about, and considered, is the key. All this is not just for clever, well-educated, rich or poor people. It is for anyone, wherever you are, wherever you start from. This is where we can all be equal and where we almost do have equal opportunity.

Let me repeat some things in Maslowian terms. First, as I keep saying, is to find out what you have within you as a person, and then how to use it. A car mechanic must fix cars, a singer needs to sing, a doctor must help people. Simple as that? Yes, almost. I paraphrased Maslow saying that 'what a person can be, he/she has to become'. It is when we do not have an aim, a purpose that is realistic and solid, that we suffer most. We feel unfulfilled, disappointed, let down, depressed, angry... We do have an innate biological need to be and we do have the potentiality to become something satisfying. Does everything that you are capable of becoming have to be reached for? Yes, but only those things that are humane, sane and realistic (Maslow dialogues, a process of self-exploration…).

Briefly then, my understanding of Maslow's 'markers' for people on the way towards self-actualisation is that they are people who share the following traits or patterns of action and thought:

*A genuine feel for and appreciation of reality within yourself, and in the world around you.

*Caution and discrimination used when dealing with unknowns… and with what you know.

*Good ability to reason and to use some reasonable logic in daily living. To see the 'truth' of anything is sometimes obvious, often not so easy. Therefore, tread with care and do not force your truth onto others. But do tell them about it, if that is appropriate.

*Human nature is not always wonderful or easy to accept. Yet, one must not despair or be crippled by it, even at times of horror. Care, yes; sink in the quagmire of guilt, fear or regret, or shame, no!

*Have a good time, as far as that is possible, and do so without pointless inhibitions and making sure that your good time does not hurt others.

*Be helpful to yourself, rather than crippled by regrets; there is nothing you can do about the past… Ah, hang on, a fine statement this last one, but not entirely true. No, you can't change the past, but perhaps you can change your attitude to it. You can learn from the past (maybe). Yes, yes, you can reframe it, rewrite it, accept it...but don't bother too much with regret; it is mostly a waste of energy.

*You do need to be creative, spontaneous and yet discriminating in your inner and outer life and actions. Therefore, and as a result of self-exploration, you must be aware of your 'programs' and beliefs. Examine these cautiously and continually as you go on, for some of these will change by necessity, and some are already keeping you from action that may be good for you.

*Your focus is on your own action, and on those of others out there in your life. Take care, though that you focus equally on out there, rather than on mere navel gazing. Self-exploring can be done only within relationships with other people and the world.

*Be serious and devoted to your work and relationships. Drop relationships that are a baggage you no longer wish to carry (but do so gently). Nurture what works for you positively and for others. Much of your energy will be spent on such living actions and that's how it ought to be. But do not fritter away your energy on rubbish, small-time junk, or on pointless actions.

*Honesty works well, yet sometimes it can be brutal. Be honest with yourself always. Be appropriately so with others, caring whether they are open to you at this moment. Sometimes your preprogrammed prejudices look true and real but they are necessarily so.

*You need alone time, a sense of healthy detachment when you are awake. I don't mean meditating, though that can be part of it. I just mean alone time to read, think, float, do nothing...

*Independence needs to be fostered, as does acceptance of one's interdependence on others. Empathy and affection for others comes with empathy for yourself. You can't have one without the other! Accepting the entire human race can be rather hard, given what some members of it do. Yet one must try to have some understanding for it all, even if you decide to fight against certain aspects of it. And fight against some things you must, if possible without violence.

*Democracy is a great and faulty ideal, but we humans have not found anything better. Therefore, foster and appreciate democracy rather than a one-sided dogmatic political, or for that matter any, ideology. For one must be wary of any and all ideologies and isms. Many have created a great deal of misery. Means do not always justify ends; ends do not always justify means.

*Humour is a large part of a self-actualising process. Laughing at self is healthy; making fun at others in a way that might hurt them is not. Yet too much 'correctness' can be a rather dry affair. Dare to see the quirky, funny side of life.

*The process of actualisation means that you will find yourself unique after all. You will come to know that you are the one and only 'you' – and beware of imitations! You can be, can strive to be original and inventive. Note you are not a special person in humanity, but you are to you and those near.

*You do need to observe the customs and laws of your society but you need not be controlled or contrived or directed by all of it. As said before, there are times to protest with power and indignation about what you know is injustice. Thus, beware of what society wants you to accept and swallow.

More or less, I think Mr Maslow would agree with all this and more. So be impatient about your progress and process, yet be kind and gentle with your life. This too is part of the purpose and process you have committed to, if you have indeed done so?

The 'Software' of Your Personality

We all carry some opposing forces within us; we have explored some of that. Who knows what one would or could do in certain circumstances that were other than what you now have. But you don't have that other; you have what you have. Thus don't worry about the what if this or that might happen. The raw energy of our opposing forces can be used – perhaps merged – towards the making of a more actualised person. Conflict will always be felt in life. We usually try to avoid feeling that; contrarily, we might try to let it be, to use it, use its drive energy to find that amalgamated position. This will not work sometimes, I am sorry to say, but it will at other times! So do not give up too easily. When it does work, you will know it; there will be a feeling of wisdom and also a feeling of almost childlike innocence when it does happen.

Maslow offered the two main streams of thought for self-actualisation: a deeper exploration and awareness of your self, and then the taking of actual actions. Nothing unusual there, everyone agrees with that. How do you start to act on a thought or feeling? It is easy: you can start by putting it out to whom and when it is appropriate. There are many 'messages' within you that cry out for action. Mostly we just get scared of trying some.

Yet again I caution, as a Zen master said: after enlightenment or self-realisation by any name, the laundry still needs to be done! Rousing as it is, do reach towards it, but remember to be satisfied with what you can do and be, once you have done what you can.

Somewhat unusual ideas concerning the possible plurality of 'self' follow. You will likely find yourself either delighted with such ideas or dead against them. Please consider them.

SELF OR SELVES?

Professor Jim Holt's book *Why Does the World Exist* should be compulsory reading for everyone. It is easy and thoroughly enlightening. *'Each person's stream of consciousness, little transient selves constantly wink in and out of existence, none of them lasting for more than an hour or so. There simply isn't any "I" or self that goes on through (let alone beyond) the waking day'...* Holt quotes Strawson, *'even though there's obviously an "I" or self at any given time.'* (Holt 2013)

The above is one splendid description, among many, of the multiple self notion, and I shall offer several others. In fact, for me the very quote itself suggests that on one hand there may not be a continuous self and on the other famous hand...*'here is obviously an I or self at any given time.'* Well, which one? Jim Holt in his marvellous book, *Why Does the World Exist*, quoted Professor Strawson and I believe Holt has accepted the possibility and probability of 'multiple selves' within the one human being. I also think several 'selves' may 'wink' in and out of existence moment to moment, yet there are also several other continuous selves that formulate and are part of us for a long time, many until we die. So I am not entirely in agreement with Strawson. My suggestion, that there are major inner 'players' or 'selves' or programs that do in fact go through each 24-hour day intact, is more along the lines of several other thinkers, like philosopher Daniel Dennett, and others I shall mention later.

Still, even some of these major selves may go, leave us, and new ones might take their place as time and experience dictates. For example, some major childish selves may disappear, and some convert a bit, mature so to speak...yet some actually stay forever. I know that some middle-aged selves are mostly still with me as are some childish ones, but not all of them. As for the selves that do 'wink in and out of existence', I am in this work far more concerned with the ones that stay in one's life. So we move on, concentrating on the stayer selves.

According to many thinkers these days, and I agree from my own experience and research, there is indeed more than one self, more than a 'singular' me that I can speak of and even relate to. Walter (2013) said that when you are talking to yourself (something we all do), the 'you' that you are speaking to is a symbol. Yes, but allow me to stretch that idea: a person, a self may also be said to be a symbol for the many personalities or programs or selves I call Me! When I check myself, or you, I am not looking at a clearly defined thing like looking at, say, a ball, which is just a ball. When dealing with myself or with you, I am looking at tremendous complexity. That complexity can be thought of as one ego-self, one that is made up of an **entire family of individuals.** Or as a bunch of in-built selves serving programs or personalities. Or as an organisation, or even as a play in a theatre! When I consider you (or me), I am looking at several various selves within the one 'me' or you!

It is commonplace when people speak of the 'baggage' they carry, that it is not only their baggage, but Mum's, Dad's, society's and so on. Cliché or not, what is this baggage actually?

'Just as your mind symbolically represents the other people in your life, it also uses this hoax (a metaphor) to represent a version of you, which makes possible an enormously powerful force in your life, this second you, who is diligently and deeply influencing your

every feeling, thought, and choice.' Walter is now speaking of at least two selves. One that speaks, and one that hears. I rather think he means the possibility of several selves.

He goes on to say:

> *'In this way the brain changes itself, commands itself, reacts to itself, reshapes itself. It somehow bootstraps self-awareness and self-determination and simultaneously generates a symbolic self to be aware of and to command (as opposed to a God or a demon who dictates orders).'*
>
> (Walter 2013)

There is, I know personally, not one clearly definable 'Ted'; I am made up of many issues, various aspects or selves. Don't worry, I am not advocating multiple personality disorder as a way of life, but rather the contrary, which is an integrated harmonious self that incorporates all my features, programs, voices, selves (by whatever word) in a harmonious self-directed whole. (Thus, neither gods nor madness needed to function well.)

While on this subject of symbolic awareness and mental commands, look at the controversial ideas of psychologist and author Julian Jaynes. Gods and demons probably were early humans' representations of multiple selves, of hearing within more than one 'voice' (Jaynes 1976). Jaynes speaks about why people of antiquity believed in prophecy, the internal voices they heard in their head. He is talking about ancient times, the dawn of human awareness as consciousness began to awaken. This, Jaynes says, was the basis and beginning of religious beliefs, of gods and spirits and so on. When people heard voices speaking to them... *'They instead believed they were listening to another all-knowing being who was observing them and their thoughts.'* Jaynes called this kind of 'old' mind 'bicameral', or two-chambered, where one chamber listened and one spoke; however, neither side (or chamber) was aware that they were part of the same brain.

'For bicameral humans, volition came as a voice that was in the nature of a neurological command,' he wrote, *'...in which the command and the action were not separated, in which to hear was to obey.'* (Jaynes 1976, 2001) In the hazy old past there was not a full consciousness, but a partial, bicameral one. It is not my interest whether Jaynes is or is not correct, but what he offers does have potential to explain some things further. These days, hearing voices is considered mental illness. I don't think Jaynes is suggesting mental illness of the ancients per se, rather that many beliefs arose in the way he described. My point then is simply to note that there are indeed right and left brains and we know by now how 'elastic' the brain can be. Now, today, the two halves of the brain 'know' one another as a total entity. That is very much consciousness. Way back then there was no such thing, and on this most of science agrees. Yet, say I, there may well be some remnants of the bicameral brain notion.

Amazing things do go wrong in the brain/mind and have been documented and explored. *The Man Who Mistook His Wife for a Hat* (Sacks 1985) and the recent books on the idea of the Elastic Brain tell much about all that can go wrong...or right about the brain. I need not go further in that direction, but Jaynes' fascinating notion (and many others' since his writing) help to move us further into our exploration of the self, or as many experts now believe, the multiple selves each of us is. And I say 'is' because I do feel like I am a unity and not a scattered plurality... So is my wife, and most of my readers.

Evolutionary psychology, for one discipline amongst many, focuses on the idea that our brains have various and different functions.

'The large number of parts of the mind can be thought of as, in some sense, being different "selves", designed to accomplish some task...'

and in addition,

'You simultaneously believe (or, at least, "believe", with quotation marks around it) many, many things that are mutually contradictory.' (Kurzban 2012)

Like I said, reader, don't worry that I am a split personality; let me assert and assure again that it is the other way around: the more of your parts, programs, selves, voices, personalities (by whatever word) you are familiar with, the better you can **integrate** and use them. Indeed, split personality cases are the very situations where various parts of the person's psyche are not well enough integrated.[32] Another heavier, philosophical way to put it: *'our brain is not a **single** uniform event but a **multilayered chain of events** in which different processes are densely coupled and interacting all the time...'* (Metzinger 2009)

To become more free as people, we need to be watching the way we are driven by our software programs (selves), what the psychologists call the defence system and what Stone and Winkelman further named as the 'Protector Controller' (Stone & Winkelman 1985). When it kicks in, the Protector Controller part of you usually activates several strong, major working programs. Many of these are the primary set-up of human beings. Now you may have noted that I introduced yet another idea, another 'metaphor', this time for the defence system: the Protector Controller. As Stone and Winkelman and many others have said, it pays to separate various aspects (programs) of the personality. There is a wonderful one-liner in therapeutic method called 'Narrative Therapy'. They say, and keep strenuously

---

[32] I shall get back to this multiple self idea later in further detail, for we can amalgamate and use more of our powers by the organised and integrated self.

pointing out, that *'you are not the problem,* **the PROBLEM is the problem***!'* The so-called problem, by the way, can be anything from a banal issue to a decision about a divorce etc. The point is certainly and at least this: you are not the problem. You 'have' a problem. Separate it out so it is easier to see and then deal with it in some way. That way you can see the problem more simply and more clearly and deal with it as an aspect of you, rather than the totality you are. Now, it may not be quite as simple or easy as I just put it. However, great clarity can be had from removing yourself from the scene of the battle where you can separate and say something that does not include thinking/feeling of yourself as THE bad fella, the problem. Again, frustrating, but I leave this for your further consideration and exploration if it is of interest.

Now, going into our main game idea and process deeper will lead us to another 'tool' of investigation and transformation. The brain commands itself and you as you. So I am told. Does it? We are exploring whether the brain/mind contains a singularity or a plurality. If plurality, then that would help to explain somewhat why one can be loving and hating at once, for example. Or why one can flick from this to that mood, and particularly why one has inner conflicts. We also have several, sometimes spontaneous and surprising responses to other people and various situations. As Hofstadter put it, '*...we are a strange loop, a supreme example of recursion, a* ***matryoshka doll of selves***' (Hofstadter 1981). I love that image, the doll within a doll within a doll... That's me and you. A marvellous metaphor that explains itself, because you can picture it. Conceptualising mental stuff into a picture that converts concepts into easy comprehension is always a tremendous gain. The next chapter follows the ideas so far with some additions.

INTRODUCING 'SUB-PERSONALITIES' (SPS) – SOME WAYS TO CONCEPTUALISE YOUR LIFE, SELF AND OTHERS.

The following is one of my (current) favourite ways of seeing life, perhaps because I am also writing novels, fiction, where there are 'characters' I need to build. Using the imagery so far, as well as what I now present, helps my writing projects. So here it is (groan, moan...) yet another metaphoric idea that might help to express the idea of several selves or sub-personalities as personal software programs, as parts of yourself. One simple notion is supposing that I am writing the story for a play or a movie called: *My Life*. I don't know whether it will be a movie, a TV series, or a theatrical play of several never-ending acts. Anyhow:

MY LIFE

Written mainly by Ted Todd (and others).
Directed and produced mainly by Ted Todd (and some others).
Starring Ted Todd, and his ensemble of sub-personalities.
Supporting actors: wife, children, dead parents and grandparents and all of you on earth.

The 'Software' of Your Personality

A review by that well-known critic Ted Todd (and others) will follow. (Wow, I am an important fella, am I not? Tickets may be booked now by buying this book.)

Imagine now that you have written a play called *My Life*. After much agonising about it, and having talked to other older 'directors' (Mum and Dad, teachers and bosses, wife or husband etc.), you have noted that the last actual directors of your life, Mr and Mrs Parents, were um...OK, but um...they had their problems and they are past directing what in any case is Your Story. They don't appear to understand this new modern-life play at hand anyway. Others who had a hand in directing you also appear not to have full understanding of the deeper meaning of the play (your life) either. So you have decided that after all only you can 'direct' the story and drama that is YOU.

Every play or movie, you will agree, needs a writer, director, several actors and other participants. Each actor-character of the drama always has their own personality; each has opinions, feelings, ideas, needs and wants; that's what makes them interesting characters. Ho, ho, ho, though, you know, as the director, that each of your 'actors' is one of your 'sub-personalities' (SPs for short). As the writer/director/producer, you are the most powerful participant in this play. YOU have the power to direct how the play is enacted, how it expresses the story-script. Or do you? Take care you do not let one of your verbose and pushy 'actors', selves or sub-personalities take over the whole play. Via the actors (your various SPs), the characters in the play must express what you as director have decided to prompt. But each actor has their own agenda, their own interpretation of this play (life). Each actor, that is each SP, wants to be the 'star' and has strong and pushy convictions about how the movie or play should be played out. Every actor (SP) brings something of their own and wants to act it out. That's why we find movies, theatre productions and books, hell, even TV, endlessly fascinating. (Or, all too often, boring.)[33] Need I spell it out further? If, for example, your inner 'Critic'[34] is directing all or too much of the action that is your life, that will be painful and limiting. So will several other perfectly user friendly SPs if they are too big for their boots!

Now a step further. As the director/producer, you are in charge. So you need to know not just the story that has been written – that would seem easy, given you wrote it. You also need to know what the characters (your SPs) you had written into the story might or could do. That's what makes actual writing and stories good when others are awful. That's what makes some lives way more satisfactory, for knowing this is having more power and freedom to be and to act. Then you need to know, as I already said, not only your main hero's personality, but also the disposition of each SP acting part. Some can act out one part, but not another. Good casting makes good plays (lives) believable and successful.

Therefore, you need to know not just the aim of the story (your life), but also the various personalities and possibilities of the actors who play the 'parts', in order to best 'cast' each player in a particular role. That is: use each SP for best results in a chosen and focused way. What you can barely know is the ultimate end of the story, given that it has not yet ended. So recall that in the end **you** are in fact the writer, director and almost all the players. You know the story, your story, so far – do you? You have, sort of, directed the play so far, as you thought best, to achieve a successful outcome. Now, if the story is garbled or unclear at the moment, if the presentation of your 'play' is without aim or confused, then a good show cannot result. Perhaps the 'production' needs deeper understanding and even some 'rewriting'. Perhaps the

---

33 The more actors and artists understand SPs, the better art will be made.
34 The 'Critic' is so common to all of us that it seems to be an absolutely necessary part of being human. Unfortunately, it is also common that, be it 'he or she', the 'Critic' is overwhelmingly too big.

The 'Software' of Your Personality

'actors' (SPs) need further explanation and direction about what is wanted from them. Possibly some 'actors' need to be replaced with others? Or maybe another angle found to clearly and usefully present the meaning and focus of the 'play'.

One interesting point needing reconsideration is that there is no conclusion to your whole story at this time. That is true and it can be viewed in two ways. One is to see what has gone on until now; the 'story' and its protagonists and outcomes stands as it does today. From here on, we said, you may have to 'rewrite several old and new chapters' and reconsider your troupe of 'actors' (SPs) and their abilities, features, needs and wants. Yet you also must remain in full charge as the 'director' of the whole event. That way you won't be a so-called 'split' personality but, rather, a more integrated, confident one.

In the kind of play-drama-comedy that we are discussing now, where no one can know what exactly will happen, you and only you have some extra know-how about the production. Your story as it unfolds day to day will channel into certain conducts, actions of yours, whatever they may be. Or else, you will ponder what had happened to your life that has flown by. (Most people seem to do a bit of that anyway.) Although you know that there are no guarantees about successful plays (life outcomes), it is also clear, is it not, that there can be some 'willed', purposeful and meaningful input by you and your SPs-'actors'.

※

So, again, no splitting of personality precisely because all these SPs will become even more integrated within you if you take on even more of the role of 'director' in your life story than you might have until now. This 'DIRECTOR' is, after all, also a sub-personality of sorts. Most of us so-called normal people manage to balance our inner programs, and thus correspondingly our outer actions, to a reasonable degree. Some cannot. Those who have insufficient integration cannot do this; they have SPs that harmfully and inappropriately 'act out'. I repeat: it is only when we are unaware of what is going on between our ears that the personality 'falls' apart, that we get into trouble, agonise, stress out, get depressed and so on. Terrorists are not to be excused, but they are an example of mistaken use of programs and belief systems (same thing). Am I oversimplifying all this? You bet I am, because this work does not need me to go any further in this direction either. Yet it is most important for the human race that people understand the basis and basics of how each of us operates.

When you do nothing but play or nothing but work, or nothing but drink, or nothing but suffer...or whatever, if and when you are totally dogmatic, or obsessive, some real-life problems do arise. The so-called personality splits, or a nervous breakdown, depression, anxiety and suchlike can arise. These splits can and do happen only because you are not familiar enough with your parts or SPs – by whatever name – and have neither enough control nor the power to choose what they (you) truly need and want. I repeat, your inner programs, selves, beliefs, voices etc. etc. can do good things or dreadful ones.

Family group?

This way is similar, but while it is not my invention, several other schools of thought touch upon it as a metaphor for our inner workings. Here is my very brief take on the greater idea. Suppose that 'I am' an entire 'family' or group of selves (SPs). My entire social and inner interactions are made up of a mix of personalities, just as families and groups are made up of various people. This is a kind of systems thinking. If I am a system or a group, then there needs to be unceasing vigilance of my inner group, in order to suit several of my inner and outer relationships.

As usual in any group, club, system, organisation, association, there will be power struggles, wants and needs, plans, good and bad ideas, and so on. And this is, all is, within the 'group' in my head! But it certainly affects what I do, say and act on out there.

So my many selves may be imagined as an entire 'internal family'. Don't put your mum's or brother's face on it instantly, for that is not what we are talking about. Suffice to say that there is a fella in my head I call the 'Critic'. His face is hard to picture. Many people say it looks like Dad's face or a teacher's face – it matters not whose face or if any (mine is a vaguely military type of face). There is also a Wise Man, a Lover, a Father, a Pusher of Work, and so on (Stone & Stone 1993). Just the very same as how the rest of the world actually operates. As in the macro, so in the micro. Go back far enough away from the earth and it becomes a small blue ball. Zoom in and it has countries, mountains, rivers, towns, villages, people, grass, bugs...and sub-personalities or selves, or programs...

What happens out there is just a larger version of what happens in here, in me![35] Think about world history. It is about large events mainly, yet if we could zoom in further, we would find a lot more going on among a lot more people than just the kings, the powerful, the rich or famous. If we could zoom down into an individual's life in, say, 1432 AD, what would we find? In any case, the point is the old one: big systems lead to and are made up of smaller and smaller system parts that make up the whole. And many have said that written and known *history is not actually about what really happened, but about what probably, maybe happened.* And it is distorted by the many writers as well. (Is that

---

35 A great deal of material is written on the subject of whether the world is 'out' there or only in here. It is another debate we won't need here, but it's a beauty. For on one hand all that you sense is within your own head/body and yet there certainly is (I think) a world out there outside of my skin.

why we used to have daily miracles and now we don't have any?) And this, dear reader, is so true of your personal history as well.

Let's strike the computer key while I'm hot: our brain/mind/memory software programs are big complex affairs, the trickiest ones in all of nature to individually explore or understand. We know so much about the brain, and enough to understand that we only know very little about the brain! Partially that is because people like the idea of simplicity; we all think that we know ourselves better than anyone else could. Yes, we do. Well, maybe. I am not always so certain. Your nearest and dearest certainly seem to know some of your parts better than you, don't they? Yes, I believe so. These are usually the programs one tends to fight against.

Our next step is to consider that our huge overarching programs that we call 'me' do need to be broken down into smaller chunks and then hypothesised, conceptualised, imagined…as usual, in order that our various programs/features should become user-friendly and at our command.

- We all have explored at least the basic 'operating system' of our body and basic abilities – babies do that, obviously, from the start.

- Our system is never without 'thought/feeling'. That set-up also helps us to learn more about ourselves and deny or mistake our ways of thinking and acting.

- We are doing this exploration right here and now, most likely because we wish to be maximising our lives. You may well be successful and good enough. Yet we may want to sort out and be rid of ill feelings, improve relationships, do better at our chosen work and so on.

The 'Software' of Your Personality

- Undertaking the journey will lead us to further recognition of more of your actual potential wants/needs and, importantly, abilities. This in turn will help to make more personally satisfying choices, decisions and actions. Like accepting what there is and how you are, perhaps? Oh, hmm, back to that? Well, um, yes and no…

ॐ

Don't believe that there are no instruction books about life; there are in truth too many of them. However, none of them are perfect, they cannot be, as each person and situation is that little bit different. But there is a tremendous amount of great info about human lives out there. Information, some (yet not all) of which you might have to apply and *adapt* to yourself. You need to find the instruction book(s), but not take on all of them right now. This you can do once you have explored your own selves and your brain/body world. It will not be denied that there is a lot of bad human instruction out there and this is very true. *Be careful*, is about all one can offer. Any get-rich-quick schemes, magical, metaphysical, religious, drug related, etc. etc. solutions and instructions are likely to be junk, and harmful. Now back to several selves, or as I prefer: sub-personalities (SPs).

SEVERAL 'SELVES'? BUT I 'FEEL' LIKE I AM JUST ME

Good thing too that you feel just like you... Still, we all experience at times that we are not just one voice, one opinion, but several competing ones. Would anyone disagree? There are several competing ideas, thoughts, and feelings within us much of the time. One is often 'divided' in the sense that while we can acknowledge our actions, feelings and thoughts, we also know that they come from many different beliefs, feelings and thoughts. Of course, one is and acts as 'just one person'; that is what we put out, and it is what each of us hopefully feels, and it acts as the 'me' we each know. But recall how often we seem divided, confused, and doubtful of our own actions, feelings and ideas – be they taken or left undone. Or how often we change our minds. Perhaps you can see already, given all the previous discussions in this book, that it does appear as if there are several of you – or more correctly several 'selves' that we've called 'programs', 'traits', 'sub-personalities' or even 'subcontractors'. Generally I like to use the expression 'sub-personalities' when debating such issues. (By the way, of course I do not mean hearing actual voices or seeing my various selves or subbies. All of them, all the subbies, are after all you.)

Carl Jung said that people like to think of themselves as one whole self, when in fact nothing could be further from the truth. By now, many philosophers and writers have suggested that the notion of unitary personhood is illusory. That, we possess 'different' selves, each with its own 'curriculum vitae', and each with its own chain of memories that reach into the past. Of course, all selves are facilitated by language.[36] This, again, is very much what I suggest, and as you can see the expertise and thinkers come from many and varied schools of thought from anthropology, archaeology, biology, philosophy, psychology, literature, and so on.

In *Do You Think What You Think You Think* by Stangroom and Baggini, philosopher Julian Baggini explores similar notions, asking whether it is actually you who thinks what you do or... did someone else? The next quote is not from a great thinker of our time: *'I have opinions of my own – strong opinions – but I don't always agree with them.'* (George W Bush) Although this sure seems funny, it is actually a truth we are all familiar with. Philosopher, scientist, writer and thinker Jim Holt (2012) notes that philosopher Derek Parfit, for example, likens the self to *'a club, one that might change its membership over time, disband altogether, and then reconvene under the same name in a different form.'* A small variation to what I proposed a few pages ago. Parfit, one of the greatest thinkers of our age, has a vision similar to fellow philosopher Daniel Dennett who in various of his books and lectures mentions that selves are not pearls found nor are they independent one from another. They are not so simply the products of the social processes that created us. Yes indeed.

We can posit then that the 'self' or 'selves' we know are not a totally steady, absolutely solid, unchangeable 'I'. The self is an ever-changing affair, one that we can know only by experiencing it and its various parts. Some thinkers are working hard on what and where the unity is or might be. Many other scientists say, and I heartily agree, that there is yet, without doubt, an underlying

---

36 Consider in addition a bilingual individual who may have at least two curricula vitae, two chains of associations, two or more sets of interpretive modes. Makes things better or harder?

unity, and it is '**memory**' that is constant and reliable enough for one to know that one is indeed me. My ME rises because I can recall my continuous life (Neisser, Bruner and others). Even the Buddha wisely stated that *'self'* is only a conventional name given to a *'set of elements'*... I love the simplicity of this.

Twenty-five years ago, I was fortunate enough to come across a particular school of the several selves notion. I am not suggesting that this is the only right way or that it is perfect as a method. After some deep study of it over many years I have taken some elements of it into my thinking and practice, having discarded various other parts of the method. Basically, the method I was introduced to is called 'Voice Dialogue' (Stone & Winkelman 1983) and it simplifies and clarifies the several selves idea...and helps to do...guess what? Yes, friends, it helps to 'conceptualise' it, you and all.

Sub-personalities (SPs) and Voice Dialogue is a process of change and consciousness.

(Stone & Winkelman 1983)

Let's look at this powerful, specific and user-friendly method just a bit more. It is called, somewhat misleadingly, 'Voice Dialogue'. It is about internal voices, not vocal cords. And it is emphatically NOT about hearing voices! Overall, it is a bit like the 'internal family idea'. I have already mentioned some of this but please persevere. Voice Dialogue, let me call it VD from now on, refers to various 'parts' of the self as 'sub-personalities', which were the same thing for our purposes as what I called your features, programs or selves.

A brief warning here is a must: while I do use the above concepts and words interchangeably, at times that cannot be done. Sometimes an SP is a smaller affair than an integrated person. Or a program may incorporate several SPs. Character traits may be a smaller unit of an SP and so on. A 'feature' at times is a big shadow or only a part of an SP. Yet, generally speaking, at this stage we need not make the main points more complex.

SPs, parts, character traits, features etc. are all exchangeable ideas even with 'programs' as I use them for our purposes in this book. I shall now stick mostly with using the 'sub-personalities' (SPs) or 'programs' to notate our discussions, as those terms are all I need for sufficient clarity.

Hal Stone and Sidra Winkelman were Jungian psychiatrists and they formulated the 'Voice Dialogue' method, which, as they said, is a process of transformation and consciousness. Somewhat earlier, Italian psychologist Roberto Assagioli formulated the idea of 'sub-personalities'. It is from the 'Voice Dialogue' method that I shall now take, with a lot of my own shortcuts, additions and alterations – what follows in the rest of this chapter. Voice Dialogue (VD) is a practical, *immediate* and user-friendly way of achieving more personal awareness. (I am very indebted to Stone and Winkelman for the teaching I have received from them personally.) Why do I say 'immediate'? Because the VD tool can be used instantly and briefly without any preamble. Once you have grasped the basics of it you can apply it to daily short- or long-term situations easily and without any drama or possible harm.

NOTE: The Voice Dialogue method did not use my 'program' idea and, as already mentioned, I have added and taken away from the whole VD system.

۶۹

Voice Dialogue calls feelings feelings, but it goes one major step further in asserting that each of our several 'sub-personalities' also has their own feelings/thoughts. Now that's a bit radical. Yet I know that my own 'Critic' tends to be an angry male. I know that when I don't feel I am getting enough love, there are some childlike pouty, sullen feelings in there, even while my adult Dr Self goes on doing well in life. Also, I have, as before, added feelings to thoughts and made one unit out of them. That was not Winkelman and Stone's idea. Back then in the 1980s and 1990s, most of the thinking trade wanted to work on feeling states and leave thoughts and thinking to a side. I never did and still do not agree with that approach.

So each 'sub-personality' is said to have its own set of feelings/thoughts, just as an individual person does. Each has, therefore, opinions, beliefs, needs and wants; yes, sir, each has a 'voice'. No, I caution again, not a voice you hear but in the other sense of 'giving voice to...' When strong feelings arise from perhaps several sub-personalities at once, then that is one explanation as to how you might feel several things at once, and confusion. Several feelings at once? Feeling/thoughts can indeed be contradictory things; we all have inner conflicts. What we are about in this book and in this particular 'consciousness' process is bringing together your personal/voices/sub-personalities/programs, features etc. – all to work in greater unison. This will admit more energy and clarity to achieve what you want – whatever that may be as long as it is decent, humane, and possible for you. When your features, feelings and energies work together with each other rather than against one another, then you use less of your limited physical and mental energy, and yet achieve more. Of course, all that can happen only if you have the right parts (SPs, programs, features, and opportunity as well) for a particular aim or goal. And then, only if they are 'activated' – called upon consciously – and are correctly aimed towards some reasonably productive aim. It is the parts that make up the whole and, as someone said, the total of the parts is actually a great deal more than each individual bit.

'Who' actually has your feelings and thoughts is an interesting question

In my household we often joke about the mysterious 'Who' person. He or she is that fella or woman who makes your socks disappear, or overcooks the meat, or leaves the door open etc. You know what I mean. Now our 'Who' also appears to be fairly inscrutable and tough. We blame all sorts of things on him/her and he never complains. Not a word. Now seriously though, let's step back for a moment into what we all know and recognise as feelings and thoughts. A reminder: I use the words feeling and thought separated only by a slash – feeling/thought; for our practical purposes, they are inseparable. Please accept this for now at least.

So when I say 'feeling/thought', who has them? Is there a one of 'I' that is my totality? Yes, kind of, but the 'I' is made up, as per previous discussions, of those particular SPs we each have. Oh by the way, they are all also a memory. A big variance arises at this point to the conventional view of the self. The difference is that in this method we must allow and view each of our own SPs as an (almost) actual entity. As Stone and Winkelman said: each of your SPs wants to be 'heard', each wants to 'assert' itself, and act, almost as if they were 'real' people...and they are real enough, they are you! So does that mean that all your feelings/thoughts are actually separate parts of your total personality? A perplexing point here, but no, not exactly separate as in unconnected. The main thing to note is that each SP is distinct in its aims and operations. Each SP believes that they have the right answers and ideas, and most tend to be even somewhat dogmatic. Each wants to do their set 'job' and each is vitally connected to the wholeness that is you. Older psychologists would have called these SPs the whole defence system. Yes, but they are more than just that.

There are some, let's say, major feeling/thought patterns, what we might term the 'heavyweights'. These are big, much used, strongly influential SPs. If you think about your major traits, you will easily recognise some of these strong ones. Our decisions about morality, ethics, beliefs etc. are usually held and practised by or from such major SPs, for example, but there are many others that are more subtle, some of lesser power and some tiny. Yet we are all humans so we all share some of these large and smaller SPs – and yet not all, and certainly not to the same degree. Meaning, the mix of SPs is what in the end constitutes what and how I act out, think, believe, feel and so on.

All right, all this may be viewed as a bit radical, huh? Treat all these above 'metaphors' seriously and yet broadly. Note that people have defence systems, just as countries do. That, defensive forces often ally with the market forces, cultures and practices of others, even at times with those of the so-called 'enemy' or problem. The same thing applies to each of us: 'alliances' are formed by one's SPs, in order to achieve something at a particular time. Alliances can change or break down. Cooperation at times is followed by sell-outs or broken deals...these go on daily in countries, groups, businesses, families, and within your own self! When I form an alliance with someone to, say, build a business, that alliance is not the same as making a loving and intimate relationship. There are similar elements, yes, but certainly not all of them. I note that it is possible to form a good business partnership and yet live in an ordinary or worse marriage... Or vice versa. Now, my example above referred to the involvement of others, one or more people. Yet all of it stands as an example to your inner selves, SPs, just as well. So let's translate just a little. Within me there is the 'Businessman' SP that used to clash with the 'Daddy' SP and even with the 'Wise Man' SP. Familiar enough to most people?

If I struggle with, say, a low self-esteem, then it will be harder to find success in private or career lives. But it's more complex, for I am struggling, as perhaps most people, with many forces within me (as well as with those out there). And I struggle on until and unless I can bring the forces (SPs) together and use them to achieve...well, whatever. So, does this mean that there are good or better, and naughty or bad SPs? Actually, no, and that is a great relief. It is more a matter of using the right SPs, let's call them 'energy patterns' for now, to do the right job.

Good and bad sub-personalities? No.

Empathically, none of these SPs – large or small – are to be thought of as either 'good' or 'bad', better or worse. No one in there inside you is trying to knowingly give you a bad time. (Even though you might feel that there is such an aspect of yourself at times when pursuing bad habits or unproductive disastrous thinking and feelings.) Each SP, however, merely does its 'job'; it has to – it is what it was 'constructed' to do, often as part of your defence system. The point is that each SP has a positive and negative polarity, and because of that, there is no need to get rid of certain SPs since usually one can turn their energies and aims towards positive outcomes. So no repression needed. (Freud would be pleased.)

The first thing then – as I keep hammering it in throughout this book – is for you to consider the following:

1. What sort of SPs do you have and 'who' does what 'job'? Note that an SP is like a feature but stronger and bigger, so to speak.

2. Considering your features, which we now may call SPs, will help to get a better feel for the SPs and help to get in touch with them. That also results in better control of the SPs.

3. In aid of what **supposed** outcomes are your present SPs operating?

4. Can SPs be turned towards more positive achievements and how?

Herewith I shall offer only a few of the more common, distinct and major SPs that we all tend to share (somewhat). I shall use Hal and Sidra Stone's sub-personality type labels, although one could use any label as long as it is constant. Please note that what follows is their interpretations and explanations of the major SPs, with my additions. The labels are taken from their book *Embracing Yourself*. (It is well worth reading, even if the title sounds a bit touchy-feely.)

Here are the main, more powerful SPs we all seem to have by any other name:

1. PROTECTOR CONTROLLER: might also be called the main defence system. This is a big fella, the strongest, the Boss. It is the gatekeeper or the umbrella, under which and in agreement with which many other SPs act. You might call him the 'chairman of the board', or the head of the inner 'family', or the director... She/he is the one who makes sure that things are done well, and that personal disasters do not happen, by laying down and sticking to certain rules that tend to be defensive. Possibly, sometimes several other SPs are unable to act because the Protector Controller/defence system may be too powerful. All SPs have to work with it, which is just as well.

The 'Software' of Your Personality

2. CRITIC: we all have this fellow. You can't be human if you haven't got an inner Critic. It is one of the most humanly shared and, worse luck, usually overly powerful SP. It looks like your biggest opponent. Yet the Critic, like all the others, has a positive and a negative side. Overly critical, it cripples the mind and actions, but right discrimination – seeing what is or is not good for one – is a positive necessity. 'He' or 'she' criticises everything we do, often crippling us, or at times saving our life.

3. PUSHER: presses us to get things done, an ambitious little lady or fella. Good thing too. But take it too far and it will be at the expense of other things in your life. Not strong enough and you will be lethargic and without much power and will achieve very little. Too strong and hell, 'you should read more, do more, get more, be more ambitious...you are not doing enough, you could do...' Surely the Pusher is a cousin of the Critic. And the two of them can do huge damage to lives or achieve sane and reasonable – or even huge – successes, in both private and working lives.

4. PEACEMAKER, or Saint: the voice of reason, rationale and smoother of competing voices. As usual, it too has positive and negative sides. Too much Saint and life becomes peace at any cost. Not enough and it's high drama, all day, every day.

5. DOUBTING Tom, Ted or Jane: always at risk, suspicious, fearful, and a deferrer; confusion is its home. Positively, it is great to question and explore things. But it's hard to live if everything is to be constantly doubted. Yet we believe so much rubbish at so many levels. The SCEPTIC is his cousin, a healthy, dependable, positive discriminator that is science and evidence orientated. 'Prove it,' says he/she. Yet if the

sceptic is overly powered he may lead to loneliness and despair.

6. LOVER: aha, it is alive and strong and needy in us all. Wants something in all of us, but at hugely varied levels. If too strong, you become narrowly focused and never satisfied. If it is not allowed enough action, you will be lonely, baffled and unfocused. The LOVER is also instinctual, needs lust, sexuality, and it is a communicator with people often looking for a strong relating orientation.

7. SLUT: ashamed, lustful, fun, pleasurable, worried, unfulfilled...write your own...but find it, don't be ashamed of it and use it, so long as it does not hurt anyone.

8. ANGRY/HATER: anger has its right place. No, it is not wrong to be angry at times. It can be a correct and proper response. Too much and it's out of control. Recall the 'Bank of Resentment'? That's where you get a big payout for even a small deposit. If you do not allow this SP to act **appropriately**, it can cost you a life. Better let out in smaller and appropriate lots than letting it blow out unreasonably. Look behind Anger and ask what and who is working with it and you will find that there can be several aspects: a hurt child from 40 years ago, a Critic that is relentless, a Lover who has never found...

9. SUPERWOMAN AND SUPERMAN: a pretender who thinks he can do anything. It is setting oneself up to fail. You can always do more, but there need to be limits. The positive side is using extra energy when needed.

10. WEAKLING: is the opposite but very negative, and it is in cahoots with the Critic and the Pusher and several others. The positive side may be that it will keep you from getting into things that are way too much for you right now.

11. SEEKER: ah, a somewhat confused and curious entity who is still looking for something more. Can become morose, depressed even, but it has to grow up, or grow out at least, of seeking nonsense out there. The Seeker is needed though, as a part that is curious about everything. The Seeker is an interesting SP as long as it seeks useful, positive and possible things, be that work or play or philosophy or experiences. Use the Seeker together with the Sceptic for better results.

12. LONE WOLF: sometimes howling at night in the vastness of the prairie is all one can do. Yet sometimes one does have to stand alone. As Clint Eastwood said in a movie, a lone man is an easy target. Yes, and yet one does need to have that feeling that I can stand alone, even if I must howl while I am doing it.

Enough for now. I recommend you start with the above list, or some of it, and see what you can relate to. Take a piece of paper or establish your own private computer file and make a list of your own, but keep it shortish. Identify your strongest seeming sub-personalities. Label them as above or with whatever name you like but stay consistent with the names. You can check it out with others as a light-hearted exercise, up to a point. You will need to explain what you are doing to a trusted other. And that's it. Simply keep the SPs in your mind as *parts of yourself, not as* YOURSELF. Each is a part. Parts can have problems. YOU can have control. Talk to the SPs as if they were someone else; in some ways they are someone else, yet each is a part of you! Again, no, you won't become a split personality, but by doing what is suggested you may well become a more integrated one, more accepting of yourself and your life.

Someone wiser than me, though I cannot recall who, once said that you may as well choose your own life! That's what life is about. However, until you know what really and truly operates you and how, until then, you can't choose and do need to be flexible about it.

&

I repeat that **every** SP has a negative and a positive side. For example, the positive side of the Pusher is that you do get things done. The negative side is when the Pusher is too heavy-handed and simply demands too much. The Pusher can drive you crazy, and even sick, working too hard, hand-in-hand with his 'cousin', the Critic. The Lover, we all like to a degree, but if it dominates, then we are likely to become less assertive than we need to be. An appropriately positive Lover is great fun and it's what the world needs, what's badly needed. The Saint is that self-sacrificing person that does it all for someone else. Too much of it and your life becomes second class and you easily become a 'Martyr'. Not a lot of positives about martyrdom. Too little of the Lover or the Carer or the…and you will find it hard to form relationships or care for others.

(See footnote[37] for some of my SPs.)

Succinctly, you need to consider whether you are 'over or under identified' with some of your SPs.

(Stone & Winkelman 1985 and later)

---

[37] As for me, I do not have a great deal of the Saint or Martyr. I do have the Wise Man or some such, that acts out. I also have some SPs I suspect are lurking in there in the dark…unidentified. Some others I have allowed more space to and a voice as I got to know them. Some I have managed to turn around and make more reasonable, like the Pusher who does push me to get things done but is no longer anxious when I slack off.

The 'Software' of Your Personality

This 'over or under identified' sentence is another of those I wish I had thought of, but I didn't. It is a most accurate and brief explanation of the way we tend to think/feel and if we do over or under identify there will be potential for problems and trouble.

Clearly, we are all aware of some of the SPs within, less so of others, and not at all of some; and that is half the problem in trying to do better for yourself or for others. But even those parts we are all too familiar with can be tricky to really understand and to use for best benefit, unless you can 'deal-talk' with them; kind of 'negotiate' with them. Further, one is forever developing new SPs. New voices may be regularly surfacing. If not, then chances are that one is very locked into a fixed style of life. This is easy to demonstrate because if you ask yourself whether 20 years ago you knew what you were going to be like today, many, or perhaps most people would have to answer, no. We have covered this in an earlier section. Now you know that several SPs were running your life back then, you might also see that several appear to have disappeared by now, right?

An interesting question might be to ponder on whether all or many of your current sub-personalities were already there in the past in some small way or form. Or whether they have actually disappeared, or just gone into hiding? I shall bravely suggest, as an example, that boredom is often experienced when no new SPs are born or when too many are not allowed to act, when one is out of touch with the SPs. Suffice to say that the potential for some of your SPs to develop or change may well have always been there. I started this section saying that this idea of *'over or under identification'* with SPs is a marvellous, fast and easy tool, so let's look at it deeper.

Over and under identification: a concept of huge importance

It simply means that one or more particular SPs are too heavy at the expense of some of the other SPs. For example, the Critic often takes over, totally freezing and souring its owner and crippling other potential and positive SP actions. If one under identifies with the Critic, then one is likely to make silly or even dangerous choices, for the Critic is the same fella that discriminates for your benefit between things useful or safe and not so.

If you over identify with, say, the Lover, then you might go for peace at all cost, you defer to all and everything, and become a doormat with few powers of assertion. Under identifying with the same SP will reduce and even cancel your ability to show and offer affection, leading to a lonely existence. It also means that you are likely to have little love for yourself. An under identified Lover is probably in cahoots with the Critic, by the way, who whispers about how you can never do anything right, and that others are not to be trusted and so on. There can be pages and pages of further examples but I shall listen to my inner SP I call DT (doubting Ted) and trust the reader to think of some.

Aspects of VOICE DIALOGUE may be practised or activated at any time because the method is self-limiting and may be focused widely or narrowly. You can stop whenever and restart at will: on the train, before you go to sleep, while waiting etc. In this process, you work on what you specifically wish to work on, taking it as far as you wish. You can start today on a specific point and even get back to it days later. It is for certain best to do it all in writing. It is a bit like journal writing, but as you can see, because it is focused, it's entirely different. Aiming it on specifics is the best way to use the method. Voice Dialogue is a 'purpose'-

built 'tool' for 'reprogramming' now, rather than during the next 30 years – or never...say the originators and many others. (I strongly suggest that this is correct.)

Reprogramming your consciousness and actual behaviour? I believe that, for all intents and purposes, these two, consciousness and behaviour, are inseparable. Some will argue with that; I won't here and now, for it is not necessary for this work of practical thought and change.

I've personally used Voice Dialogue – or something by that kind of methodology – as an overall process of transformation that suits many of my other practical ideas and it has worked well for me. It has not been a great effort; in fact, it has become a sort of personal philosophy that I can filter things, my life, through. For one thing, I said it was the immediacy of use that makes this framework a good one. For the other, it is the fact that just knowing how the method works and using that somewhat in daily thought and actions brings an almost automatic improvement to aspects of living. No torturous schemes need be involved here, not once you comprehend the idea in at least a broad way.

Naturally, not everything suits everyone. Voice Dialogue proper has some odd ideas too, just as most thought-provoking ideas do when it comes to transformation of self, or reprogramming by whatever means.[38]

---

38 Work on yourself always needs to be done with a focus if you want to build new achievements of any sort. Or if you wish to tackle old pains. Most psychological methods are usually a long, slow process, often showing meagre results or temporary ones. Though therapy is not officially offered as a temporary bandaid, it usually does create that kind of effect, and often a fallacious one. Therapy can be useful or just another 'false program' that solves little, or worse, it leads up yet another 'as if' path.

Sub-personalities can also be viewed as subcontractors

Here is yet another metaphoric view. Now this is almost a metaphor about a metaphor, as we compare SPs with 'subcontractors'. You know, you are building your own house (self) but your wife (Lover and Pusher) says you need a licensed electrician (Sparky) and a bricklayer (Worker). Yes, I am being a touch fanciful.

Your SPs really are kind of like subcontractors within you, 'hired' by you to do a particular 'job', so to speak, because you needed a job done! Needed a job done? Like all contractors, your plumber, or electrician or fridge repairman, they can be compared to internal subbies; they all have a certain amount of knowledge and power. Yet they all do what they do, and not much else. Your plumber will ruin your wall, but won't plaster it, for example. They all want to get just their own job done. Yes, your SPs want 'action' of themselves, as it were; each hardwired SP (important in your psyche) has a 'life' of its own. However, (unlike when you call a plumber) your internal subbies pop up and get to work, sometimes with, but rather often without, your awareness or request.

We wish to take a little more control of all this. Ask yourself who is 'driving' your life/car at the time when you are on the street thinking about your work or your play, or somebody you love, or a book you have just read, or a movie you have just seen. Who or what feels good or bad exactly? Who is pushing you to do more… or less? Who in there is arguing with yourself? Is it exactly the same person (SP) who suddenly loses, as it were, that particular portion of your very kind, civilised and nice personality when something threatens? The same person who would not hurt a fly but will suddenly turn into a raging maniac because of some unexpected small threat, say, a car moving on the wrong side of

The 'Software' of Your Personality

you? Then you have rage and fear about a disaster that did not even actually eventuate. You have momentarily turned into a 'killer', so to speak. An overly strong term, perhaps, but there he/she is, an evidently aggressive part of you in there somewhere who often appears to be the same as your Mr Chicken, the scared part...or is it? And it or I should say 'they' come out in response to a threat. That is their 'job'. The aggression or the high level of fear was not really called for; it was not necessary, yet it flew out. And the less aware you are of it all, the more all sorts of unpleasant things may occur. This is the 'I lost my temper and did something that I now regret' situation many of us experience. This 'they' are your uncontrolled parts working against you.

One night at around 10 pm, I was driving home from a human relationships workshop I facilitated. I was happy with the outcomes. Turning a corner a bit fast made another car come to a slightly screeching stop at a roundabout. My fault, yes, my mind was elsewhere. I waved apologetically as a young woman got out of her car waving a baseball bat and screaming at me for what I had done. 'Sorry, sorry,' I muttered, wanting to move on, and with shaking hands I drove on. She followed me. Perhaps she was going in the same direction, I thought with a beating heart, I mean, she was clearly loaded and dangerous. As we drove she finally turned away into a street. I went on for another two blocks, relieved, but then something flooded me; blood flushed through me suddenly, and now I was furious. I screeched around and went back to now follow her... What was I going to do? Follow her home and what? Luckily, as I instantly realised the 'Angry-crazy' fella was acting out, the rush of blood to the head left as fast as it had come. Once I calmed down, I wondered what that was all about for either of us. No, I couldn't solve it, but, yes, I had saved myself from taking stupid actions.

Think of events in your life, or ponder on mine, about what and 'who' was representing the young woman, or me, for the very few minutes of this road rage. I ask again figuratively: who is driving your car (your life)? Is it that elegant businesswoman I see or the scared kid dressed up as a businessperson? Is it a man who does not really care about what he looks like, for whom cars are just something used to go from place A to B? Is it an imaginary racing driver who actually is a camera salesperson? Is it somebody who wants to be seen as successful? Is it somebody who thinks that the colour red on his car will suit you so much that others will look at and notice you? Not one of these several 'parts' of you is all you are. You are much more than all that. And yet?

Another situation: who is playing when you are playing? Is it you, the managing director, or the ex factory hand? Is it the child that you were and have regained or kept? Who is drinking too much? Who is negotiating? Who is meditating? Who is making love? Which part or parts of you are doing all these things? What is success? Is success dollars, peace or love – or all of these? None of these? Who in there, inside your brain/body, is driving your beliefs? You? Oh, really you? Or is it just what was pummelled into you as a child and since then is a mere part member of your total being?

Enough now. You get the idea: investigate and hear your 'selves'. No, this is not analysis, heaven forbid. You ask, you listen, you ponder/feel. That's it. You might or might not take action. Fine, it's up to you.

A few more salient points

Many people told me during workshops on relationships, or counselling, and even at group training sessions on selling and marketing, that they did not find it easy to imagine sub-personalities as stand-up entities. Strangely, we can all imagine Santa Claus, a pink elephant, a fire-breathing monster, or an angel, or even God! Yet we have trouble playfully envisaging a part of ourselves? It is fairly obvious that this is the product of Western socio-cultural upbringing, and particularly that of English-speaking societies. But never mind that. Let's get on with it. If you are reading this book, then I know you can do it.

I suggest that if you can't picture a particular SP, then first try and find a living example, perhaps of a person you know. For, say, the 'Critic', an important 'top dog SP', I for example picture an old male teacher who used to chase me around the classroom with a ruler and called me an absolute dickhead. That will do for starters. I call him simply 'Critic'. These days I speak to an inner critic whose face is easy for me to see, because it is my own younger face, one I know only too well. Or imagine your aunty Nell who was a deferring doormat, but a lovely, loving (perhaps boring too) person…or picture a judge you have seen in a favourite TV show. Borrow from wherever you can. I emphasise that it is most helpful in this practice to have a 'picture' of who you are internally talking to, but keep it constant.

Unexpected feelings/thoughts, indeed SPs, can rise surprisingly.

You are in the movies and you've been quite happy on the day. In the movie the little boy's dog dies and you have tears rising to your eyes. In another scene, the child loses a toy – your eyes go wet again. Perhaps the cavalry arrives to save the person who was kidnapped by the baddies, and your heart lifts. Clearly, there are feelings of which we are not always aware of, and which come to the surface unexpectedly, and often not appropriately. We are, after all, constantly stimulated by what we experience.

Perhaps you are not very brave, but in one particular situation you forget yourself (underline 'forget') and you jump in and do something unexpectedly brave to help someone else. Alternatively, you are very brave – you jump out of airplanes, you run up 54 floors of the building – but you are scared of falling in love, or you are scared of dogs or spiders. Or you are in love, but you have many arguments, or you never have arguments, but you are also never in love. Maybe you have resigned yourself to the realities of life, but you dream about other things and the strength of some of these dreams, and I mean daydreams, surprises you. SPs rise at times to your consciousness, surprising you, that is just as it is for human beings.

Sometimes you envision realistic things, but you do not do anything about them, because you don't feel that you are able to. You might feel/think that you are locked into your life such as it is. You may believe that there is nothing else you could do or be. Perhaps so, and maybe not. You feel now as though ('as if') this is how it is, and it can't be helped. That's OK if you are happy enough and comfortable with it. Alternatively, you fight against who and how you are, constantly feeling/thinking that life is unsatisfactory. Your reality may well feel as if you are locked in without control or choice. Sometimes you have decided on taking some new or different action, but you never quite get around to actually doing it, beyond grass cutting.

You are so flat out, extra busy, every minute of the day is taken up. When you finally sit down you feel/think that you have earned the right to just sit there and do nothing. Oh good. Or you cannot just sit and do nothing, or play games. You fritter away your time, you make plans, you are a Walter Mitty? You have imagination, you have ideas, you could do the lot, you have the education and the technical expertise and money is not the problem. Or it is. Yet still, not much happens. Somehow, so many people never get around to taking the right actions that they would like to take, sometimes for the better.

Or else you have tried something you were not equipped to do; you set yourself up to fail, so to speak. Perhaps you had a good go, but somehow things did not work out. Bad luck and

The 'Software' of Your Personality

circumstances? Maybe so. The treasurer made an announcement that ruined your plans, the Australian dollar went up or down, it rained, it was a drought…enough already. Why do all these things happen the way they happen? **I have an answer.**

No real answer is entirely possible, only perhaps partial ones. Forget the 'why' questions and tackle these: How much of what has happened to you is due to outside of you, and how much to inside of you? How much do you have control of? Likely we will never exactly know but consider the following:

1. We can govern a great deal more of our lives.

2. We have no control of a great deal of our lives.

3. Therefore, concentrate on what you may be able to control.

(I don't like the word 'control', it is overly powerful, but you know what I mean.)

The point is that everyone has experienced the internal power of feelings and thoughts, that there is indeed a lot of push and strength in several of your various SPs. Underlying them, part of them, are your 'belief' systems. I repeat endlessly, oh poor reader, that each of these alive programs, beliefs, feelings, features are SPs and they have rules, wants and needs. Thus each SP by necessity pushes, or rejects, energises as it were, in order to put itself into action. Like all dogmatic people, each of your SPs thoroughly believes that they and only they have the right answers and actions. And this, as we know already, can work for or against you.

We do not consciously think of doing our lives just this way, or see it as such, any more than we think about how we are driving our car. The sub-personalities are the software programs of your mind after all, and they simply come to life instantly in answer to particular given situations which are sensory input perceptions. The subbies are by now, by today, this minute, on auto-action, programmed to kick in when certain things happen, when your synapses register something.

SPs can and often do conflict, and possibly even ought to!

If every SP just does what it does, then if there is a conflict between any two or more, there is the rising of what we feel as and call confusion or pain or whatever. And it does certainly happen that both suitable and unsuitable SPs to a particular situation kick in. That is in fact very much the human condition. I will even go so far as to say that we are biologically programmed and set to be this way. Sometimes SPs (you) act out, rightly so or else by, shall we say, 'mistake'. What else can explain sudden unexpected feelings and thoughts, particularly strong ones? We could write a long and sad story about my father's disappearance when I was five years old and we do need to give that story some internal air and room. Some, but not years of often circular, silly and counterintuitive analysis like: how do I feel about that? How the devil indeed. Bad and sad, true enough, and now let's move on, that's how. I mean, so bloody what by now, 40 years later.

A rush of 'love' to the head, or a cold feeling of fear or sadness, or gladness…whatever arises that we usually think of as kind of an 'automatic' mood change at times needs a bit of consideration. Sometimes more or at other times less or none. We already do all this anyway; what I suggest simply is that one does it on a more educated and conceptual basis.

BELIEFS, VALUES, ETHICS, MORALITY AND OTHER SUSPICIOUS ISSUES!

Watch out, your sub-personalities are using them.

Don't worry, a major exposé of belief systems, morals and ethics is **not** forthcoming. I will merely touch upon some of your main SPs and point towards what these might use, abuse, or authorise, that is, how the SPs deal with such issues as beliefs, ethics and morality.

Imagine an apex or triangle. There is one of three possible ideas/sides:

1. A belief in God or some sort of spiritual ideology.
2. No belief in any such thing.
3. Like many others you don't believe in religion, but still have some God belief.

Under each apex are many possible derivatives, but they tend to be somewhat set and belong to the main heading. I suggested that there are – basically – three main belief things (or groupings of things) that you might 'believe' in. Keeping it simple is all we need. We could put together a longer list; however, all we need right now is to have a straight and easy, even simple, understanding of the idea. So, which of the three basic positions you have makes a huge difference to your behaviour and life.

1. **Some sort of spiritual ideology and God beliefs.** If strong enough and dogmatic, such beliefs will constrict and cover much freedom of action or thought, unless the individual is a hypocrite – which most humans are. (Yes, me too.) Unfortunately, for example, most religions are not even compatible with democracy. Religions are also not so compatible with most of human nature either. Are we all sinners really? Is my newborn granddaughter a sinner? She does not look like one... Mostly, religion denies at least some of other religions' belief systems. I think that it is clear to see that the many and mostly outdated religious rules act mainly to control individuals. To keep them in the system, and to further the faith. Control needs certain rules, regulations, hierarchical systems, and the churches provide that. Your SPs were born out of your early and later beliefs, comprehensions, experiences etc., so your SPs were constructed by beliefs you were stuffed with. This is a circular, self-feeding situation that many, even most of us people struggle with, for or against.

2. **No belief in God or religious systems.** The broad spectrum of socio-cultural, political and social and moral beliefs of your particular society and culture are held without the need for an authority beyond the laws of the land. Politics, be that democracy or whatever form, the many currently acceptable moral and ethical mores and rules, science, education, technology and so on all can and do form a coherent enough whole for an individual to 'believe' in, and practise in a moral and ethical way. Neither with or without God makes all of what we believe and practise necessarily either all good or all bad, but in a relatively democratic society at least one can

choose between one or another belief. In any case though, we all tend to believe in some form of 'social contract'.

3. **No belief in organised religion but some strong or vague feeling or idea of a God of some sort.** I think perhaps the majority of people in Western societies belong to this grouping (?). In this lot we tend to be closer to point number 2 as far as ethics and morality are concerned.

From the above groups, each person constructs their own (later) personal belief systems, morals, ethics etc., as their own way of life, a way of dealing with the inputs from the world. The point is to see that your particular beliefs, attitudes, dogma, opinions, theories and principles do drive, and have constructed, some of your SPs who are thus 'indoctrinated' and 'learned'. They become part of you and then push and sell whatever they have and are. Again: they have formed and constructed your values, ethics, morality and beliefs and they were formed by them. So your various beliefs by now are actual SPs and vice versa! It is not that there is anything wrong with any of this necessarily... UNLESS...!

Unless some of your beliefs etc. are too dangerously 'heavy'. Naturally, I am not referring to beliefs on the small, banal scale, like whether you believe in chocolate or swimming in salt water. We are talking about real issues of values, ethics, morality and so on. These also affect politics, actions you take or leave, and even what career you choose to pursue.

When there is too much separation and conflict between certain of your SPs, that is when you might become neurotic, ill or even a psychopath or sociopath. Think on this: how could a loving Nazi father kill other people's children? Terrorists like Nazis have an ill ability to separate, split off, wall off various of their inner subbies' forces. In this way they have SPs that are not integrated, and are able to act entirely on their own. For example, terrorists killing innocent children at a marketplace. We can assuredly say that these are people who have over identified with their ANGER, say, and are also aiding and abetting that, curiously, with a God belief as a rule. Without integration of your SPs into a coherent enough system, we can be killers, bad people, unsuccessful, depressed...or suffer neurosis and psychosis, mental breakdown and eventually total madness. The way to beat the system and to be healthy is to 'know' your parts and integrate them into a positive coherent force of wholeness that is YOU. Have a look at virtually anything you dislike, hate, or are afraid of. At the bottom of it all, you will find an SP, a 'belief system', or principle of some sort that has often come by indoctrination from someone else.

So, dear readers, belief systems are Us, they are SPs, they need to be questioned and watched. The more dogmatic you feel about them, the more likely they are to cause you or someone else harm.

Our language usage is tricky. We often say we 'believe' when we 'know' something, and we sometimes say we 'know' when we merely 'believe'. Don't mix up these ideas; it is bad for you not to use the correct word. Similarly, we sometimes say that we 'feel' instead of saying we 'think', and vice versa. It matters which word you use.

Accepting or rejecting our own sub-personalities is called 'over or under identification' with some of these parts

Rehash: while we are likely familiar with several of our SPs, we certainly are less or not at all familiar with others. Both the known and unknown need to be better identified and put to positive use. Some SPs we know and like, or fight against – sometimes doing both, in a reasonable manner. Others, those we dislike because they hurt and/or work against us, we try to be rid of. I have come to see that getting rid of something you are and have been all these years is a tricky and mostly time-consuming affair that does not truly work. Rather, in my scheme we do not aim to get rid of parts of us but learn to use them positively. So there are SPs we are familiar enough with. The point is that the SPs we are not aware of work just the same behind the 'scenes' of our mind. They may be working for or against us, for or against our wishes, needs and wants. Or may be working confusingly, which often might account for what we commonly term as depression.

My task now is to explore more of what happens when we either **over or under identify with** or completely reject some of our sub-personalities.

What happens by default (so to speak) is that we want to 'over identify' with what each of us believes and calls 'good' SPs, the ones we believe to be and were taught to think of as 'good'. We identify correctly or otherwise also with the (seemingly) useful 'feel good' ones. We tend to reject SPs we have decided are the 'bad' ones. We? Oh cherished reader, do recall that 'we' or 'me' is a huge program that's been programmed by Mum and Dad and society. Most if not all of our 'default' situation and thus decisions come from the socio-cultural situation around us. Sometimes, more usage of the baddies may be just what we need, but are uncomfortable to employ. Powers of assertion, for example. So many people are loath to use them and are unable to do so. The other side of healthy assertion is always being terribly polite. Indeed, obviously it is arbitrary and subjective what we call a bad or good SP. In fact, I remind again that all SPs have positive and negative polarities, good and bad sides.

If you are a true orthodox religious believer, then you will likely deny or push away the existence of your erotic SPs. If you are a thief, then you over identify with someone in there who believes that 'the world owes you because...' If you are a businessperson, you identify with 'negotiating', 'marketing', 'selling' etc. as good concepts, and you will be outraged at my suggestion that all these can be and often are manipulative lies. (That'd be on the negative end, and yet again they certainly also have positive attributes.) If you are a people helper you will likely do that at some cost to you, like trying never to get angry, say, or not having enough time for yourself. If you over identify with anger/aggression as the only way to get on, then you may find yourself a bit alienated or in a lot of angry and dangerous situations. Over identification with say your 'Pusher' will lead to doing too much work at some cost to yourself and family. Under identifying with your 'Softie' is likely to mean that you will have trouble showing feelings for others. And so on and on. It is not neuroscience working out whether you are over or under identified with certain of your SPs and features. Just hear yourself and others who often point them out to you.

The crux of the matter is that sometimes (often?) we do not know whether we are over or under identifying with some of our SPs. Let's just say that anything held overly strongly and in a dogmatic fashion is likely to be an over identification. Almost anything that is feared or rejected is likely to be under identification. Both need investigating. And these two are not separated issues but sides of the same coin. Over identification of one brings with it necessarily an under identification of another SP.

Mainly at an early life stage, what we were told to reject and had disallowed became strange and even fearful. What we idealised as the right way to be got stronger and stronger. Both may have squeezed out other life possibilities and decisions. If we over identified to our religious beliefs, then we are likely to dogmatically hold on to ideas and values that our religion has taught us. Some people do that at great costs, and do so even when finding that much of it has not worked for them. Entire communities of women suffer from this, for example birth control, abortion, euthanasia, denial of sexuality and so on, and not only women suffer but as a consequence men as well.

Most people hold vague and confused and rather muddled beliefs, morality and ethics of all sorts, not only religious ones. They have to act out whatever we were plugged into by our parents and society. (I am not blaming parents or even the society for this; to do that would be useless.) We know already that your SPs, programs/thoughts/feelings – all these that you have nurtured and believe you had constructed – often belong to the past, parents and society. Migrants really experience this phenomenon again, when arriving in a new country, as a shock at first hand, and fast. From other countries they bring many ideologies, ways of being, but their children growing up here discard or alter a great deal of it simply because the circumstances in, say, Iran bear little or no resemblance to our Australian society.

> *'Only on arrival, at this end or that, would he assume or be assigned a purpose, and then he would be himself, or one of his selves again.'*
>
> (The Innocent, a novel by Ian McEwan, 2005)

Well then, let's look at what happened and is happening to your perhaps now outdated, or thus far rejected, yet powerful SPs and see what 'personalities' – what SPs – they had grown into. I have space only to consider a few obvious ones, those that many of us in Western societies at least appear to share. These SPs, by the way, are as a rule the ones we have a tendency to either over or under identify with. Over and under identification can – as I said before – mostly be traced back to the things that we were told to either do, think, believe, feel, or have, as a must. Or, the opposite, the 'don't do that' – don't accept, don't have, do not even think, do not even feel that way. The 'no', the negative ones, were usually the 'naughty' ones, or the 'bad' ones like not eating with your fingers, and always being polite and never arguing with Mum or Dad and so on, masturbation and sex, and so on. Then you also imbibed perhaps racist slogans, anti-women jokes and behaviours, and so on. The positive ones you were pressed to identify with were mostly taking on your parents' and their society's 'good' – the approved behaviours like politeness, belief system of sorts, so-called honesty, footy, fairness, and so on. Alas, so many of these turned out to be hypocritical and limiting or outright lies.

Now this, all this, is a problem, firstly because it is unavoidable. It is also necessary for each of us to fit into our society so we must learn the 'rules'. Yet what we learn as good or bad can change, and does change, and some things, beliefs, ideas were never what they were held up to be. In Hungary, hating Jews in the 1940s was considered the proper attitude. In America still not everyone sees black people as equals. Many people stifled their sexuality at great cost to self and to others. Many families have been destroyed by a father who worked too much, or alternatively did nothing... Values and beliefs are touchy and tricky, and as I often noted, they are arbitrary, subject to change and often misunderstood in any case. And even the saner values and beliefs can be hypocritical. Just consider how often we lie to the kids while we tell them to be honest. Or how often we tell each other not to feel the way we do... What silly nonsense and yet some of all this is also the way things are for us people. So then, mine is not a statement of Do Not Do It (whatever), but rather, take care of what and when you do.

Much human tragedy comes from not understanding all this. Many, even all, the people I know seem to have some or great understanding of it and yet so many do not have enough. For many of the values/beliefs we hold are nonsense, hypocritical, unhealthy or simply ridiculous. Yes, some are useful and necessary. By now, most adults realise that repression, denial is a bit like the jack-in-the-box toy: the more you push down, the bigger the jump…and this can be as bad as its opposite, the letting it all hang out, as they used to say in the 1970s. It is obvious to most adults that if you keep your anger in long enough and often enough, it is likely to blow up inappropriately, at the wrong place, towards the wrong people. It is obvious to many that if you keep loving the 'wrong' person, you just get your head kicked in. Yet it happens: alcoholics' wives often take many years before they leave, if ever. What SPs is an alcoholic's spouse over identified with? (Several, I believe.)

Your active and acting SPs are alive and strong and will direct your actions, positive and/or negative – I repeat – with or without your awareness of them! Deny (under identify) and repress an SP and it will energise, it will get stronger, it will counter-react (jack-in-the-box). Similarly, deny, repress a nation of people and they will react. Over identify with an SP like, say, 'always telling the whole truth', or always showing your anger, and you won't be too popular at times with some people. Alternatively, under identifying with assertion and anger will make you a 'goody-two-shoes' (?), and it will deliver things you did not want. Always lie about everything, always tell the truth? Neither will be a great way to live. Life is not an 'always' or 'never' situation, but a mix and the making of sensitive and appropriate decisions.

By the way, those parts of your personality that are kept down, hidden, pushed away are the ones that cost you extra physical and mental energy

What then should one do about some of the SPs that want to do things not all that socially brilliant, or even lawful? Or actions that seem not ethical or morally correct? Or actions that are not even particularly nice, even as you see it? Well, it would take several books to answer my own questions in detail, subjective as they are in regard to what is or is not a repression: an over or under identification. Suffice to say that many of the, shall we say, uncomfortable SPs can be tamed or transmuted into productive energies as I have proposed now too often. (That is, if they need, you need, conversion.) To start with, and at the very least, you need to get to know them better, 'acknowledge' and even 'honour' them, as it were. The early Greeks worshipped many gods (somewhat similar to current day Hinduism). Each Greek person and household had a chosen deity, but people knew that they must honour _all_ the other gods. Honouring all your SPs is the same sort of idea, which is science rather than a 'peeled balloon' (Mum answered this when I asked what's for dinner?).

One thing for certain is that being familiar with how you really feel/act can take the teeth out of the potentially nastier or hard to live with SPs. It is those people who are out of touch with their SPs who commit crimes and take immoral actions. If I know some of my not so nice or inappropriate behaviours, then I can be on guard against them lest they should bubble up at the wrong time and place. If I am familiar with my lazy side, then I can better activate the opposite, perhaps the 'Pusher'. If I know my Pusher well, and he is over active I can ask for time-out for my inner 'child' that wants to play.

The 'Software' of Your Personality

The English words 'illusion', 'delusion' and 'collusion' all have the Latin root of 'ludere', which means to play. Thus, illusion implies playing false with perception, delusion implies playing false with thoughts and feelings, and collusion, playing false together with either yourself or/and with someone else, to support the illusions and delusions. Such movements happen more when one is not familiar with one's own, and thus other people's, sub-personalities.

To reiterate: watch out for whatever conviction you hold too dogmatically. Treat that not as 'bad' – tut-tut – but simply be aware and deal with it. Note what you are most afraid of or cautious about – and explore it. Give it a name, such as the Pusher, the Critic, the Carer, the Slut, or whatever, because they are easier to call up that way, and to deal with. Many philosophers and psychologists agree that the so-called 'middle way' in life is sane and reasonable. Allow room and energy therefore for all you are, for all your SPs. Chop the wood while you have an axe in your hand; when you feel or think something, consider going into it deeper right away.

PS. One does not chop wood all day, every day, forever either.

CREATIVE LIVING IS MEANING AND PURPOSE.

One indicator of creativity is when concepts, thoughts, words, or objects that don't normally go together are joined in novel ways – like in metaphors (yes, again) – and thus result in something fresh, newish, or even amazing. Living creatively includes careers, relationships, child care, time management, ecology, and even banal stuff like cooking or exercise...in other words, I am including a well-rounded way of living.

Creativity, to start with, is imaginative communications with yourself. Inventiveness always incorporates an element of 'playing' with concepts, words, ideas. Originality, ingenuity and inventiveness of all sorts may be even more important than sex as the most central force, need and indeed obligation in human lives. Our personal and social survival is ultimately about the positive or negative usage of human intellectual powers.

Of course, simply playing with ideas and words and concepts does not necessarily bring about fresh perceptions or brilliant ideas. But without frolicking and participating therein, there is little chance of allowing the self to break through the preset programs we live with (we are). It is probably everyone's experience that if you brainstorm ideas with several other people in a playful manner, you have a better chance of finding creative solutions. (Or just a lot of great fun and nonsense.) We can also do, and indeed need to do, inner and imaginative thinking/feeling on our own.

The neural connections in our brains that are not used lie dormant or they die out like unused paths in the bush. Those paths grow and are healthier when more creative input is happening. Creative, inventive living is not only more fun, but it is a healthy way to be, even if it is not aimed at producing something big. Then again, people need to become HUMAN BEINGS rather than only human doings, and that takes some continual imaginative reinventing of yourself!

We are all familiar with boredom, and many of us at times have fallen into a 'rut'. There may be several things interacting at these times. The moment you can rise up to think/feel differently, you are on the way to another level of existence. Such a move, for example, is to seriously and consciously consider your personal traits as SPs with all that this implies. Your unused programs (SPs) are fading bush tracks, and are at times overgrown and 'delete' themselves. Other SPs somehow develop and are constructed within you without you even noticing it. What you want, in any case, is some control, the ability to decide which programs to keep, use, or be rid of. All this was suggested in various ways before, so this creativity chapter is yet another different angle and way to tackle the whole thought of this book. The paths 'more or less travelled' is a metaphor I really like. Going off the well-travelled paths in search of new territories may take some effort, but it is likely to lead to more creativity and riches, and less boredom. The brain/mind wants to set like jelly, wants to hardwire your experiences for ease of later use. Just as well, for doing that is a must, up to a point. However, the dirt roads and the struggle that led you to where you are now might be lost and forgotten. Perhaps this is one reason why mental anguish remains, sometimes without the accurate (or any) real memory of how it got there. That is another psychological excursion I shall not now pursue. Let us dig in that creativity jungle a little further.

Many people know the famous words of Robert Frost about the road not chosen. The road less travelled could indeed work out well, or badly; it can be scary and yet make all the difference... As you might know, explorers and pioneers often got arrows in their backs. But many moved on to create better lives as well. One can and does need to be taking well-calculated and realistic for you risks.

During the creative endeavour, communications between you and you – or others – seems to flow very well at times because the people you are communicating with are more receptive. Fortunately, most people are receptive to creative input, at least up to the point where it clashes with their over identified SPs (watch out for that warning signal). So a new piece of art, song, business, anything newish, if it is truly creative is often successful and welcomed by many and rubbished by many as well. Such was the 'devil's own' music, rock and roll, invented in the 1960s. Or the birth control pill. Many hated it; some loved it. Or communism, Chinese, Russian or Hungarian style etc. etc.

Life is created by two people. Creative activity is enormous in early childhood. As we get educated, most of us lose the ability we may have had when under 12 or so of age. I won't go into what is or is not good about education today except to say that the high pressure on students means that they need to learn given material. This is or would be good if at the same time students also learned to use the material creatively where possible. Or at least to think about it in such way. It is notable after all that people who do use creative ideas are often very successful. I'll also posit that creative people are likely to feel better about their lives.

The 'Software' of Your Personality

ॐ

Let's look at what happens when you are communicating within just yourself. Most people would not say 'I am communicating with myself', would they? Yet I suggest that thinking of it this way is a slightly different concept and better focuses the mind to the task of what we usually term as 'I'm thinking'. I remind the reader that there is not one self in there, but several selves or channels or SPs. Thus we, and the SPs, often 'weigh up' contradictory wants and needs and agonise about what to do. This is familiar to anyone.

In order for your creativity to flow, you need to be receptive, and in order to be receptive, you probably need to access 'playing' – frolicking with your SPs. This is like playing with the idea of noticing your metaphors, the sub-personality ideas, or the PC analogy. Bowman and Peat in their book *Science, Order and Creativity* (2000) say that creative activity is not to be regarded as a problem to be solved, but to be played for the play itself. Meaning that in creative thinking/playing nothing is taken for granted and everything is put up for re-evaluation. Just as Malcolm Turnbull said when he became the Australian PM, 'everything is on the table', and I wish he kept with that but he did not. The idea of 'what if?' thinking will be familiar to many people. It is a contrasting question to what I called 'as if'.

Even 'what if?' thinking might put a certain amount of brakes on creative thought, because it asks, sometimes too early, for presumed outcomes. This perhaps cannot be helped, but must be watched vigilantly. At first, just inventing new possibilities is all one looks for; the outcomes can be considered later. Ah, poor us though, it seems virtually impossible for us to think of anything without at the same time thinking of the presumed outcomes like, 'If I do this, will X or will Y happen?' And just as well, when you were going out into the forest full of sabre-toothed tigers 10,000 years ago. Also just as well to a degree now, for one big and silly decision can ruin your life. Yet we must take chances, well-informed ones, and it is not always easy to know whether we are or are not well informed.

All that I've been suggesting might sound like serious work. I can hear you saying 'oh God, I have even more to do'. And it can be work, so the short answer is yes, and no, as usual. Still, it can also be very satisfying – if, and when once you get an idea right. Then, you check for outcomes. If results are for the better, then you will feel less stressed about what you do and more focused on what actually matters. And things pay off. Then it all becomes a more automated affair and you will be using those of your most appropriate features (SPs) that best suit the need or job on hand.

By the way, you do need to be clear about what is suggested here, but no, you don't have to be perfect about any of it. Playfully enjoy the learning, the understanding and the arguments I offer. Discard some and accept others (with care...). Use what is suggested, but do not turn it into another false dogma, as it were. And creative thinking should not take huge amounts of time either, depending of course on what it is about. A scientific affair will take way longer than to build the new kitchen, or how to improve your income by 20% or to refresh an old relating pattern.

Imaginative thinking works and moves forward rather like the scientific model of thinking. Simply put: an idea is followed by a conceptualisation of some sort, enabling one to propose something that might be acted upon. The idea is then explored in some ways as to its relevance, implications, and outcomes. The very important step is the taking of actual action. Equally important, however, is to always evaluate the results or outcomes in several ways, such as:

Are there any results at all?

Are the results what was wanted?

Are the outcomes not what was wanted, but satisfactorily in that direction?

Are the outcomes positive or actually negative, and of course, what that suggests? If the outcomes are negative, the whole set-up may be re-explored as to how the results came to be negative, and the whole circuit may then be repeated with some changes. Or thrown in the trash can. (Excuse the rather oversimplified explanation of what science does to achieve, explain and create.) By the way, if we get a negative result, we tend to explore what has gone wrong and that is good. However, as individuals we rarely explore success, and carefully consider what has gone right!

We can keep learning, changing, and overriding the primal commands of our DNA; this is widely agreed on by many thinkers. Individuals should shape and construct the landscape of their lives – creatively. When we action a new idea, we always bring together old familiar know-how and new sparks. We bring the old to the newly creative ideas, since if we did not use old experiences, known expertise and perception, we could not possibly be thinking of new versions. In any case, at some moment there has to be a drive, indeed a commitment from proposal to action and to evaluation.

This brings us back to the conscious and unconscious modes of knowledge. We do not 'think' about how to drive a car consciously, except when something goes wrong. We do not think about how to ride a bicycle once we know how to do it, or about how to sweat while riding. Both happen on 'automatic' of sorts. We do not think or consider how many apples we have if we pick up two in the left hand and two in the right; all that has become unconscious or, as I prefer, 'automatic' knowledge. In his book *Flourish*, Martin Seligman (2011) said that the more components of a task you have on automatic, the more time you have left over to do the 'heavy lifting'. Surely, this is true on both the small and the very large scale.

Once a creative idea is implemented, if it works and if it is what we have set out to achieve, then we have to 'bed' it in for it to become 'automatic' knowledge.

> *We could not possibly live without being committed to certain assumptions about the world and ourselves. The ideas or knowledge that we take as accepted assumptions and (automatic) knowledge do not take up a great deal of energy or time. Thus any new idea or behaviour that can be turned into 'automatic knowledge' will indeed free the mind to consider creativity.*

Change is constant, so they keep saying...

We have to be very careful that we do not take any of the assumptions we have now as correct forever, without further questioning. All is in constant change. People change biologically, physically and mentally; circumstances and situations change. Our desires, needs, wants, goals, aims also change. Perhaps this is why we sometimes surprise ourselves about our actions, values and belief systems. Things we have held as unassailable at some point may surface as opposite to what we now want and think. In fact, what has changed is that other aspects in our lives have moved on and the assumptions that we have held about them are simply no longer valid or applicable now.

If we hang on to old, perhaps outdated or unproductive ideas inflexibly, we may well be wasting our time and energy; life and time is better spent in looking at them creatively. It is clear to every adult that what I called the scientific model is in fact what happens anyway (to a degree) in daily lives: we think of doing something (who knows why, or perhaps we set out to think it, either way) and we consider our possible actions. Then we take – or leave – such actions, and finally evaluate the results. So there is nothing unusual in the idea; indeed the philosophies of science have clearly arisen from the ideas of personal experience.

Doing something new, really new, may or may not be diametrically opposed to what has been done before. One of the problems that one encounters with creative thought, action or evaluation is that we will easily fall for the 'this must be good because it is so different to what I have done before'. This of course is equally as untrue as doing pretty much what you have done before with a minor alteration that you now believe to have magical value.

I repeat with some extension that: *'People do, or think, or even feel more and more of what has never (truly) worked for them.'* It happens all the time: that is to say, instead of finding new solutions or new ways of acting or achieving what we want, we tend to just kind of repaint the old room.

Incoming new knowledge is usually mixed with past experience, via the filter of creativity. This rarely happens simply through good luck. I think it happens so rarely, that when it does happen, we know that it has happened, as it usually carries with it some most interesting results, usually (I think) of a positive nature. Sometimes to a worrying degree. We have said several times before that we have unconscious defence mechanisms against new ideas. Against anything that might threaten our current equilibrium, value system, beliefs or plans, i.e. our current programs, SPs. The problem was, you know, that at least a great proportion of these defences (SPs) are indeed unconscious. And they may well be fundamentally important defences. (If old ideas and defences were not so fundamentally important, we probably would not be holding them so tightly.)[39]

Einstein, that extremely creative genius, said words to the effect that creative acts come from the opposing, from the pushing against another point of view, and that this is the law of differentiation. To me this can mean that by consciously using opposing ideas from people, or those held by my own SPs, creative action is likely to result.

Finally, and I think obviously, practising small creative acts is likely to build bigger ones. We see how creative small children are, and we see how in old age we lose that sense of creative action. Some of the loss is due to reduced physical or mental ability; therefore, one must – as usual – keep exercising body and mind. To do this at an older age, there is already the need to be creative.

---

39 The craziness of some organisations comes from such above cited reasons and is multiplied by itself. I think there is a strong feeling in individuals to impose or to hold on to their defences, ideals and systems, and whether they know those or not, there is an underlying belief that they do know.

FINALLY

> *'The word "ecstasy" derives from the Greek for "to stand outside of". To stand outside of what? Of oneself.'*
> From *Betraying Spinoza: the Renegade Jew Who Gave Us Modernity* by Rebecca Goldstein.

Meaning, yet again, that to objectively see who and how you are, and what you must do, you need what only great awareness can bring.

As said before, we simply must take some things for granted; indeed, we cannot be checking out everything on a momentary basis. We simply must take some things in life for granted, and live with the surprises that happen from time to time. Fine. So don't bother to examine the things you feel are meaningless or banal, or those that we take for granted until, and if, you find that you need to? Or simply want to? Hmm and um, and all the other arrghs and ums... Because the point is this: if you are satisfied and happy, then perhaps leave it alone. If otherwise, if you still have something you want to do or become, then perhaps tackle it and constantly. It is, we are, life is a *narrative*. Perhaps we can change the underlying story and write new chapters. That is also part of what we may call creative change.

And so, friends, I am arriving towards the end of this particular range of thoughts and feelings that I have long wanted to put forward. I agree with psychologist Carl Rogers:

'I have gradually come to one negative conclusion about the good life. It seems to me that the good life is not any fixed state. It is not, in my estimation, a state of virtue, or contentment, or nirvana, or happiness. It is not a condition in which the individual is adjusted or fulfilled or actualized. To use psychological terms, it is not a state of drive-reduction, or tension-reduction, or homeostasis. **The good life is a process, not a state of being.** *It is a direction not a destination.'* (Rogers 1961)

Once again we have the metaphor: 'life is a way of travelling' rather than one of ever arriving at a final **desti-station**...(not a misspelling). **The process is the product**. And this way of travelling is, it needs to be, an attentive one. It needs to be seen as a 'narrative' that can be 'rewritten' at will and thoroughly understood, and 'edited' at times. You simply must become more attentive to yourself first and foremost, for you can know others only as well as you know yourself. You can understand others only to the degree you can comprehend yourself...and vice versa.

ཨོཾ

Now I will try to briefly summarise, trying to press the whole of my material here into a husk

There is no soul or little person in your head directing the operation of your life. *'No one is pushing the Reboot button, no transcendental technician of subjectivity...'* You are a *'dynamical self-organization'*, an *'Ego Machine'* (Metzinger 2009). You, reader, you really are IT, on your own and yet connected and relating to everyone and everything. It is all about you, doing or not what you call living your life. There is in my experience no God concept out there that will bring the goodies or save you from whatever. There is just humanity, good, bad and indifferent.

The 'Software' of Your Personality

You need to have a strong, viable and workable concept of who you are and how you operate: of what you think/feel. I offered several metaphors for how to rethink, reform, rewrite, reprogram the 'narrative' that is you. Perhaps you need a new working concept of yourself and of others, possibly not. One big item was the question: is there just one of you there? Yes, of course you are You, but I suggested – as so many current thinkers do these days – that the 'me' we know is several selves: SPs, sub-personalities, programs, subcontractors, if you like. Another concept I offered was the 'Literary Editor of Life Narratives'. All these and many others are more than just metaphors and analogies; they are actual tools you can use by simply making the decision to use them. Take some idea that appeals from one area and another from elsewhere. Use one or several. Not too many.

No need to chuck out, delete all you are; good heavens, if you are reading this book, you must be relatively sane and OK already. Simply take from here what might serve you better. No need to 'reboot' all of your human computer.

Along our journey, we considered a lot of outdated nonsensical ideas about human lives. Outdated data and behaviours, old ways that were never true or positive...or maybe they were back then, but are not now. Like dogmatically held beliefs, racist or doubtful ethics and morality, or other outdated and perhaps repressed parts of you. We considered choice and decision making. We have looked at the human condition in general and personal, and we contemplated creative living. All in aid of what is most important for you to be familiar with: your true 'features', your SPs, so you can find and build your purposes, aims and goals. You do need to know as precisely as possible the outcomes and possible benefits that you are looking for in your life today, this week, this year and on into the future.

'What a person must or could be...' (Maslow) is what he or she needs to find out. That is the purpose and meaning of life: to know who, what and how you are. To keep exploring that. Life has no meaning or purpose other than this giant quest that you are. Your Purpose and Meaning is living Your Life as well as possible! The process is the product, the trip itself is the thing for there is no destination.

Where will you go from here? What will you do? Remember that you need not be perfect or always come first, for it is often the second 'mouse' that gets to eat the cheese...

BIBLIOGRAPHY

I offer a (not exactly academic) bibliography from which you might choose, or not, for further reading. Most, if not all, of these books and publications can be purchased from Amazon and other like resellers as both online eBooks or in hard copy. Sage Publications is another wonderful source of both heavy and lighter but serious material on human lives (and all else).

I believe there is enough, some would say too much, material in my book for some time if you care to do more than just a read-through. Still, there is a great deal of brilliant thinking from many contemporary writers, and some of it is easy reading and yet very enlightening.

Anderson, L 2006, 'Analytic autoethnography', *Journal of Contemporary Ethnography*, vol. 35.

Atkins, P 2003, *Galileo's finger*, Oxford University Press, USA.

Atkins, P 2011, *On being*, Oxford University Press, Amazon online.

Baggini, J 2011, *The ego trick*, Granta Books, UK, and Amazon Kindle.

Bamberg, M & Andrews, M (eds) 2004, *Considering counter narratives: narrating, resisting, making sense*, John Benjamin, Amsterdam.

Barclay, 1994

Barthes, R 1975, *The pleasure of the text*, HarperCollins, New York.

Barthes, R 1977, *Image–music–text*, Fontana Press, London, UK.

Barthes, R 2000, *A Roland Barthes reader*, S Sontag (ed.), Vintage Classics, London.Behar, R 1996, *The vulnerable observer: anthropology that breaks your heart*, Beacon Press, Boston, USA.

Bellows, S 1990, Romanes lecture, 'The distracted public' (excerpt), viewed August 2009.

Bercaw, N 1996, 'Gendering the master narrative', University of North Carolina Press, USA.

Bochner, A 2001, 'Narrative's virtues', *Qualitative Inquiry*, vol. 7, no. 2, pp. 131–157.

Bochner, AP & Ellis, C 1996, 'Talking over ethnography', in C Ellis and AP Bochner (eds), *Composing ethnography: alternative forms of qualitative writing*, AltaMira, California.

Bochner, AP & Ellis, C 2003, 'An introduction to the arts and narrative research: art as inquiry', *Qualitative Inquiry*, vol. 9, no. 4, pp. 506–514.

Bohm D and Peat FD 2000, *Science, order and creativity*, Routledge, Taylor & Francis Ltd, United Kingdom.

Borges, JL 1979, *The book of sand*, Penguin Books, Sydney.

Borges, JL 1981, *Labyrinths*, King Penguin, New York.

Bragg, M 2009, 'Melvyn Bragg on autobiographical fiction', *Sunday Times*, February 2009, https://www.thetimes.co.uk/article/melvyn-bragg-on-autobiographical-fiction-s23jl6ppf72 , viewed 2009.

Braiterman, Z 2010, 'Against Holocaust-Sublime: naive reference and the generation of memory', *History and Memory*, vol. 12, no. 2, Fall/Winter 2000, pp. 7–28, viewed November 2010, http://muse.jhu.edu/journals/ham/summary/v012/12.2braiterman.html.

Brilliant, A 1987, *I try to take one day at a time but sometimes several days attack me at once*, Woodbridge Press, Santa Barbara, California.

Brooks, M 1998, A CBS interview, CBS Interactive 2011.Bruner, J 1985a, *Actual minds, possible worlds*, Harvard University Press, Cambridge, MA.

Bruner, J 1985b, 'Narrative and paradigmatic modes of thought', in E Eisner (ed.), *Learning and teaching the ways of knowing: eighty-fourth yearbook of the National Society for the Study of Education*, Part II, Chicago University Press, Chicago.

Bruner, J 1990, *Acts of meaning*, Harvard University Press, Cambridge, MA.

Bruner, J 1996, *The culture of education*, Harvard University Press, Cambridge, MA.

Bruner, J 2004, 'Life narratives', *Social Research Magazine,* vol. 71, no. 3, pp. 691–709.

Bruner, J 2006, *Narrative, learning and culture*, New Social Science Monographs, Copenhagen Business School, Copenhagen.

Buck, PS 2013, *The eternal wonder*, Amazon.

Bullough, RV, Jnr, & Pinnegar S 2001, 'Guidelines for quality in autobiographical forms of self-study research', *Educational Researcher*, vol. 30, no. 3, pp. 13–21.

Campbell, J 1993, *The hero with a thousand faces*, Fontana Press, Great Britain.

Corey, FC 1998, 'The personal: against the master narrative', in SJ Dailey (ed.), *The future of performance studies: visions and revisions*, National Communications Association, US.

Cox, J & Stromquist, S (eds) 1998, *Contesting the master narrative: essays in social history*, University of Iowa Press, Iowa.

Dawkins, R 2006, *The selfish gene* (3rd edition), Oxford University Press.

Djerassi, C 2001, 'Carl Djerassi reflects on the Pill as it meets its 50th birthday', Stanford News Service, viewed October 2010, http://news.stanford.edu/pr/01/thismanspill295.html .

Doring, T 2006, 'Edward Said and the fiction of autobiography', *Wasafiri,* vol. 21, pp. 71–78.

Eakin, PJ 1999, *How our lives become stories,* Cornell University Press, New York, USA.

Eco, U 1997, *Kant and the platypus,* Harcourt, Orlando, USA.

Eco, U 2006, *On literature,* Vintage Books, London.

Erikson, E 2001, *The Erik Erikson reader,* W.W. Norton & Co., USA.

Feldman, C 2006, 'Ambivalent identities in nations as "Hardened" groups: France and the US in 2005', *Narrative learning and culture,* New Social Science Monographs, Copenhagen.

Fivush, R & Haden, CA (eds) 2003, *Autobiographical memory and the construction of a narrative self: developmental and cultural perspectives,* Psychology Press, Erlbaum, USA.

Goldstein, RN 2009, *Betraying Spinoza,* Amazon.

Herman, D (ed.) 2003, *Narrative theory and the cognitive sciences,* University of Chicago Press, Chicago.

Herman, D 2009, *Basic elements of narrative,* Wiley-Blackwell, London, UK.

Hofstadter, DR & Dennett, DC 1981, *The mind's I: fantasies and reflections on self and soul,* Bantam Books, USA.

Holt, J 2012, *Why does the world exist?* W.W. Norton & Co., USA, Amazon.

Horney, K 1999, *Our inner conflicts,* Routledge, London.

Hutcheon, L 1994, *Irony's edge: the theory of politics of irony,* Routledge, New York.

Irving, J 2000, *My movie business: a memoir*, Black Swan, London, UK.

Jaynes, J [1976, 2001], *The origin of consciousness in the breakdown of the bicameral mind*, Houghton Mifflin.

Kerkyasharian, S 1998, *Multiculturalism in Australia – today and tomorrow*, Ethnic Affairs Commission of NSW, Ashfield, NSW.

Kessel, S, Cole, P & Johnson, D 1992, 'The self as a center of narrative gravity', in S Kessel, P Cole & D Johnson (eds), *A self divided: a review of self and consciousness: multiple perspectives*, Lawrence Erlbaum Associates, Hillsdale, New Jersey.

Khrishnamurti, J 1972, *You are the world*, Harper & Row, New York.Kotz, D 2010, 'Birth control pill turns 50: 7 ways it changed lives', US News Company, viewed May 2010, http://health.usnews.com/health-news/womens-health/articles/2010/05/07/birth-control-pill-turns-50-7-ways-it-changed-lives .

Kuhn, TS 1970, *The structure of scientific revolutions*, University of Chicago Press, Chicago.

Kundera, M 1984, *The unbearable lightness of being*, Faber & Faber, London.

Kundera, M 1988, *The art of the novel*, Faber &Faber, London.

Kurzban, R 2012, *Why everyone (else) is a hypocrite: evolution and the modular mind*, Princeton University Press, USA.

Kushner, HS 1978, *When bad things happen to good people*, Random House, USA.

Lakoff, G & Johnson, M 1980, *Metaphors we live by*, University of Chicago Press, Chicago.

Lee, C 1996

Lem, S 1983, *His master's voice*, Harcourt Brace Jovanovich Publishers, New York.Linde, C 2001, "Narrative and social tacit knowledge", *Journal of Knowledge Management*, Special

Issue on Tacit Knowledge and Active Learning, 5(2).Lutz, C 1995, 'Culture and consciousness: a problem in the anthropology of knowledge' in S Kessel, PM Cole & D Johnson (eds), *A self divided: a review of self and consciousness: multiple perspectives*, Lawrence Erlbaum Associates, New Jersey.

Lyotard, J-F 1995, *The postmodern condition: a report on knowledge*, Manchester University Press, Manchester.

McAdams, DP 1985, 1993, *The stories we live by*, Guilford Press, New York.

McAdams, DP 2008, 'Personal narratives and the life story', in OP John, RW Robins & LA Pervin (eds), *Handbook of personality: theory and research,* Guilford Press, New York.

McCarthy, J 2007, *Dennett and Ricoeur on the narrative self*, Humanity Books, New York.

MacIntyre, A 1967, 'The idea of a social science', *Aristotelian Society Supplement*, XLI.

MacIntyre, A 1984, 'The virtues, the unity of a human life and the concept of tradition' in A MacIntyre, *After virtue*, University of Notre Dame Press, Paris.

Maslow, A 1943–1968, Quotes from various of his books and writing. See Wikipedia for details of books and articles, https://en.wikipedia.org/wiki/Abraham_Maslow . Also Maslow online quotes.

Metzinger, T 2009, *The ego tunnel*, Basic Books, New York, Amazon Kindle.

Morgan, A 2000, *What is narrative therapy?*, Dulwich Centre Publications, Adelaide.

Morris, P 1996, *Patrick Modiano*, Berg, Washington DC.

Morrison, T 1970, *The bluest eye*, Holt, Rinehart and Winston, Austin, Texas.

Moyers, B 1989, 'A world of ideas: exposing the master narrative', Interview with Toni Morrison, viewed March 2011, www.oberlin.edu/acs/books/bluesteye.htm.

Mumford, S & Anjum, RL 2013, *Causation: a very short introduction*, Amazon Kindle.

Neisser, U 1994, 'Self narratives: true and false' in U Neisser & R Fivush (eds), *The remembering self*, Cambridge University Press, Cambridge.

Neisser, U (ed.) 2006, *The perceived self*, Cambridge University Press, Cambridge.

Neisser, U & Fivush, R (eds) 1994, *The remembering self*, Cambridge University Press, Cambridge.

Ochs, E & Capps, L 1996, 'Narrating the self', *Annual review of Anthropology*, vol. 25, pp. 19–43.

Olendzki, A 2015, *Unlimiting mind: the radically experiential psychology of Buddhism*, Amazon.

Parry, A 1991, 'A universe of stories', *Family Process*, vol.30, pp. 37–54.

Parry, A & Doan, RE 1994, *Story re-visions*, Guilford Press, New York.

Pinker, S 1994, *The language instinct*, William Morrow and Company, New York.

Polkinghorne, DE 1988, *Narrative knowing and the human sciences*, University of New York, Albany.

Popkin, JD 2003, 'Holocaust memories, historians' memoirs: first-person narrative and the memory of the Holocaust', *History and Memory*, vol. 15, no. 1, Spring/Summer 2003, pp. 49–84.

Richardson, B 2009, *Recent concepts of narrative and the narratives of narrative theory*, University of Maryland, Washington DC.

Ricoeur, P 1991a, 'Life in quest of narratives', in D Wood (ed.), *On Paul Ricoeur*, Routledge, London.

Ricoeur, P 1991b, 'What is a text?', in MJ Valdes (ed.), *A Ricoeur reader*, University of Toronto Press, Toronto.

Ricoeur, P 1992, *Oneself as another*, Chicago University Press, Chicago.

Rogers, CR 1961, *On becoming a person*, Amazon Kindle.

Schlink, B 1995, *The reader*, Vintage International, New York.

Seligman M 2011

Stone, H & Stone, S 1993, *Embracing your inner critic*, Harper-Collins, New York.

Stone, H & Winkelman, S 1983–85, *Embracing heaven and earth*, DeVorss and Company, California.Todd, E 2013, 'Narratives, self and identity', exegesis for a PhD thesis, Swinburne University Online.

Wajnryb, R 2001, *The silence: how tragedy shapes talk*, Allen & Unwin, Sydney, NSW.

Walter, C 1998, 2013, *Last ape standing*, Walker Books, Amazon.

White, M 1995, *Re-authoring lives*, Dulwich Centre publications, Adelaide, Australia.

White, M & Epston, D 1990, *Narrative means to therapeutic ends*, W.W. Norton & Co., New York.

Wilson, EO 1978, *On human nature*, Harvard University Press, USA.

Wilson, RA 1983, *Prometheus rising*, New Falcon Publications, USA.

Wylie, H & Pare, D 2001, 'Whose story is it anyway?', *Mosaic: A Journal for the Interdisciplinary Study of Literature*, vol. 34, no. 1, pp. 153–172.

Yalom, ID 2002, *The gift of therapy*, HarperCollins, New York.

www.ingramcontent.com/pod-product-compliance
Lightning Source LLC
Chambersburg PA
CBHW071155300426
44113CB00009B/1222